A PEOPLE'S HISTORY OF SPORTS IN THE UNITED STATES

ALSO BY DAVE ZIRIN

Welcome to the Terrordome:
The Pain, Politics, and Promise of Sports

Muhammad Ali Handbook

What's My Name, Fool?
Sports and Resistance in the United States

A PEOPLE'S HISTORY OF SPORTS IN THE UNITED STATES

250 Years of Politics, Protest, People, and Play

Dave Zirin

THE NEW PRESS

NEW YORK
LONDON

Requests for permission to reproduce selections from this book
should be mailed to: Permissions Department, The New Press,
38 Greene Street, New York, NY 10013.

Published in the United States by The New Press, New York, 2008
Distributed by W. W. Norton & Company, Inc., New York

LIBRARY OF CONGRESS CATALOGING-IN-PUBLICATION DATA

Zirin, Dave.
A people's history of sports in the United States : from bull-baiting to Barry Bonds—
250 years of politics, protest, people, and play / Dave Zirin.
p. cm.
Includes bibliographical references and index.
ISBN 978-1-59558-100-6 (hc)
1. Sports—Political aspects—United States—History. 2. Sports—
Social aspects—United States—History. I. Title.
GV706.35.Z567 2008
306.4'830973—dc22   2008020420

The New Press was established in 1990 as a not-for-profit alternative to the large,
commercial publishing houses currently dominating the book publishing industry.
The New Press operates in the public interest rather than for private gain, and is
committed to publishing, in innovative ways, works of educational, cultural, and
community value that are often deemed insufficiently profitable.

www.thenewpress.com

Composition by dix!

Printed in the United States of America

2   4   6   8   10   9   7   5   3   1

To Michele, Sasha Jane, and
Baby Jacob. The Dream Team.

Contents

Series Preface

Turning history on its head opens up whole new worlds of possibility. Once, historians looked only at society's upper crust: the leaders and others who made the headlines and whose words and deeds survived as historical truth. In our lifetimes, this has begun to change. Shifting history's lens from the upper rungs to the lower, we are learning more than ever about the masses of people who did the work that made society tick.

Not surprisingly, as the lens shifts the basic narratives change as well. The history of men and women of all classes, colors, and cultures reveals an astonishing degree of struggle and independent political action. Everyday people played complicated historical roles, and they developed highly sophisticated and often very different political ideas from the people who ruled them. Sometimes their accomplishments left tangible traces; other times, the traces are invisible but no less real. They left their mark on our institutions, our folkways and language, on our political habits and vocabulary. We are only now beginning to excavate this multifaceted history.

The New Press People's History Series roams far and wide through human history, revisiting old stories in new ways, and introducing altogether new accounts of the struggles of common people to make their own history. Taking the lives and viewpoints of common people as its point of departure, the series reexamines subjects as different as the American Revolution, the history of sports, the history of American art, the Mexican Revolution, and the rise of the Third World.

A people's history does more than add to the catalogue of what we already know. These books will shake up readers' understanding of the past—just as common people throughout history have shaken up their always changeable worlds.

Howard Zinn
Boston, 2000

Preface

The great Howard Cosell in a scathing critique of the sports world once said "rule number one of the jockocracy" was that sports and politics could never mix. Sports had to be dumbed down and quarantined from that nasty netherworld where political ideas and social concerns threatened to ruin the party. Debate was to be confined to "less filling" versus "tastes great."

Today major sports columnists rain down many a verbal blow anytime an athlete takes a political stand. They can be worse when people outside the sports world try to say their piece—for example, when Jesse Jackson criticized hiring practices in the athletic department at the University of Alabama. They argue that sports and politics don't belong in the same zip code, the same country, the same universe. It's not just sports columnists—it's the conventional wisdom throughout your local newspaper. Even E. J. Dionne, the house liberal of the *Washington Post*, wrote in 2003, "Most of us who love sports want to forget about politics when we watch games. Sports, like so many other voluntary activities, creates connections across political lines. All Americans who are rooting for the Red Sox in the playoffs are my friends this month, no matter what their ideology."

Dionne's starting point is that sports are apolitical, neutral space. The problem with Dionne, the sports page, and everyone who tries to segregate these two worlds is that they are trafficking in myth. They want us to believe that sports and politics together are as painful a mash-up as Mitt Romney getting cornrows or Hillary Clinton cutting a salsa album. It is certainly easy to understand why this is so readily accepted. Many of us watch ESPN to forget at all costs what they are doing on C-SPAN.

But in an era where the building of publicly funded stadiums has become a substitute for anything resembling an urban policy; in a time when local governments build these monuments to corporate greed on the taxpayers' dime, siphoning off millions of dollars into commercial enterprise while schools, hospitals, and bridges decay, one can hardly say that sports exists in a world separate from politics. When the sports page—with its lurid tales of steroids, Michael Vick, referee gambling, and high-profile sexual harassment suits—no longer can be contained in the sports page, then clearly we need some kind of framework to take on and separate what we love and hate about sports so we can challenge it to change.

But sports are more than just a sounding board for war, graft, and mind-numbing moralism. It can also be a place of inspiration that doesn't transcend the political but becomes the political, a place where we see our own dreams and aspirations played out in dynamic Technicolor. Politics are remote and alien to the vast majority of people. But the playing field is where we can project our every thought, hope, and fear. We want to believe fiercely that this is the one place where ability alone determines how we are judged. If you can play, you will play, no matter your color, class, or gender. This is why boxers such as Joe Louis and the great Muhammad Ali, Olympic stars such as Wilma Rudolph and Jim Thorpe, tennis players such as Billie Jean King and the Williams sisters, and even golf's Tiger Woods (although he would never want the title) are viewed, consciously or not, as political beings—carriers of the dream that the playing field for all of us might be made a little more level.

This volume is an effort to resuscitate the political heart that beats in the sports world—to have a history that critically examines the political forces as well as the political power at work in the world of sports. It also stands proudly with the tradition of progressive dissenters in sports, people who have attempted to use the world of sports as a platform to advance ideas of resistance. These are people who have not allowed the politics of modern sport in the United States to be the province of those who financially control it—and those in government who would so casually exploit the platform. This book is dedicated to all rebel athletes. From five-foot jockeys to seven-foot hoopsters, they are the giants upon whose shoulders this hidden history rests.

Acknowledgments

First and foremost I need to recognize every sport, team, individual and athletic protest that didn't make the final cut. There were many. Anything that ended up on the cutting room floor falls on me alone. Let me know what you think I missed and maybe we can petition The New Press for a Volume II.

What survived was what I thought were the high points of the sports/politics collision. I also somehow survived, but would have been a stain on the side of the road if not for the people below.

It's a simple fact that without Andy Hsiao, who believed in the book from day one, and was still working on it in remote locales on day one thousand, there would be no book. Everyone else at The New Press, especially Ellen Adler, Marc Favreau, Maury Botton, and Jason Ng also fought for this book to make it to print. And a special mention to Sue Warga, whom I have never met, but had the unenviable task of copy editing—and taming—the manuscript. I owe you a drink.

Thanks also to the folks outside The New Press who helped with research: David Thurston, Alex Billet, and Travis Vogan were immeasurably helpful, especially David whose early advice about an embryonic draft shaped the book decisively for (I believe) the better.

There are writers who lent me support and inspiration, whether they knew it or not: Robert Lipsyte, Lester Rodney, Bill Rhoden, David Steele, Kevin Blackistone, Christine Brennan, David Aldridge, Will Leitch, DK Wilson, Mike "Mizzo" Tillery, Scoop Jackson, Jemele Hill, and the late Ralph Wiley.

Thanks to the independent media that gave this kind of sports writing a chance, particularly the people of Pacifica: Amy Goodman, Andrea Lewis, Amy Allison, Esther Armah, and Deepa Fernandes.

There are a community of authors and academics in the North American Society for the Sociology of Sport who also helped me. Their work is required reading for those who want to reclaim sports. And the Macalester triad of Peter Rachleff, Clay Steinman, and Leola Johnson, who put the fightin' in Fighting Scots.

And there are the editors and producers who both employ and tolerate me: BJ Schecter, Ben Osborne, Susan Price, Nick Goldberg, Gary Spiecker, Katrina vanden Heuvel, Steven Wells, Peter Rothberg, Joan Connell, "Hard Core" Richard Garner, Roane Carey, Matt Rothschild, Alan Maass, Elizabeth Schulte, Michael Goodfriend, David Goodfriend, Mark Walsh, Ari B, and Jeremiah Tittle on the wheels of schlemiel.

Thanks are due also to the people at Haymarket Books for their support throughout: Anthony Arnove, Julie Fain, Elizabeth Terzakis, Rachel Cohen, and Sarah Macaraeg.

Then there's my family. Michele and Sasha. My mother Jane and father Jim, Annie, Jason, Amira and Izzy, Marlene, Peter, Maggie, Michael, Susan, Ed, Bryan, Denise. Meme and Pop Pop. And the Carons, my emissaries to the Terrordome. Also thank you Uncle Robert for being there when we needed you. To my grandparents: Morris Zirin and Kate Zirin, Silvia Rubin, and the indomitable Alexander Rubin. All my love and deepest respect.

And to the athletes—the true jocks for justice that inspire a greater understanding of sports and society: John Carlos, Rubin Carter, Scott Fujita, Tommie Smith, Vivian Stringer, Lee Evans, Etan Thomas, Jim Bouton, Bill "Spaceman" Lee, Eddie Mustafa Muhammad, David Meggyesy, Troy Vincent, Jeff "Snowman" Monson, Toni Smith, Anthony Prior, Dr. Phil Shinnick, Joakim Noah, John Coursey, Shaun Harkin,

Sarah Knopf, Doug Harris, Steve Yellen, and Rus Bradburd. Keep bring-ing the heat.

Lastly, the greatest debt in this sports book is to Howard Zinn. Thank you for teaching us that we can write our own people's history. And thank you for showing us that we can use history to fight for the future.

· 1 ·

Until the Twentieth Century

Before they played, they danced. The Choctaw tribe would prepare as long as four months before a lacrosse match. Everyone planned, everyone readied themselves, and before the ball was dropped, everyone danced. The dance involved everyone who was willing and able: men and women, young and old. They would shake lacrosse sticks to the heavens, each side asking for a little boost from the gods, while food and drink were heartily consumed.

Once the game began, the players distinguished themselves from the dancers. They took the moccasins from their feet and a scrap of clothing encircled their waist. But wrapped around the swatch of cloth was an ornately woven belt. Extending from the back of the belt was a "tail" made of animal hair and feathers. Around their heads, they wore multihued headdresses made up of elaborate quills and cloth. But all of this was mellow compared to the play itself. An Anglo observer named George Catlin watched, his jaw on the floor.

> In these desperate struggles for the ball, when it is *up* . . . (where hundreds are running together and leaping, actually over each other's heads, and darting between their adversaries' legs, tripping

and throwing, and foiling each other in every possible manner, and every voice raised to the highest key, in shrill yelps and barks)! there are rapid successions of feats and of incidents, that astonish and amuse far beyond the conception of any one who has not had the singular good luck to witness them.

It was sport as he had never seen it; it both excited and repelled him. Excitation and repulsion: despite all the changes over time, our reaction to the spectacle of sports has remained remarkably constant.[1]

Native Americans played far more than lacrosse. They also took part in what we would recognize as forms of wrestling, football, racing, and hunting. The primary purpose was fun, but they also served a variety of other functions. Sports were a method of community training in agricultural or military skills. They also formed part of religious ceremony. The divisions between these functions were flagrantly ill-defined. Even when people's roles were separated into spectator and participant, the spectators were as engaged as any game crowd at the World Series.[2]

As the passengers of the *Mayflower* stumbled upon these games in the New World, they must have felt sledgehammered by the irony of it all. It was these very games that were emblematic of what many of the settlers—the Puritans—were attempting to escape.

Too Pure for Sports

King James of England loved his sports. In his "Kings Majesties Declaration to His Subjects concerning lawfull Sports to bee used," also known as the *Book of Sports* (1618), the king saw a national value—and a safety valve—in play. He wrote, "Our pleasure likewise is, Our good people be not disturbed, letted, or discouraged from any lawful reaction, Such as dancing, either of men or women, Archery for men, leaping, vaulting, or any such harmlesse, Recreation, nor from having of May Games, Whitsun Ales, and Morris-dances, and the setting up of Maypoles, and other sports."[3]

James believed that restricting sport "cannot but breed a great discontentment in Our people's hearts." He feared that an absence of sports would mean more time not in the church but in the alehouses, where people would be subject to all kinds of "idle and discontented speeches."[4]

But James's view that sports were essential was also quite mercenary: "The other inconvenience is that this prohibition barreth the common and meaner sort of people from using such exercises as may make their bodies more able for warre, when Wee or our successors shall have occasion to use them."[5] This is the seventeenth-century version of Dwight Eisenhower's famed dictum, "The true mission of American sports is to prepare young men for war."[6]

Puritans, however, were horrified by this encouragement of what they believed to be base debauchery. Puritan leader Thomas Hall said in 1660:

> If I would debauch a people, and draw them from God and his worship to superstition and Idolatry, I would take this course; I would open this gap to them, they should have Floralia and Saturnalia, they should have feast upon feast (as 'tis in Popery), they should have wakes to prophane the Lord's day, they should have May-Games, and Christmas-revels, with dancing, drinking, whoring, potting, piping, gaming, till they were made dissolute, and fit to receive any superstition, and easily drawn to bee of any, or of no religion."[7]

Magistrates in Massachusetts and other New England colonies sought to quell the influence of sports when they legislated against such wicked games as shuffleboard and lawn bowling.[8]

But even the Puritans were conflicted by this unyielding view. No less a Puritan than John Winthrop wrote about his own internal struggles with the role of sport. "When I had some tyme abstained from such worldly delights as my heart most desired, I grewe melancholick and uncomfortable. . . . I grewe unto a great dullnesse and discontent: which being at last perceived, I examined my heart, and findinge it needfull to recreate my mind with some outward recreation, I yielded unto it, and by a moderate exercise herein was much refreshed."[9]

A glacial change in attitudes was starting to seep in as early as the seventeenth century. The question raised—and still unanswered—by these nouveau Puritans was whether sports could be moderated or needed to be banished.

As Thomas Gouge in his *Young Man's Guide Through the Wilderness of This World to the Heavenly Canaan* wrote in 1672, "[Games] should be as Sauces to your Meat, to sharpen your appetite onto the duties of your Calling, and not to glut yourselves with them."[10]

New modes of play also arose, especially as the first glimmerings of a consumer society appeared early in the eighteenth century. Merchants sold toys and card tables, dancing instructors began to give lessons, and taverns and pubs sponsored games. The proprietor of Boston's British Coffee House advertised in 1714 that a bowling green now adjoined his establishment, where "all Gentlemen, Merchants, and others, that have a mind to Recreate themselves, shall be accommodated."[11]

But another way of looking at sports—as neither harmless diversion or corrupting debauchery—was on the rise among the new private ownership class. A leading periodical, *London Magazine*, wrote, "'Tis well known that such Diversions are chiefly enjoy'd by the common People; who being fatigued by labouring continually for a sorry Living, find a Relaxation highly necessary for them."[12] And no less an observer than Adam Smith argued in *The Wealth of Nations* that sports helped check the power of "fanatical" religious sects, for fun and games helped quell the alienation that made such "disruptive" groups attractive.[13]

What was behind these arguments? It's not too far-fetched to say that elites were starting to see in sports the importance—if not the beauty— that ordinary people already saw. The conquerors of the New World could sense that this was not merely fun and games but could play a necessary role in the developing modern society, transmitting values and providing a release from the workweek.

The Dirty South

The southern colonies carried little of the conflicted guilt of the northern Puritans. The aristocracy in places such as Virginia and the Carolinas molded their lives in European noble terms of building a leisured paradise. They envisioned an easy and bountiful life on fresh and fertile soil. The English heritage of fairs, feast days, and sports became the tangible expression of their aspirations.

In this culture, horse racing became the most popular, best organized, and most important American sport from the colonial era well into the nineteenth century. In addition to horse races, which could run over the course of a week, fox and quail hunts were a part of this life. But unlike the blue-blooded culture in Britain, the new southern aristocracy—these forerunners of Ted Turner—would also organize bloody cockfights, bare-knuckled boxing, and eye-gouging matches as well. These contests brought together wealthy and poor whites—almost exclusively male—in a common audience.

Sports became a way the colonies formed an independent—white—identity apart from Britain. By the eve of the Revolution, several wealthy men, northern and southern, ran their horses in a circuit of races from Leedstown, Virginia, through Annapolis, Philadelphia, New Jersey, and New York. Similarly, the rabid passion of new elites was cockfighting, something that would be unheard of in old Europe. Inheritances could be won or lost by the fighting spirit of angry chickens.[14]

The Other America: Sports in Bondage

For slaves, life was not foxhunts and horse races (unless they were charged with the actual care and maintenance of the animals). In fact, the entire conception of play among slaves on a colonial plantation was as different from whites' as bondage was from freedom. Games in slave quarters were played by boys and girls, men and women. Most common were those that required nothing in the way of equipment, such as races and dances. Some of these games and dances were geared to honor deities, while others were secular. Other games reflected the precariousness of their lives. If they played dodgeball, then no one would be eliminated. Some historians have attributed this to the desire to escape the reality that a family member could be "eliminated" by being sold at random.[15]

Plantation owners actively promoted sports as a way to direct energies and create harmony in bondage. It is for this very reason that the great abolitionist and former slave Frederick Douglass saw no joy in sports. Douglass didn't believe it could be a source of comfort or cultural expression. Instead, he was a merciless foe of anything that aided the harmony of plantation life. "To make a contented slave, you must make a thoughtless one. It is necessary to darken his moral and mental vision, and, as far as possible, to annihilate his power of reason. He must be able to detect no inconsistencies in slavery. The man that takes his earnings, must be able to convince him that he has a perfect right to do so. It must not depend upon mere force; the slave must know no Higher Law than his master's will. The whole relationship must not only demonstrate, to his mind, its necessity, but its absolute rightfulness."[16]

In the period before the American Revolution, there are some clear points of similarity between sports throughout the New World, whether in the Puritan Northeast, the wilder Virginia, or on a plantation. In each place, sports proved to be unconquerable: a balm against the harshness of the new climes, a source of community, and a means of escapism. It blossomed in the face of religiosity, political argument, and outright legal repression. It would prove to continue to be irrepressible in the years to come.

Sports and the American Revolution

As the tensions with the British crown deepened in the eighteenth century and calls for revolution spread from statehouses to public houses (pubs), delegates to the First Continental Congress urged people to "discountenance and discourage every species of extravagance and dissipation, especially horse-racing, and all kinds of gambling, cock fighting, exhibitions of shows, plays, and other expensive diversions and amusements."[17]

By the eve of battle, the colonies seemed transformed, with sports having receded dramatically into the background. As one Philadelphian put it, "The troublous times have come. . . . Everything bears a warlike aspect. We hear no more of races, of cockfighting . . . bullbaiting or bearbaiting; these men have something else to think of, they discuss the war views, they prepare for war."[18]

But sports actually spread and flourished during the Revolutionary

War in the battle regiments themselves, where they helped stave off boredom. General George Washington himself instructed his military leaders to defy the official rules and look the other way while soldiers played cards and all other kinds of homemade games at the front. (He did take a harder line against gambling, but it is evocative that amidst the freezing temperatures and deprivation of war, gambling was even an issue.)[19]

Class After the Revolution

From the beginning the Founding Fathers who designed these United States were acutely aware of the question of class. "All communities divide themselves into the few and the many," said Alexander Hamilton. "The first are the rich and the well-born, the other the mass of the people. The voice of the people has been said to be voice of God; and however generally this maxim has been quoted and believed, it is not true in fact. The people are turbulent and changing; they seldom judge or determine right. Give therefore to the first class a distinct permanent share in the government. . . . Can a democratic assembly who annually revolve in the mass of the people be supposed steadily to pursue the public good? Nothing but a permanent body can check the imprudence of democracy."[20] At the Constitutional Convention, Hamilton's commitment to the "the grand American experiment" was apparent when he suggested a president and Senate chosen for life.

Fellow Founding Father James Madison wrote in *The Federalist Papers* that the new nation must be organized to make sure "a rage for paper money, for an abolition of debts, for an equal division of property, or for any other improper or wicked project, will be less apt to pervade the whole body of the Union than a particular member of it."[21]

The United States had consolidated, but with unresolved questions that future generations would fight and die over. The questions of slavery, women's suffrage, and whether people without property could have a say in their country still would require answers.

In the decades after the Revolution, the United States reflected this polarized reality and exacerbated the divisions that had been accepted as natural. The country began an industrial push, immigrants swelled the population, Indians were exterminated. Profound polarization meant that the games of the day were ever more polarized as well.

Sports reflected every tension. The games played among the working many became more brutal than—and more segregated from—those of their wealthy counterparts. Bull baiting was an early favorite among the rural poor, with rat baiting its urban complement.

Here is one anonymous description of an early bull-baiting affair that took place in Baltimore:

> The bull was a fine, well-bred creature; seven or eight dogs were turned loose on him at once. They soon tore his ears off, and shockingly lacerated his head which made the poor thing bellow hideously and run about in every direction to the length of his chain, maddened with pain. In ten minutes he had killed one dog and lamed others; when I turned away in disgust.[22]

"Rat baiting" involved no "fine, well-bred creatures." Born in New York City (fitting, somehow), rat baiting would involve putting one hundred rats in a pit eight feet long. Then a dog would be dropped in the middle and watchers would bet on how many the poor pooch could kill in a given period of time.

This, in all its glory, was sports "from below," and the new northern elites were horrified by what they saw. The view that would define the twentieth century—that there were good sports, which bred correct American values, and bad sports—had not yet emerged. All sport was clearly and demonstrably sin. One could just count the rats to see that.

But in North and South, among black and white, sports became a necessary release for those denied a seat at Alexander Hamilton's table. New ideas about sports were direct reflections of how the country was changing. In 1790, there were roughly four million people in the United States, most living less than fifty miles from the Atlantic Ocean. By 1830, there were thirteen million, and by 1840, four and a half million had gone over the Appalachians and into the Mississippi Valley.[23]

In 1842, journalist Horace Greeley recounted with horror a boxing match that ended in death. The two-hour-and-forty-three-minute fight was, in Greeley's view, a case of someone being "immolated on the altar of sport." What turned Greeley's stomach particularly was that the atrocity was not shocking but expected.

> Let none say that his death was accidental. He openly avowed, on starting to the battleground, that he went to "win or die." He tied a black handkerchief to his post in the ring as his colors, to evince the same determination. Not one of the fifteen hundred who quietly looked on could have been ignorant that his life was the fearful stake of the contest.

Further roiling Greeley's senses was the way the spectacle was consumed:

> How shall we speak of the getters up and encouragers of this fight?—the gamblers, the brothelmakers, and keepers of flash groggeries, who were ever the chief patrons of "the ring," and who were the choice spirits of this festival of fiends? They were in raptures as the well-aimed, deadly blows descended heavily upon the face and neck of the doomed victim, transforming the image of God into a livid and loathsome ruin.

But Greeley's motives were not merely outrage. He made it a point to write that "the originators and fosterers of pugilism in this country are almost entirely foreigners by birth." Greeley's venom was also aimed at public officials. "Who licenses foreigners of at best suspicious character to keep houses of public entertainment in our city? If those pugilistic grog shops are kept without licenses, whose duty is it to close them? Why is it not done?"[24]

The kind of anger Greeley expressed was reinforced from the pulpit. An 1851 edition of *Congregationist* magazine preached:

> Let our readers, one and all, remember that we were sent into the world, not for sport and amusement, but for labor; not to enjoy and

please ourselves, but to serve and glorify God, and be useful to our fellow men. That is the great object and end of life. In pursuing this end, God has indeed permitted us all needful diversion and recreation. . . . But the great end of life after all is work. . . . The Christian fathers have a tradition that John Baptist, when a boy— being requested by some other boys to join them in play—replied, "I came into this world not for sport." Whether the Baptist ever said this, we are unable to decide. But whether he did or not, it is a remarkable saying. It is a true saying—however cutting may be the reproof which it carries to not a few of our fellow men. It is a saying which we may all with propriety adopt. "We came into this world not for sport." We were sent here for a higher and nobler object.[25]

Yet sports couldn't be legislated or moralized out of existence. What could be achieved in the South, however, were laws to make sure they didn't become a point of fraternization for black slaves and the white poor. The plantocracy, whose wealth had grown in comparison to that of poor southern whites, acted upon Frederick Douglass's words that they "separate both to conquer each."

In his multivolume history of blacks in sport called *A Hard Road to Glory*, Arthur Ashe wrote,

The southern states adopted so-called "Black Codes" to regulate social interaction among whites, slaves, and free blacks. Whites and blacks rubbed elbows at cockfights and horse races but seldom at any other sports events. In 1830, North Carolina passed a law stating "that is shall not be lawful for any white person or free Negro, or mulatto, or persons of mixed blood to play at any game of cards, dice, nine-pins, and any game of chance or hazard whether for money, liquor, or property or not, with any slave or slaves."[26]

The first tide of immigrants was arriving from Europe and brought their own traditions of play into the cities. At the same time, Native Americans with their own games and traditions were being vanquished.

In 1820, 120,000 Indians lived east of the Mississippi. By 1844, fewer than 30,000 remained. Those who survived invasion and disease had been forced under the shadow of genocide to migrate westward.

Lewis Cass, secretary of war, wrote in an 1830 article in *North American Review* that Americans must not regret "the progress of civilization and improvement, the triumph of industry and art, by which these regions have been reclaimed, and over which freedom, religion, and science are extending their sway."

Though he would have preferred this be done with "a smaller sacrifice; that the aboriginal population had accommodated themselves to the inevitable change of their condition . . . such a wish is in vain. A barbarous people, depending for subsistence upon the scanty and precarious supplies furnished by the chase, cannot live in contact with a civilized community."[27]

Women Want Off the Sidelines

The position of women pushed them to fight for their own political space. Thomas Jefferson said with condescension typical of the era that women were "too wise to wrinkle their foreheads with politics."[28]

The first women's rights convention in history took place at Seneca Falls in 1840. This was the home of the conference's key organizer, Elizabeth Cady Stanton. Her isolation and anger at the reality of second-class citizenship spurred her actions.

> The general discontent I felt with woman's portion as wife, mother, housekeeper, physician, and spiritual guide, the chaotic condition into which everything fell without her constant supervision, and the wearied, anxious look of the majority of women, impressed me with the strong feeling that some active measures should be taken to remedy the wrongs of society in general and of women in particular . . . all I had read of the legal status of women, and the oppression I saw everywhere, together swept across my soul. . . . I could not see what to do or where to begin—my only thought was a public meeting for protest and discussion.[29]

It was at Seneca Falls that the onetime slave Sojourner Truth would make a famous speech in which she said:

> That man over there says that woman needs to be helped into carriages and lifted over ditches. . . . Nobody ever helps me into carriages, or over mud-puddles or gives me any best place. And ain't I a woman? Look at my arm! I have ploughed, and planted, and gathered into barns, and no man could head me! And ain't I a woman? I would work as much and eat as much as a man, when I could get it, and bear the lash as well. And ain't I a woman? I have borne thirteen children and seen em most all sold off to slavery, and when I cried out with my mother's grief, none but Jesus heard me! And ain't I a woman?[30]

From these early times, sports was a way for women to rebel. One writer in an 1878 edition of the *American Christian Review* diagrammed the twelve-step downfall of any woman who dared engage in the sinful world of croquet.

1. A social party.
2. Social and play party.
3. Croquet party.
4. Picnic and croquet party.
5. Picnic, croquet and dance.
6. Absence from church.
7. Imprudent or immoral conduct.
8. Exclusion from the church.
9. A runaway-match.
10. Poverty and discontent.
11. Shame and disgrace.
12. Ruin.[31]

Despite these perils, women's colleges after the Civil War began to offer athletic options. Sports also came to symbolize the movement for suffrage. The development of the rubber tire and growth of the bicycle craze was widely accepted as a tool for women's liberation. In 1895, twenty-five years before women won the right to vote, suffragette Elizabeth Cady Stanton wrote, "Many a woman is riding to suffrage on a bicycle."

Susan B. Anthony agreed, saying,

Let me tell you what I think of bicycling. I think it has done more to emancipate women than anything else in the world: It gives women a feeling of freedom and self-reliance. I stand and rejoice every time I see a woman ride by on a wheel. The picture of free, untrammeled womanhood.[32]

Indeed, Stanton and Anthony recognized that women's right to physical play was essential and inextricable from citizenship. In a piece for the women's magazine *The Lily*, Stanton wholeheartedly rejected claims of a man's "physical superiority," writing, "We cannot say what the woman might be physically, if the girl were allowed all the freedom of the boy, in romping, swimming, climbing, playing ball."[33] By the turn of the century, many proponents emerged for women in sports. In 1901, Anne O'Hagan wrote:

With the single exception of the improvement in the legal status of women, their entrance into the realm of sports is the most cheering thing that has happened to them in the century just past. In the first place, there is the question of health. The general adoption of athletic sports by women meant the gradual disappearance of the swooning damsel of old romance, and of that very real creature, the lady who delighted, a decade or so ago, to describe herself as "high strung," which, being properly interpreted, meant uncontrolled and difficult to live with. Women who didn't like athletics were formed to take them up in self defense; and exercise meant firmer muscles, better circulation, a more equable temper, and the dethronement of the "nervous headache" from its high place in feminine regard.[34]

The Emergence of Baseball and the Birth of Nostalgia

Like jazz and the johnnycake, baseball was uniquely born and bred in the United States. The earliest form of baseball was called "rounders." It was played informally by working-class children in cities at the turn of the nineteenth century. It was also called "round ball," "sting ball," "soak ball," "burn ball," "town ball," the "Massachusetts Game," and sometimes even "base ball." The rules were ever malleable. A base could be a rock, a bat, an ax handle, a ball, or some shredded rubber.[35]

In 1845 the game took its great leap forward through the work of a man named Alexander Cartwright. As the country urbanized in this period, particularly the North, there was a broader thirst for rules and some sense of order. Gone for Cartwright would be the baseball of ragged children, in its place something for adults that could resemble clean entertainment and exercise. The national pastime, which many link to the pastoral, was created to tame the city. Cartwright wanted a city game without the anarchy of the city.

Cartwright, a bank teller and volunteer fireman, represented the striving middle class of the new urban centers. He founded the Knickerbocker Base Ball Club of New York, a group of young men (described as "gentlemen" in one account) that gathered after church on Sundays to play the sport according to Cartwright's ever-evolving rules. When the Knickerbockers were formed on September 23, 1845, membership was offered to "those whose sedentary habits required recreation." To the Knickerbockers, being a good player wasn't as important as having "the reputation of a gentleman."[36]

Cartwright was baseball's Prometheus, inventing out of whole cloth concepts such as tagging the runner instead of pegging him with the ball, using actual canvas bases, the shortstop, a batting order, the foul ball, and three strikes and three outs. He also dressed his team in natty flannel shirts, caps, and baggy pantaloons, creating a style that would outlive some of his other concepts, such as banning the use of gloves.[37]

The first "organized" game took place on June 19, 1846, just across the river from Manhattan, at Elysian Fields in Hoboken, New Jersey.

Carwright's team lost 23 to 1 even though he was also the umpire since only he knew all the rules.[38]

Cartwright's baseball was meant to be a different kind of endeavor than the bare-knuckled boxing, betting, and rowdy exhibitions associated with sport. As Ron McCullough writes in his book *From Cartwright to Shoeless Joe,*

> There were no grandstands (and no admission fees); you would either stand and watch the game from along the sidelines or park your horse and carriage in the outfield and observe from there (there were no outfield walls). Sometimes a tent or pavilion would be erected for the ladies, to shield them from the hot sun . . . The crowd was generally quiet and mannerly. Instead of cheering or boos, you would usually hear only polite applause and an occasional "Well done" when a particularly good play was made.[39]

In May 1857, the Knickerbockers met with reps from other clubs to codify the rules. The names of the other clubs present that day signified the national ascension and manifest confidence such as Empire, Eagle, Gotham, and Excelsior. The game's absence of a defined time structure, the leisurely pace, and the green diamond all spoke to a lost agrarian past many in the cities would remember wistfully. In other words, nostalgia existed at the game's birth.[40]

It was thought for decades that baseball's creator was a prominent Union general named Abner Doubleday who in his pre-martial days was said to have invented the sport. But this was myth. Neither his personal effects (letters, notes) nor his 1893 obituary in the *New York Times* makes mention of baseball. The tale was born when Albert Spalding, of Spalding sporting goods, put together a panel to declare how the sport began. Spalding, a former pitcher, team owner, and antiunion zealot, trumpeted that the game's roots lay in Cooperstown, New York, a bucolic all-American postcard of a place. Doubleday, a veteran who graduated from West Point and fought Indians, Mexicans, and Confederates, seemed as good a choice as any to be the founder. The myth was powerful enough and repeated enough that Cooperstown is now the site of the baseball hall of fame. There is no evidence Doubleday ever even set foot in Cooperstown.[41]

The best thing to happen to baseball was actually the Civil War. The intermingling of soldiers from geographically diverse regions and the boredom in between battles led to the spread of the game. The Civil War brought together people of different ethnicities and immigrant groups in the Union army, allowing regional games, particularly baseball, to spread after the war into every nook and cranny of the country. As Albert Spalding later wrote, "The sport had its baptism when our country was in the preliminary agonies of a fratricidal conflict. Its early evolution was among the men, both North and South, who, during the war of the 1860s, played the game to relieve the monotony of camp life in those years of melancholy struggle. It was the medium by which, in the days following the 'late unpleasantness,' a million warriors and their sons, from both belligerent sections, passed naturally, easily, gracefully from a state of bitter battling to one of perfect peace. . . . Baseball, I repeat, is war! And the playing of the game is a battle in which every contestant is a commanding general, who, having a field of occupation, must defend it; who, having gained an advantage, must hold it by the employment of every faculty of his brain and body, by every resource of his mind and muscle."[42]

Some soldiers would take bats and balls to training after enlisting or being drafted. In letters home, they would write of these games as bright spots in a bleak time. Private Alpheris B. Parker of the Tenth Massachusetts wrote: "The parade ground has been a busy place for a week or so past, ball-playing having become a mania in camp. Officer and men forget, for a time, the differences in rank and indulge in the invigorating sport with a schoolboy's ardor."[43]

George Putnam, a Union soldier, wrote with dark humor how one game suffered an abrupt end when their outfielders were attacked by incoming musket balls. "Suddenly there was a scattering of fire, which three outfielders caught the brunt; the centerfield was hit and was captured, left and right field managed to get back to our lines. The attack . . . was repelled without serious difficulty, but we had lost not only our centerfield, but . . . the only baseball in Alexandria, Texas."[44]

A Civil War Ends

After the Civil War, the smashing of the plantocracy laid the groundwork for industrialization to go national—and the country suffered the tumultuous birth pangs of the new unfettered capitalism. As Howard Zinn wrote:

> The cities . . . were death traps of typhus, tuberculosis, hunger, and fire. In New York, 100,000 people lived in the cellars of the slums; 12,000 women worked in houses of prostitution to keep from starving; the garbage, lying 2 feet deep in the streets, was alive with rats. In Philadelphia, while the rich got fresh water from the Schuylkill River, everyone else drank from the Delaware, into which 13 million gallons of sewage were dumped every day. In the Great Chicago Fire in 1871, the tenements fell so fast, one after another, that people said it sounded like an earthquake.[45]

Gustavus Myers, discussing the growth of the Astor family fortune, wrote,

> Is it not murder when, compelled by want, people are forced to fester in squalid, germ-filled tenements, where the sunlight never enters and where disease finds a prolific breeding-place? Untold thousands went to their deaths in these unspeakable places. Yet, so far as the Law was concerned, the rents collected by the Astors, as well as by other landlords, were honestly made. The whole institution of Law saw nothing out of the way in these conditions, and very significantly so, because, to repeat over and over again, Law did not represent the ethics or ideals of advanced humanity; it exactly reflected, as a pool reflects the sky, the demands and self-interest of the growing propertied classes.[46]

Unfettered capitalism also saw, for better and worse, the beginning of sports' commercialization. The manufacturing and marketing of sporting goods such as cricket bats, bows and arrows, billiard tables, and hunting and fishing gear also began around midcentury.

The Spindle-Shanked

During this era of industry, there began a fear among the new barons that they were raising slothful children completely unprepared to navigate the hardscrabble industrial world. Their concern bordered on the hysterical. *Harper's Monthly* sounded the alarm, calling this young generation "an apathetic-brained, a pale pasty-faced, narrow-chested, spindle-shanked, dwarfed race—mere walking manikins to advertise the last-cut of the fashionable tailor."[47] Oliver Wendell Holmes wrote in the *Atlantic Monthly* in 1858, "I am satisfied that such a set of black-coated, stiff-jointed, soft-muscled, paste-complexioned youth as we can boast in our Atlantic cities never before sprang from the loins of Anglo-Saxon lineage."[48]

Since putting their children to work was not a option, sports was seen as the way to put some calluses on their hands. This signaled the shift of conventional wisdom by the moral guardians of the republic. Instead of seeing sports as an immoral waste of time and an express lane to sin, they began to separate "good sports," which taught obeisance to authority, values, godliness, and could toughen up these petal-picking pasty-faces, from bad sports such as cockfighting and rat baiting. This new ethos was called "Muscular Christianity."[49] Elite schools such as Amherst, Brown, Harvard, Williams, and Yale initiated intercollegiate games. Prominent Protestant churches even began to build bowling alleys into their basements.[50]

In support of the new Muscular Christianity, Thomas Wentworth Higginson delivered an influential sermon titled "Saints and Their Bodies." He thundered, "Sentimentalists wither away like blanched potato-plants in the cellar; and then comes some vigorous youth from his outdoor work or play, and grasps the rudder of the age, as he grasped the oar, the bat, or the plough handle."[51]

But even at the beginnings of modern sport, Muscular Christianity meant different things to different people. Higginson was a supporter of John Brown's raid on Harpers Ferry and believed in abolition by any means necessary. Holmes was on the other side, believing that social stability should be the end, organized athletics the means.

Baseball After the Civil War

Baseball, with its appeals to nostalgia, normalcy, timelessness, and orientation on the upwardly mobile, took national hold after soldiers returned from the Civil War to their hometowns. The sport was proudly backward-looking, harking back to a "simpler time" before the world spun off its axis. Albert Spalding wrote:

> Neither our wives, our sisters, our daughters, nor our sweethearts may play baseball on the field. They may play cricket, but seldom do; they may play lawn tennis, and win championships; they may play basketball, and achieve laurels; they may play golf, and receive trophies; but baseball is too strenuous for womankind, except as she may take part in grandstand, with applause for the brilliant play, with waving kerchief to the hero of the three bagger, and, since she is ever a loyal partisan to the home team, with smiles of derision for the umpire when he gives us the worst of it, and, for the same reason, with occasional perfectly decorous demonstrations when it becomes necessary to rattle the opposing pitcher.[52]

But baseball was not immune to the "robber baron" mentality pervading the country. Entrepreneurs looked at baseball and saw dollar signs. Contests began to be advertised, marketed, and sold to the public. Game tickets ranged from a quarter to a shocking five dollars, and crowds were beginning to gather in the thousands. In the robber baron tradition, no players were paid despite the big money. As McCullough writes, "The idea that someone could actually make a living by playing some sort of game was preposterous."[53]

This changed in 1869 when the Cincinnati Red Stockings fielded a team with an annual payroll of $9,300. The Red Stockings worked for their money. They traveled nearly 12,000 miles and played before crowds totaling more than 200,000 people. Total gate receipts were $29,724.87; salaries and expenses, $29,726.26; net profit, $1.39.[54]

Gone were the days of Cartwright's gentlemen. Now gambling, drinking, and taunting were part of the experience. Women were given special enclosed canvas-covered seating. Baseball had become a game for the masses. In late August 1867, a team called the Mutuals traveled to Washington to meet with President Andrew Johnson at the White House. Perhaps oblivious to irony, Johnson, the man who oversaw the defeat of Radical Reconstruction in the South, declared baseball the "national game" even though it was not unusual at this time for "mixed matches" to take place where black teams would play white teams.[55]

Order Comes to Baseball

National game or not, the sport was floundering: graft, open cheating, and utter disorganization pervaded the game. It mirrored the way the early years of industry thrashed about in similar anarchy. This changed, in baseball at least, in 1876, when William Hulbert formed the National League of Professional Baseball Clubs. The National League's initial salvos were executed with a reformer's zeal. The league banned open gambling and liquor sales at games. It pledged to expel clubs that failed to stick to schedules, and it even prohibited the playing of league games on Sunday.[56]

The desire for order extended to labor-management relations. In 1879, the owners unanimously agreed to that they should be allowed to "reserve" five players for the next season. This was the birth of what came to be known as the reserve clause. The clause was eventually extended to cover all major league players, virtually binding a player to the same club for life. In 1887, almost ninety years before the issue of the reserve clause would be finally settled, John Montgomery Ward wrote a piece where he asked the question *Is the Base-Ball Player a Chattel*.

In the enactment of the reserve-rule the clubs were probably influenced by three considerations: they wished to make the business of base-ball more permanent, they meant to reduce salaries, and they meant to secure a monopoly of the game. . . . The effect of this was that a player reserved was forced to sign with the club reserving him, or quit playing ball altogether. . . . There is now no escape for the player. . . . Like a fugitive-slave law, the reserve-rule denies him a harbor or a livelihood, and carries him back, bound and shackled, to the club from which he attempted to escape. We have, then, the curious result of a contract which on its face is for seven months being binding for life. . . . These are, in part, the relations which exist between base-ball players and the associations by which they are employed. Is there a base-ball official who will claim them to be governed by any semblance of equity? Is it surprising that players begin to protest, and think it necessary to combine for mutual protection?[57]

Business was booming. Publishers of major daily newspapers, such as Charles A. Dana, William Randolph Hearst, and Joseph Pulitzer, increased circulation by creating regular sports sections with separate scribes: the creation of the sportswriter. By the 1880s, professional baseball was a $10-million-a-year enterprise.[58]

Rebellion Comes to Baseball

This was an era of not only robber barons but revolt, and baseball was not immune. In 1885, Billy Voltz, a minor league manager from Chattanooga, founded the National Brotherhood of Professional Base Ball Players, the first players' union. Their president was the aforementioned John Montgomery Ward, who also held a law degree from Columbia Law College. After negotiations failed to address salaries and the reserve clause, "Ward led the Brotherhood in open revolution at the end of the 1889 season."[59]

A large swath of players, furious about ownership's lack of desire to take their demands seriously, split and formed their own separate enterprise, called the Players' League, in 1890. Their slogan was "Fire the boss!" As sports historians Elliott Gorn and Warren Goldstein describe,

For a year, seven cities had two teams each, and the Players' League teams generally outdrew their National League rivals. Most athletes jumped to the Players' League, and the new teams were joint-ownership ventures between rich backers and the players themselves. Albert Spalding, now part owner of the National League Chicago franchise, denounced the players as anarchists and revolutionaries. Insofar as players (workers) attempted to take back control of their labor from owners, theirs was indeed a radical step. The old owners, however, had deeper pockets than the athletes; they outlasted their former employees, and when the dust settled, both the American Association and the Players' League collapsed, allowing the consolidation of the National League into a twelve-team organization.[60]

One writer called the entire Players' League exercise "a slave's revolt."[61] It is ironic that he would use the term, since one issue the first players' union failed to address was the most pressing issue of its time: the systematic expulsion of black players from the game.

Moses Fleetwood Walker

Moses Fleetwood Walker's promising baseball career was pounded to dust not by ownership but by the white players themselves. In 1887, future Hall of Famer Adrian "Cap" Anson refused to allow his team to play against Newark unless Walker and George Stovey were benched. Anson's team issued the following letter:

> Dear Sir:
>   We the undersigned, do hereby warn you not to put up Walker, the Negro catcher, the days you play in Richmond, as we could mention the names of seventy-five determined men who have sworn to mob Walker, if he comes on the grounds in a suit. We hope you will listen to our words of warning, so there will be no trouble, and if you do not, there certainly will be. We only write this to prevent much bloodshed, as you alone can prevent.[62]

As William Rhoden wrote "Billy Voltz refused to concede, and even sent Walker, who was scheduled to have an off day, to right field. He told Anson that if Chicago pulled out, Toledo wouldn't pay the guarantee. Anson backed down and the game was played. . . . At a game in Syracuse, Walker took the day off and sat in the dugout in street clothes. The Toronto manager asked Walker to leave the stadium. Heated words were exchanged. According to one account, Walker was surrounded by fans and allegedly brandished a loaded revolver and threatened to put a hole in someone in the crowd. He was arrested but released, and the next day he was in Syracuse's lineup."[63]

But Walker—even though he is now a baseball footnote and most fans think Jackie Robinson was the first African American player—didn't fade into obscurity. The son of an Ohio doctor, Walker went to Oberlin College, a school with roots in the abolitionist movement. (Oberlin will make a reappearance later in this book, as it was the only school that would offer Olympic gold medal winner Tommie Smith a job after the 1968 Olympics.) Walker went on to both run a hotel and become an inventor of early movie cameras. He was also a spokesperson for the idea that the only way blacks could escape white supremacy would be to secede from America. At age fifty-one, in 1908, he wrote the pamphlet *Our Home Colony,* a scathing indictment of the "race problem" in the United States:

> The annals of civilized history will not show [the white man's] equal in cruelty and inhumanity. That this people could suddenly change from such a character to a humane and Christian disposition in relation to the Negro is against the very nature and constitution of man. We see no possible hope that the Negro will ever secure the enjoyment of this social freedom and equality. Without it, he can never expect full and complete development.[64]

Walker called for a mass exodus to Liberia, an idea rooted in his long-worn pessimism about the incurability of white supremacy. The only solution to "the Negro problem or if you prefer, the white man's problem" is "the wholesale emigration of the Negro from America. . . . We do not believe in the wholesale deportation of the Negro at the present time. . . . But the time is fast approaching when the Negroes at the very least must leave the Southern states." In Walker we see a precursor to the Garveyite movement of the 1920s. In other sections of Walker's work, he writes bracingly about everything from the effect of white dolls on young black girls to the inhumanity of lynchings. The sham of baseball's "level playing field" created a man with no illusions in the promise of America. His baseball experience produced enduring scars.[65]

The forceful excising from the league of black players led to tragicomic episodes of managers trying by any means to get the best talent on the field. Hall of Fame Baltimore Orioles manager John "The Little General" McGraw signed an African American player named Charley Grant. But this bit of ancestral knowledge was kept between McGraw and Grant. McGraw instead told the press that the Orioles had signed the great Cherokee sports star "Tokohoma." Unfortunately, McGraw's plan fell apart when friends of Grant saw him on the field and went en masse to the team hotel to celebrate his triumph.[66]

These episodes had repercussions far beyond Walker, Charley Grant, and the other handful of African American ballplayers. The whitening of the national pastime became a living symbol of the exclusion of blacks from all walks of public life. It also created what came to be known as baseball's "color line," which stubbornly endured until 1947.

Booms and Busts

But while the ruling elite were worried about their sons' spindly shanks, they had bigger concerns in the streets. This was an era of marginal booms and crushing busts for everyone not named Astor, Vanderbilt, Rockefeller, Carnegie, Mellon, Gould, or Morgan.

Economic depression hit in 1877. In the sweltering summer of that year, drinking water and sewage intermingled, killing large numbers, disproportionately children. The *New York Times* wrote: "Already the cry of the dying children begins to be heard. . . . Soon, to judge from the past, there will be a thousand deaths of infants per week in the city." In the first week of July 139 babies died in Baltimore.[67]

This was also the year of the general strike. When the great railroad strikes of 1877 were over, a hundred people were dead, a thousand people had gone to jail, a hundred thousand workers had gone on strike, and sympathy actions had sprouted among the unemployed.[68]

The tumult was a harbinger of transformation. From 1860 to 1900 the population of the United States grew from 31 million to 75 million; now 20 million people lived west of the Mississippi, and the number of farms grew from 2 million to 6 million. New York grew from 850,000 to 4 million, Chicago from 110,000 to 2 million, Philadelphia from 650,000 to 1.5 million.[69]

With overcrowded cities came conflict. In 1884, women's assemblies of textile workers and hat makers went on strike. The following year in New York, cloak and shirt makers, both men and women (holding separate meetings but acting together), went on strike. The *New York World* called it "a revolt for bread and butter." They won higher wages and shorter hours.[70]

The year 1893 saw an economic crisis that rocked the country. After years of unfettered growth, the walls tumbled down: 642 banks and 16,000 businesses shut their doors. Out of 15 million workers, 3 million were unemployed. Rage reigned.[71] As the *Chicago Times* described the railroad strike of 1894:

> To say that the mob went wild is but a weak expression. . . . The command to charge was given. . . . From that moment only bayonets were used. . . . A dozen men in the front line of rioters received bayonet wounds. . . . Tearing up cobble stones, the mob made a determined charge. . . . the word was passed along the line for each officer to take care of himself. One by one, as occasion demanded, they fired point blank into the crowd. . . . The police followed with their clubs. A wire fence inclosed the track. The rioters had forgotten it; when they turned to fly they were caught in a trap. The police were not inclined to be merciful, and driving the mob against the barbed wires clubbed it unmercifully. . . . The crowd outside the fence rallied to the assistance of the rioters. The shower of stones was incessant. The ground over which the fight had occurred was like a battlefield. The men shot by the troops and police lay about like logs.[72]

Clearly more was needed than rifles and bayonets to assuage such a restive populace. The "values of sport" were also central to this project.

Young Man, There's No Need to Feel Down

The organization that most strongly espoused the "values of sport" was the Young Men's Christian Association, the YMCA. Founded first in England in 1844, and reaching North America in 1851, the Y became the place for acculturation and a bulwark against rebellion. By 1869, San Francisco, Washington, D.C., and New York City all had YMCA gymnasiums. Within twenty-five years, there were 261 Y gyms scattered across America. The Y adopted the inverted triangle as its emblem in 1895, signifying the three components of fully developed man: mind, body, and spirit.[73]

"Wholesome athletics certainly were part of a social control movement designed to channel people, especially working-class and immigrant youths, into safe activities," Gorn and Goldstein write. "By the end of the century, many reformers believed that sports could be a socially stabilizing force that would help Americanize foreigners, pacify angry workers, clear the streets of delinquents, and stem the tide of radicalism. Sports could deflect tensions away from an oppressive social structure and channel energy into safe activities that taught the modern industrial values of hard work, cooperation, and self-discipline, and thereby help secure social order."[74]

Horse Racing

In the nineteenth century, horse racing was perhaps the most popular sport in the United States. It was also a sport dominated by African Americans. The first Kentucky Derby, also known as the "Run for the Roses," took place on May 17, 1875, in front of ten thousand spectators. Of the fifteen jockeys, fourteen were black. White riders at this time generally did not challenge the black jockeys' preeminence because of the stigma attached to working a "slave job." As Rhoden writes, "The position of a black who rode for wealthy racing stables after the Civil War was quite similar to that of a slave who rode for his master. . . . The black jockeys were hirelings who rode primarily for someone else's business."[75]

The most famous horseman, the Michael Jordan of the stables, was

Isaac Murphy. Murphy made his riding debut in 1875 at the tender age of fourteen, just five days after that first Kentucky Derby. After three years, Murphy was one of the highest-paid athletes in the country. His annual income was roughly $20,000—nearly more than the entire payroll of Cap Anson's Chicago White Stockings. But the period at the end of the nineteenth century was so rife with reaction that Murphy's dominance represented a threat to the ideas of white supremacy.[76]

In 1889, after another day of dominance for the black jockeys, the *New York Herald* wrote, "The sons of Ham outrode the children of Japhet with a vengeance, for not a single white was successful in guiding a winner past the judges. It was a field day for the dusky riders and they forced their Caucasian competitors to take positions in the background."[77]

A headline in an 1890 issue of *Spirit of the Times* remarked on the disturbing truth that "all the best jockeys of the West are colored."[78] Isaac Murphy himself commented, "I am disgusted with the way they treated me in the East during the summer. When I won it was all right, but when I lost they would say, 'There's that nigger, drunk again.' I tell you, I'm disgusted and soured on the whole business."[79]

Two years before Murphy died in 1896, the Jockey Club was formed as the national administrative arm of the horse racing industry. Its central purpose was to license jockeys on an annual basis. After the Jockey Club came into being, black jockeys just weren't reregistered, and horse owners received the message from their brethren to not even try to protest. Even riding a horse well was too much for whites to stomach in the public sphere.[80]

Boxing

No sport has chewed up athletes (especially black athletes) and spit them out quite the way boxing has. The first boxers in the United States were slaves. Southern plantation owners amused themselves by putting together their strongest chattel and having them fight it out while wearing iron collars.[81]

But after the abolition of slavery, boxing was unique among sports because, unlike every other major athletic venture, it was desegregated—

except when white boxers refused to step in the ring with black opponents. Boxing champion John L. Sullivan, for example, refused to fight black contenders, claiming that he owed it to his fans not to "sully the white race," a policy that conveniently kept him from facing arguably the finest boxer of the 1880s, the Australian Peter Jackson.[82]

Promoters didn't promote integrated bouts because they were in any way progressive. Quite the contrary. The brutality of the sport itself gave promoters a stage to make a buck off the rampant racism in American society. Unwittingly, these early fight financiers opened up space where the white supremacist ideas of society could be challenged. As the *Chicago Tribune* wrote about a contest between a black fighter, George Dixon, and a white fighter, Jack Skelly, "White fans winced every time Dixon landed on Skelly. The sight was repugnant to some men from the South. A darky is alright in his place here, but the idea of sitting quietly by and seeing a colored boy pommel a white lad grates on southerners."[83]

The *New Orleans Times-Democrat* put it much more bluntly: "What with bruises, lacerations and coagulated blood, Skelly's nose, mouth, and eye presented a horrible spectacle . . . some even turned away their heads in disgust . . . at that face already disfigured past recognition. . . . It was a mistake to match a negro and a white man, a mistake to bring the races together on any terms of equality, even in the prize ring. . . . It was not pleasant to see a white man applaud a negro for knocking another white man out."[84]

Charles A. Dana, of the *New York Sun*, wrote:

We are in the midst of a growing menace. The black man is rapidly forging to the front ranks in athletics, especially in the field of fisticuffs. We are in the midst of a black rise against white supremacy. . . . Less than a year ago [black Australian] Peter Jackson could have whipped the world—[Jim] Corbett, [Robert] Fitzsimmons, . . . but the white race is saved from having at the head of pugilism a Negro. . . . There are two Negroes in the ring today who can thrash any white man breathing in their respective classes: George Dixon and Joe Walcott. If the negro is capable of developing such prowess in those divisions of boxing, what is going to stop him from making the same progress in the heavier ranks?

What America needs now is another John L. Sullivan. . . . How is it that these sable champions spring up all at once? Is it because they are far and away better than their white brethren or is the Caucasian race deteriorating? . . . Wake up you pugilists of the white race! Are you going to permit yourself to be passed by the black race? . . . Some say that the 'colored brother' is not a man of the highest courage, but I doubt that. . . . He has always been made to believe that he belongs to an inferior race. . . . But . . . the Negro has evinced as much courage in combat as the white man.[85]

Women's Hoops

Early women's basketball, played on elite campuses, was a very rough-and-tumble operation. Freed from their corsets, they let their elbows fly freely as well. This caused a reaction sharper than those elbows. As Susan Cahn writes in the book *Coming on Strong*:

> Smith College Athletic Director Senda Berenson, shocked by both the rough play and the negative publicity it generated, resolved to introduce stricter regulations for women's play . . . in 1899 she organized a National Women's Basketball Committee under APEA auspices. Through the Spalding sporting goods company, the committee issued its first official women's rulebook in 1901. The rules allowed players to dribble the ball only one time (later three bounces were allowed) and prohibited physical contact and any effort to hinder the shooter. By contrast, the five player "boys' rules," played by boys, men, and girls or women who had not encountered the new rules, allowed all players to run the full court and placed fewer restrictions on dribbling or on guarding the offensive player.

Sports for women—particularly upper-class women—were tied to more than physical expression.[86]

For women in this era, exercise and games were a privilege, a sign of status. If a woman played golf, rode horses, or played tennis, it meant she belonged to a new citadel of status: the country club. In 1894, journalist Caspar Whitney wrote a paean to this institution in *Harper's New Monthly*:

> Who shall deny the country club to have been a veritable blessing, what with its sport and pleasure and health-giving properties that have brushed the cobwebs from weary brains, and given us blue sky, green grass, and restful shade in exchange for smoke-laden atmosphere, parboiled pavements, and the never ceasing glare and racket of the city? And womankind too has partaken of country-club as she should of all blessings, in relaxation from the petty trials of housekeeping, and the parade and deceits of society, while the hue of health has deepened in her cheeks. It has been a wholesome growth all round.[87]

Theodore Roosevelt

Out of this era of Muscular Christianity came its most prominent spokesperson: Theodore Roosevelt. In his piece "Professionalism in Sports," published in 1890, the thirty-one-year-old Rough Rider wrote, "There is a certain tendency . . . to underestimate or overlook the need of the virile, masterful qualities of the heart and mind. . . . There is no better way of counteracting this tendency than by encouraging bodily exercise, and especially the sports which develop such qualities as courage, resolution, and endurance."[88]

In 1893, in "The Value of Athletic Training," Roosevelt proclaimed:

> In a perfectly peaceful and commercial civilization such as ours there is always a danger of laying too little stress upon the more virile virtues—upon the virtues which go to make up a race of statesmen and soldiers, of pioneers and explorers by land and sea, of bridge-builders and road-makers, of commonwealth-builders— in short, upon those virtues for the lack of which, whether in an individual or in a nation, no amount of refinement and learning of gentleness and culture, can possibly atone. These are the very

qualities which are fostered by vigorous manly out-of-door sports.[89]

All of the "masterful nations" in history, Roosevelt declared, encouraged rugged sports. Athletic training could help revitalize commercial America and build a new Anglo-Saxon superrace. Albert Spalding agreed—and saw baseball as a way to do it:

Baseball has "followed the flag." It followed the flag to the front in the [eighteen-] sixties and received then an impetus which has carried it to half a century of wondrous growth and prosperity. It has followed the flag to Alaska, where, under the midnight sun, it is played on Arctic ice. It has followed the flag to the Hawaiian Islands, and at once supplanted every other form of athletics in popularity. It has followed the flag to the Philippines, to Porto Rico, and to Cuba, and wherever a ship floating the Stars and Stripes finds anchorage today, somewhere on a nearby shore the American National Game is in progress.[90]

The game did follow the flag. It also followed an imperial expansion that strongly influenced how games were taught and played throughout the United States.

· 2 ·

Rough Riding

Today sports often resembles a substitute for war. In 1900, America's most prominent athletic spokesperson wanted war to begin to substitute for sports. The man was Teddy Roosevelt, and at age forty-two, before he was chosen to run as William McKinley's vice president, he was already a known figure. A member of one of the country's most prominent families, TR was known as a leading proponent of "Muscular Christianity." But more than anything else, he was catapulted to the vice presidency by his stature as a war celebrity, someone whom the media had already burnished in a golden hue after he organized the Rough Riders in the Spanish-American War. The myth of the Rough Riders, built around Teddy's fame, was that they were a gentlemen's corps of tremendous effectiveness. Reality was harsher: three-quarters of all Rough Riders either died, were wounded, or were struck by disease, and Teddy himself caught malaria.[1]

In 1897, a year before the Rough Riders saw action, Roosevelt wrote, "In strict confidence . . . I should welcome almost any war, for I think this country needs one."[2] The itch to conquer was not his alone. This was the age of empire. As the *Washington Post* editorialized right before the Spanish-American War, "A new consciousness seems to have come upon us—the consciousness of strength—and with it a new appetite, the yearning to show our strength. . . . Ambition, interest, land hunger, pride, the mere joy of fighting, whatever it may be, we are animated by a new sensation. We are face to face with a strange destiny. The taste of Empire is in the mouth of the people even as the taste of blood in the jungle."[3] And Indiana senator Albert Beveridge bellowed in 1897, "American factories are making more than the American people can use; American soil is producing more than they can consume. Fate has written our policy for us; the trade of the world must and shall be ours."[4]

But it was Teddy Roosevelt, his love of war matched only by his love of sport, who best exemplified the new mood. And in the wake of the assassination of William McKinley, the forty-two-year-old Roosevelt became the youngest president in the country's history. As he told the Naval War College: "All the great masterful races have been fighting races. . . . No triumph of peace is quite so great as the supreme triumph of war."[5]

The philosopher William James, who became one of the leading anti-imperialists of his time, wrote a scathing assessment of Roosevelt's character, describing him as a man who "gushes over war as the ideal condition of human society, for the manly strenuousness which it involves, and treats peace as a condition of blubberlike and swollen ignobility, fit only for huckstering weaklings, dwelling in the gray twilight and heedless of the higher life."[6]

In the tragic absence of a permanent state of imperial war, Roosevelt became the great promoter of having the federal government fund sports programs as a cornerstone of the new American century. Just as King James feared that the absence of sports would leave his subjects unprepared for "warre," Roosevelt saw masculinity and Muscular Christianity as symbiotic with a nation poised to conquer.

In 1903, he encouraged the launching of the Public Schools Athletic League—for boys only, of course—with the financial backing of some of America's most prominent bankers and industrialists. In seven years, seventeen cities adopted versions of the program. The mission statement of the PSAL was to "provide opportunities for educating students in physical fitness, character development and socialization skills through an athletic program that fosters teamwork, discipline and sportsmanship."[7]

Football

But Roosevelt—and the ethos of Muscular Christianity—saw a higher function for sports than merely keeping the urban poor in fighting shape. Just as their fathers had used sports to keep them from becoming "spindle-shanked," Roosevelt's generation imparted that same idea to their own children of privilege. Teddy's particular love was football. As he wrote in "The American Boy," "In life, as in a foot-ball game, the principle to follow is: Hit the line hard; don't foul and don't shirk, but hit the line hard."[8]

Before this period, football at the elite colleges bore no resemblance to the game today. The sport dates back to 1869, when Princeton and Rutgers played the inaugural intercollegiate game. Harvard and Yale started their black-and-blue-blooded rivalry in 1875, and the following year, four Ivy League schools formed the Intercollegiate Football Association to standardize rules. But the word *rules* overstates the degree of order on the field. The games had more in common with the bull- and rat-baiting days of yore than anything one would expect to come out of the Ivy League. Games tended to have all the poetry and artistry of a drunken brawl. The results were deadly. As sportswriter Dan Daly put it, "Modern football, we tend to forget, was born in a funeral parlor." In 1905, eighteen players died resulting from injuries on the field. It was so bad that in 1906, Roosevelt himself threatened to have the sport banned.[9] Despite efforts to clean up the sport, which included the formation of the National Collegiate Athletic Association (NCAA), thirty-three college players died in 1910.[10]

The man who started to turn football away from something resembling outtakes from *Braveheart* was a part-time coach and professor at Yale named Walter Camp. His ideas took several decades to emerge from the New Haven campus, but by 1892, at the age of thirty-three, Camp was already being called the "father of American football." He introduced everything from the forward pass and the line of scrimmage to the idea of teams fielding eleven men per side. Many today see in football a kind of war game with pads. But Camp's model for how to order the game was based not on the military model but on the factory model. It was the imposed discipline of early industrial life that shaped football. As president and chairman of the New Haven Clock Company, Camp had firsthand knowledge of the factory system. Football should be a place, he believed, to teach order and obedience.[11]

As Michael Oriard wrote in *Reading Football*, there was a direct correlation between Frederick Taylor's "four elements of scientific management (Science, Harmony, Cooperation, and Maximum Output) otherwise known as Taylorism, and Camp's principles of 'team work, strategy, and tactics.' Such parallels are more than coincidence. Walter Camp's professional life was lived in a modern manufacturing enterprise."[12]

Camp wrote, "Finding a weak spot through which a play can be made, feeling out the line with experimental attempts, concealing the real strength [until] everything is ripe for the big push, then letting drive where least expected, what is this, an outline of football or business tactics?" This made a winner out of Yale in the early years of football.[13]

Camp preached the gospel of football around the country in countless sermons, articles, and coaching retreats. He wasn't only selling a sport, but a way of life. "Camp was instrumental through writing and lecturing in attaching an almost mythical atmosphere of manliness and heroism to the game not previously known in American team sports," wrote Richard P. Borkowski.[14]

Camp delivered the sport from the violent pathology of elite northeastern colleges, making it something that had a national following. The first Thanksgiving game between Harvard and Yale, played in New York City, drew only 5,000 fans. But by 1884 that figure was 10,000, and by the late 1880s the Thanksgiving games were buzzworthy events. In the early 1890s crowds of 30,000–40,000 people were the norm.[15]

The sport was machismo for the middle classes. Future Olympic chieftain Avery Brundage wrote as a young man, "No better place than a football field could be chosen to test out a man. Here a fellow is stripped of most of the finer little things contributed by ages of civilization, and his virgin nature is exposed to the hot fire of battle. It is man against man, and there is no more thorough mode of exposing one's true self."[16]

Yale's yearly football receipts grew to $100,000 by the end of the nineteenth century, more than its law school or medical school budget and one-eighth of the entire school budget. King Football had taken the throne.[17]

Football and the Shaping of Paul Robeson

This early era of football forged one of the enduring freedom fighters of the twentieth century, Paul Robeson. Robeson is best known as an actor, singer, and political activist, but he was also one of the finest football players ever to come out of the state of New Jersey. Robeson achieved this stature at Rutgers University. He was only the third African American student in the history of the school and during his years of study was the only black student on campus.[18]

The segregation of the day was so intense that Paul Robeson, football hero and one of the great defining voices of the century, couldn't join the Rutgers glee club. His coach, George Foster Sanford, was thrilled at the prospect of having a player with Robeson's skill, but half his thirty-man team had pledged not to play if a "Negro" joined the team.

"On my first day of scrimmage," Robeson remembered years later, "they set about making sure I would not get on their team. One boy slugged me in the face and smashed my nose—an injury that has been a trouble to me as a singer ever since. And then as I was down, flat on my back, another boy got me with his knee. He just came over and dropped his knee into my upper body, dislocating my right shoulder. At the age of seventeen, that was tough going—a broken nose, a dislocated shoulder, a split lip, two swollen eyes and plenty of other cuts and bruises."[19] Robeson was laid up for a week and a half but returned to the field determined to hit back:

I made a tackle and was on the ground, my right hand extended beyond the pile-up and palm down. . . . A boy came over and stepped down hard on my hand. He meant to break the bones. The bones held, but the cleats of his shoes took every single one of the finger-nails off of my right hand. The next play again came right at my defensive end position; the whole backfield came at me. In rage, I swept out my arms . . . [and the] interference just seemed to fall down. Then there was only the ball carrier; I wanted to kill him. . . . I actually had him up above my head. . . . I was going to smash him so hard to the ground that . . . he'd break right in two.[20]

It was then that Coach Sanford put Robeson on the varsity. It was also then that Robeson's teammates stopped trying to "kill him." His teammates moved further toward begrudging acceptance when the team was shut out at the hands of rival Princeton in a game where Robeson rode the bench.

When Rutgers played West Virginia later that year, Robeson dominated on both sides of the ball. West Virginia's coach yelled at his players, "Any player who can take the beating that Robeson has taken from you, giving as good as he's gotten and without squealing, is not Black. *He's a white man!* Now go back out there and play like hell—and give him a break!"[21]

Robeson understood the challenges and welcomed them. "When I was out on a football field or in a classroom or anywhere else, I wasn't just there on my own. I was the representative of a lot of Negro boys who wanted to play football, who wanted to go to college; and as their representative, I had to show that I could take whatever they handed out. . . . This was part of our struggle."[22]

James D. Carr, Rutgers' first African American student, a Phi Beta Kappa who graduated in 1892, wrote to school president William H.S. Demarest. Carr warned with prescience about Robeson's possible future move toward revolutionary politics:

I am deeply moved at the injustice done to a student of Rutgers in good and regular standing of good moral character and splendid mental equipment—one of the best athletes ever developed at Rutgers—who, because guilty of a skin not colored as their own, was excluded from the honorable field of athletic encounter, as one inferior. . . . Not only he, but his race as well was deprived of the opportunity of showing its athletic ability, and, perhaps, its athletic superiority. . . . Can you imagine his thoughts and feelings when, in contemplative mood, he reflects in the years to come that his Alma Mater faltered and quailed when the test came, and that she preferred the holding of an athletic game to the maintenance of her honor and principle?[23]

Once Robeson achieved both in the classroom and on the football field, the university was all too quick to pat itself on the back for its remarkable openmindedness in "embracing" him. The school newspaper, the *Targum*, ran an editorial following Robeson's graduation that read:

Individuals occasionally complain that there is no equality for members of the colored race in the United States. It is true that what is generally known as social equality has not been granted by the majority of whites. . . . But one fact which deserves consideration, and is too frequently neglected, is that equality does exist . . . for those colored men and women who struggle for success. Look at Paul Robeson, former All-American football player and one of four men tapped for the senior honor society when he was an undergraduate at Rutgers. What other nation has a record of encouraging Negro achievement even remotely comparable to the record of the United States? This is something to be emphasized through the length and breadth of the land. For when dictators of red radicalism and Black reaction really concentrate on splitting America internally, they will no doubt start by making fancy promises to the colored people—telling them that they have been oppressed.[24]

The irony is that Robeson came to look to "red radicalism" as a way to fight racism.

World War I
Sports tend to make their most jarring transformations in periods of war. During the American Revolution, sports receded to the background of

daily life but were critical among Washington's troops in fighting the boredom of base camp. After the Civil War, sports that were previously regional spread across the nation. World War I accelerated sports through a similar period of transition.

The war itself was deeply unpopular. Six weeks after the declaration of war, the government expected 1 million men to sign up and fight— but only 73,000 had enlisted. Congress then instituted conscription to make up the difference.[25]

The right to free speech was also sharply abridged. Eugene Debs, the labor leader and socialist who had run for president four times, was given a ten-year sentence for his 1918 speech in Canton, Ohio, where he said, "They tell us that we live in a great free republic; that our institutions are democratic; that we are a free and self-governing people. That is too much, even for a joke. . . . Wars throughout history have been waged for conquest and plunder. . . . And that is war in a nutshell. The master class has always declared the wars; the subject class has always fought the battles."[26]

In his closing remarks to the jury at his trial, Debs said, "Your honor, years ago I recognized my kinship with all living beings, and I made up my mind that I was not one bit better than the meanest on earth. I said then, and I say now, that while there is a lower class, I am in it; while there is a criminal element, I am of it; while there is a soul in prison, I am not free." In 1920, running for president on the Socialist Party platform from prison, Debs received 13 percent of the popular vote.[27]

As President Woodrow Wilson continued his unpopular prosecution of his "war to end all wars," he saw sports as a critical way to prepare future troops. There were voices that thought sports should be suspended for the duration of the war, but Wilson strongly believed otherwise. "I hope that the normal course of college sports will be continued," he said, ". . . as a real contribution to the national defense." This is exactly what happened.[28]

For the first time in American history, sports were formally linked to military preparedness. Write Gorn and Goldstein:

Athletics now would be sanctioned and even financed by the federal government. Recreational experts assured the nation that by playing baseball and football, by boxing and exercising, young American men would be fit enough for war. . . . But not until World War I were athletic training and competition systematically adopted for troop morale, hygiene, and physical readiness for war. Recreation professionals greeted these developments enthusiastically. . . . The celebration went even further, as the AEF [American Expeditionary Forces] championships slid over into the Inter-Allied Games (also known as the Military Olympics) in Joinville, France, in the summer of 1919, an astonishing extravaganza staged in the midst of postwar devastation which nevertheless drew something like half a million spectators over two weeks.[29]

Walter Camp, by now nearly sixty, became athletic director of the navy.

Jack Johnson

For African Americans, this was a time of terror. Hollywood gave them D.W. Griffith's *Birth of a Nation*, a Ku Klux Klan propaganda film (based on a play called *The Klansman*) that President Wilson enthusiastically screened in the White House in 1915, calling it "history writ by lightning." The Klan achieved a remarkable resurgence, using *Birth of a Nation* to recruit. Not surprisingly, this was a period that saw lynchings reach epidemic proportions. In 1919 alone, one estimate is that there were eighty-three lynchings in the United States.[30]

The place for African Americans was precarious; for African American athletes, it was no less so. The color line in baseball was entrenched. African American jockeys had been rooted out of their sport. In football, Yale's great African American player Fritz Pollard was told after one game, "You're a nigger, but you're the best goddamned football player I ever saw." That was a high point.[31]

For African American women, Olympic official Norman Cox lobbied that "the Committee should create a special category of competition for them—the unfairly advantaged 'hermaphrodites' who regularly defeated 'normal women,' those less skilled 'child-bearing types' with "largish breasts, wide hips [and] knocked knees."[32]

This was the era of deeply racist pseudoscience. The attitude was not only that blacks were mentally inferior to whites, but also that they were physically inferior to whites. Blacks were cast as too lazy and too undisciplined ever to be taken seriously as athletes. In the midst of these ideological rapids stood Jack Johnson.

When Johnson became the first heavyweight boxing champion with black skin in 1908, his victory created a serious crisis in the conventional wisdom about race. The media whipped up a frenzy around the need for "a great white hope" (a phrase coined by author Jack London) to restore order to the boxing world—and the world in general. Former champion Jim Jeffries was coaxed out of retirement and said, "I am going into this fight for the sole purpose of proving that a white man is better than a Negro."[33]

In the weeks before their fight, Johnson—in marked contrast to the standard African American posture of the day—was more than willing to be heard. In a July 4, 1910, *Philadelphia Inquirer* story titled "Jack Johnson Believes He's Jeff's Master," he is quoted as saying, "I honestly believe that in pugilism I am Jeffries' master, and it is my purpose to demonstrate this in the most decisive way possible. . . . Let me say in conclusion that I believe the meeting between Mr. Jeffries and myself will be a great test of strength, skill, and endurance. The tap of the gong will be music to me."[34]

This might seem today like something Dame Judi Dench would say to Helen Mirren before the Oscars, but at the time it was verbal fireworks. Another piece that day in the *Dallas Morning News*, titled "Negroes Praying for Johnson," says, "Some others fear trouble if he [Johnson] wins and are consequently boosting Jeffries. . . . For the first time Independence Day will be enjoyed as a real holiday by the negroes tomorrow."[35]

In the black press, the backing of Johnson was without equivocation. On February 4, 1910, a cartoon on the front page of the African American newspaper the *Chicago Defender* showed Johnson and Jeffries in the ring, with Johnson surrounded by ominous spirits bearing names such as "Race Hatred," "Prejudice," and "Negro Persecution." The caption read, "He Will Have Them All to Beat."[36]

In the lead-up to the fight, the *Defender* commented, "On the arid plains of the Sage Brush State the white man and the negro will settle the mooted question of supremacy. . . . When the smoke of the battle clears away, and when the din of mingled cheers and groans have died away . . . there will be deep mourning throughout the domains of Uncle Sam over Jeffries inability."[37]

At the fight itself, the ringside band played "All Coons Look Alike to Me," and the all-white crowd chanted, "Kill the nigger." In an early incarnation of the information superhighway, young children working as "telegram runners" ran through urban environs every round calling out the rounds.[38] But Johnson was faster, stronger, and smarter than Jeffries. He knocked Jeffries out with ease.

"More than 25,000 people had gathered to watch the fight," Johnson wrote in his autobiography, "and as I looked about me, and scanned that sea of white faces I felt the auspiciousness of the occasion. There were few men of my own race among the spectators. I realized that my victory in this event meant more than on any previous occasion. It wasn't just the championship that was at stake—it was my own honor, and in a degree the honor of my own race. . . . The 'white hope' had failed."[39]

It is no exaggeration to say that the failure of the "white hope" caused a full-blown ideological crisis. "That Mr. Johnson should so lightly and carelessly punch the head of Mr. Jeffries," wrote the *New York World*, "must come as a shock to every devoted believer in the supremacy of the Anglo-Saxon race."[40]

After Johnson's victory, there were race riots around the country—in Illinois, Missouri, New York, Ohio, Pennsylvania, Colorado, Texas, and Washington, D.C. Most of the riots consisted of white lynch mobs attacking blacks, and blacks fighting back. One hundred fifty-one people died. This reaction to a boxing match was the most widespread racial uprising that the United States had ever seen—or ever would see until the assassination of civil rights leader Dr. Martin Luther King Jr.

Right-wing and religious organizations immediately moved to ban boxing. Congress actually passed a law banning boxing films.[41]

Even some black leaders, such as Booker T. Washington, pushed Johnson to condemn African Americans for rioting, and to toe the line. But Johnson remained defiant. For this mortal sin—and a variety of venal ones—he faced harrassment and persecution for most of his life. He was forced into exile in 1913 on the trumped-up charge of transporting a white woman across state lines for prostitution. As Johnson wrote in his autobiography, as soon as he defeated Jeffries, "from that minute on, the hunt for the 'white hope' was redoubled, and when it proceeded with so little success other methods were taken to dispose of me."[42]

Washington, who believed that blacks should abstain from any kind of agitation and focus on low-level economic development, couldn't stand Johnson. As he said with unvarnished scorn:

I can only say at this time, that this is another illustration of the almost irreparable injury that a wrong action on the part of a single individual may do to a whole race. It shows the folly of those persons who think that they alone will be held responsible for the evil that they do. Especially is this true in the case of the Negro in the United States today. No one can do so much injury to the Negro race as the Negro himself. This will seem to many persons unjust, but no one can doubt that it is true. What makes the situation seem a little worse in this case, is the fact that it was the white man, not the black man who has given Jack Johnson the kind of prominence he has enjoyed up to now and put him, in other words, in a position where he has been able to bring humiliation upon the whole race of which he is a member.[43]

Washington's contempt for Johnson didn't stop him from setting aside a special assembly room at his Tuskegee Institute to hear special telegraphic reports of Johnson's fights.[44]

But Johnson to the mass of his people was no devil. He was becoming folklore. In the words of a ditty sung to the tune of a spiritual:

Amaze an' Grace, how sweet it sounds,
Jack Johnson knocked Jim Jeffries down.
Jim Jeffries jumped up an' hit Jack on the chin,
An' then Jack knocked him down agin.
The Yankees hold the play,
The white man pulls the trigger;
But it make no difference what the white man say,
The world champion's still a nigger.[45]

Another who differed from the Booker T. Washington view of Johnson was Washington's great rival W.E.B. Du Bois. Du Bois, a towering intellectual, was one of the first to try to put the moralizing about "violence" in sports—and the street violence associated with Jack Johnson—in some sort of context. As he wrote in the *Crisis*, the organ of the NAACP, in 1914:

There is today some brutality connected with boxing, but as compared with football and boat racing it may be seriously questioned whether boxing deserves to be put in a separate class by reason of its cruelty. Certainly it is a highly civilized pastime as compared with the international game of war which produces so many 'heroes' and 'national monuments'. Boxing has fallen into disfavor— into very great disfavor. . . . The cause is clear: Jack Johnson . . . has out-sparred an Irishman. He did it with little brutality, the utmost fairness and great good nature. He did not 'knock' his opponent senseless. Apparently he did not even try. Neither he nor his race invented prize fighting or particularly like it. Why then this thrill of national disgust? Because Johnson is black. Of course some pretend to object to Mr. Johnson's character. But we have yet to hear, in the case of White America, that marital troubles have disqualified prize fighters or ball players or even statesmen. It comes down, then, after all to this unforgivable blackness.[46]

Du Bois also differed from Washington on the essence of sports itself, wanting African Americans to engage more fully in the nation's expanding sporting life. He wrote, "I have long noted with silent apprehension a distinct tendency among us, to depreciate and belittle and sneer at means of recreation, to consider amusement as the peculiar property of the devil, and to look upon even its legitimate pursuit as time wasted and energy misspent."[47]

Black Sox

It was in 1912 that Jack Johnson was charged with taking his lover (and later wife) Lucille Cameron across state lines for "immoral purposes," a violation of the Mann Act. The presiding judge was a man named Kenesaw Mountain Landis. Landis was not done passing judgment on the world of sports. In 1919, eight members of the Chicago White Sox—known for eternity as the Black Sox—were accused of conspiring to throw the World Series. Although they were cleared in a court of law, they were damned with a lifetime ban put down by a new creation: the baseball commissioner. This first commissioner was Kenesaw Mountain Landis. In the wake of the World Series, the owners wanted someone to exercise total control over the game and rescue its integrity in the eyes of the public. Judge Landis certainly had earned his bones in the eyes of the ownership class. In 1918, he sat in judgment of Big Bill Haywood and about one hundred other members of the revolutionary union the Industrial Workers of the World, or "Wobblies," for violating the Espionage Act of 1917. While Landis oversaw their harsh sentences and even deportations, most of his decisions were either reversed on appeal or nullified by presidential pardon.[48]

As *Washington Post* columnist Shirley Povich described the reclusive and all-powerful commissioner, "There is a man of mystery. Mysterious in the manner that he so completely dominates his associates, who, in his present undertaking, are his employers. He not only tells then what to do, but how to do it and when. And he makes them like it."[49]

Landis's influence grew even more powerful toward the end of his reign in 1944. As we will see, he was a major obstacle to ending baseball's color line. But in 1920, it was the Black Sox who felt his wrath. The great Shoeless Joe Jackson, a lifetime .356 hitter who batted .375 and committed no errors in the World Series he was supposed to have thrown, never played again.

The year 1919 also saw two massive reforms that put a terrific stamp on the years to come: women's suffrage and prohibition. The 1920s would be defined in many ways by the desire of women to be heard and the desire of a nation recovering from war and upheaval to have a drink.

· 3 ·

Sports and Leisure

The 1920s were known as the Jazz Age, a time of hard partying and weary disaffection. The decade began, however, not with groan of cynicism but with an international challenge to power. In the wake of World War I, millions of people in every corner on earth demanded change. The *Nation* magazine wrote:

The most extraordinary phenomenon of the present time . . . is the unprecedented revolt of the rank and file. . . .

In Russia it has dethroned the Czar. . . . In Korea and India and Egypt and Ireland it keeps up an unyielding resistance to political tyranny. In England it brought about the railway strike, against the judgement of the men's own executives. In Seattle and San Francisco it has resulted in the stevedores' recent refusal to handle arms or supplies destined for the overthrow of the Soviet Government. In one district of Illinois it manifested itself in a resolution of striking miners, unanimously requesting their state executive "to go to Hell." In Pittsburgh, according to Mr. [Samuel] Gompers, it compelled the reluctant American Federation officers to call the steel strike, lest the control pass into the hands of the I.W.W.'s and other "radicals." In New York, it brought about the longshoremen's strike and kept the men out in defiance of union officials, and caused the upheaval in the printing trade, which the international officers, even though the employers worked hand in glove with them, were completely unable to control.

The common man . . . losing faith in the old leadership, has experienced a new access of self-confidence, or at least a new recklessness, a readiness to take chances on his own account . . . authority cannot any longer be imposed from above; it comes automatically from below.[1]

But this period of revolt met with a terrible backlash as the federal government used its wartime powers to crush dissent. The backlash was spearheaded by Attorney General A. Mitchell Palmer, who led what were known as the Palmer Raids. That summer, eight bombs went off around the country, including one in front of Palmer's home. Thousands were rounded up and hundreds were deported, including anarchist and women's rights activist Emma Goldman. Much of this was done under the guise of "anticommunism." In one day in 1920, five thousand to ten thousand members of the U.S. Communist Party were jailed in thirty cities.[2]

In his essay "The Case Against the Reds," Palmer charged that "tongues of revolutionary heat were licking the alt[a]rs of the churches, leaping into the belfry of the school bell, crawling into the sacred corners of American homes, seeking to replace marriage vows with libertine laws, burning up the foundations of society."[3]

The combination of an economic boom and a nation fatigued by conflict and war created conditions that made the Palmer Raids possible: hundreds of thousands of urban dwellers identified as part of a "lost generation" that rejected traditional society. This lost generation ostensibly rejected politics, but their libertarian, antipolitical ethos created social space both for women and gays and lesbians that would not be seen again until the 1960s.

As one Jazz Age song went,

Masculine women, feminine men
Which is the rooster, which is the hen?
It's hard to tell 'em apart today! And say!
Sister is busy learning to shave,
Brother just loves his permanent wave,
It's hard to tell 'em apart today! Hey, hey!
Girls were girls and boys were boys when I was a tot,
Now we don't know who is who, or even what's what!
Knickers and trousers, baggy and wide,
Nobody knows who's walking inside,
Those masculine women and feminine men![4]

There was a new woman on the urban scene, known as the "flapper." Precocious and identifiable through a shorter bob haircut, the flapper set traditional gender roles on their ear. In a 1925 article in the *New Republic* called "Flapper Jane," journalist Bruce Bliven expresses the confusion people felt about the age and this new kind of young woman.

Jane is 19. . . . This Jane, being 19, is a flapper, though she urgently denies that she is a member of the younger generation. The younger generation, she will tell you, is aged 15 to 17; and she professes to be decidedly shocked at the things they do and say. That is a fact which would interest her minister, if he knew it—poor man, he knows so little! For he regards Jane as a perfectly horrible example of wild youth—paint, cigarettes, cocktails, petting parties—oooh! Yet if the younger generation shocks her as she says, query: how wild is Jane?

. . . Generally speaking, however, it is safe to say that as regards the wildness of youth there is a good deal more smoke than fire. Anyhow, the new Era of Undressing, as already suggested, has spread far beyond the boundaries of Jane's group. The fashion is followed by hordes of unquestionably monogamous matrons, including many who join heartily in the general ululations as to what young people are coming to. Attempts to link the new freedom

with prohibition, with the automobile, the decline of Fundamen-
talism, are certainly without foundation. These may be accessory,
and indeed almost certainly are, but only after the fact.

That fact is, as Jane says, that women to-day are shaking off the
shreds and patches of their age-old servitude. "Feminism" has won
a victory so nearly complete that we have even forgotten the fierce
challenge which once inhered in the very word. Women have
highly resolved that they are just as good as men, and intend to be
treated so. They don't mean to have any more unwanted children.
They don't intend to be debarred from any profession or occupation which they choose to enter. They clearly mean (even though
not all of them yet realize it) that in the great game of sexual selec-
tion they shall no longer be forced to play the role, simulated or
real, of helpless quarry. If they want to wear their heads shaven, as
a symbol of defiance against the former fate which for three mil-
lennia forced them to dress their heavy locks according to male de-
crees, they will have their way. If they should elect to go naked
nothing is more certain than that naked they will go, while from
the sidelines to which he has been relegated mere man is vouch-
safed permission only to pipe a feeble Hurrah![5]

Many of the culturati, still reeling from World War I, proudly
adopted the label "anti-American." At their pinnacle was Baltimore's
H.L. Mencken, who wrote in his classic essay "On Being an American,"

Here the business of getting a living . . . is enormously easier than
it is in any other Christian land—so easy, in fact, that an educated
and forehanded man who fails at it must actually make deliberate
efforts to that end. Here the general average of intelligence, of
knowledge, of competence, of integrity, of self-respect, of honor is
so low that any man who knows his trade, does not fear ghosts, has
read fifty good books, and practices the common decencies stands
out as brilliantly as a wart on a bald head, and is thrown willy-nilly
into a meager and exclusive aristocracy. And here, more than anywhere else I know of or have heard of, the daily panorama of

human existence, of private and communal folly—the unending procession of governmental extortions and chicaneries, of commercial brigandages and throat-slittings, of theological buffooneries, of aesthetic ribaldries, of legal swindles and harlotries, of miscellaneous rogueries, villainies, imbecilities, grotesqueries, and extravagances—is so inordinately gross and preposterous, so perfectly brought up to the highest conceivable amperage, so steadily enriched with an almost fabulous daring and originality, that only the man who was born with a petrified diaphragm can fail to laugh himself to sleep every night, and to awake every morning with all the eager, unflagging expectation of a Sunday-school superintendent touring the Paris peep-shows.[6]

Mencken's style influenced many writers, including African American radical author Richard Wright. In his autobiographical *Black Boy*, Wright writes of Mencken,

I was jarred and shocked by the clear, clean, sweeping sentences. . . . Why did he write like that? I pictured the man as a raging demon, slashing with his pen . . . denouncing everything American . . . laughing . . . mocking God, authority. . . . This man was fighting, fighting with words. He was using words as a weapon, using them as one would use a club. . . . I read on and what amazed me was not what he said, but how on earth anybody had the courage to say it."[7]

The new mass media and celebrity culture created icons out of people who in decades previous would have been pariahs: Mencken, F. Scott Fitzgerald, and the flapper were discussed in broadsheets and tabloids. The Jazz Age was a time of flux.

The Sport of Celebrity

The celebrity culture found a much more comfortable home in the world of sports. Mencken hailed from the city of Baltimore. The 1920s also saw the rise of another child of Charm City: George Herman "Babe"

Ruth. Ruth is credited with saving baseball after the 1919 Black Sox scandal, especially after a monster 1920 season when he hit fifty-four home runs, a total that exceeded the number of homers for every other team on the big leagues except for the Philadelphia Phillies. His slugging percentage of .847 that year stood as an untouchable record until Barry Bonds surpassed it in 2001.[8]

Ruth's towering home runs were not the only feat turning him into an icon. The new mass media, exemplified by radio and the newsreel, were creating a new kind of sports celebrity. It wasn't just Ruth's home runs. It was his beatific face. It was his nicknames: "The Great Bambino," "The Big Bam," "The Sultan of Swat." It was his famed gluttony, celebrated in a period of excess. The age has in many ways been exemplified by what Babe Ruth is reputed to have said when he was asked if it was appropriate he should be making more than the president: "Why not? I'm having a better year than he is!"[9]

During this golden age of sports, Ruth was one of several of the new sporting heroes. Others such as boxers Jack Dempsey and Gene Tunney, football star Red Grange, and golfer Bobby Jones were also made mythic.

Their celebrity was ornately constructed by a new breed of sports columnist. Replacing the tabloid gutter dwellers of the shiny sheets were sportswriters who were lyrical and even literary. The Mount Rushmore of these poetical pundits of the 1920s was occupied by Heywood Broun, Damon Runyon, Paul Gallico, and Grantland Rice. They were lyrical and literary. They were also about as subtle as a blowtorch.

Rice is best known perhaps for nicknaming Notre Dame's football backfield the "Four Horsemen" (as in the Four Horsemen of the Apocalypse) for the *New York Herald Tribune*.

Outlined against a blue-gray October sky the Four Horsemen rode again. In dramatic lore they are known as Famine, Pestilence, Destruction and Death. These are only aliases. Their real names are Stuhldreher, Miller, Crowley and Layden. They formed the crest of the South Bend cyclone before which another fighting Army team was swept over the precipice at the Polo Grounds this afternoon as 55,000 spectators peered down upon the bewildering panorama spread out upon the green plain below.[10]

Washington Post columnist Shirley Povich wrote of Rice, "He was the first to prove, I think, that sportswriters could actually write, at least one of them."[11]

Rice's style of sportswriting did more than just provide some of the most memorable newspaper prose of the century. It served to create out-sized heroes out of ordinary jocks. It transported athletes from the realm of the tangible to the legendary. These writers were the Greek chorus for the people who would become the gods of the twenty-first century. They collectively helped cement the separation between the professional and the spectator. Rice didn't just write that Hall of Fame pitcher Dizzy Dean had a great fastball. He wrote:

Yes, it's Dean, Dean, Dean,
He's a beggar with a bullet through your spleen,
Though at times some bat has flayed you,
by the Texas sun that made you,
you're a better man than bats are, Dizzy Dean.[12]

In the world of Rice and company, a prerequisite to achieving this kind of status was being white and having an xy chromosome pair.

Hard Road, No Glory

The dark period for African Americans that surrounded the ascendancy of Jack Johnson continued into the 1920s. The Ku Klux Klan grew to four and a half million members and even spread out of the South and took root in the North and Midwest. The acceptance of both racial violence and the ideas of white supremacy led to the growth of Marcus Garvey and the Universal Negro Improvement Association and African Communities League (UNIA-ACL) and calls to go "back to Africa." At its peak, the UNIA boasted as many as four million members. The majority of blacks had no interest in going back at all. What they wanted was a sense of pride and community in a dehumanizing world. The fathers of both Malcolm X and Muhammad Ali were influenced by Garvey's teachings.[13]

In the world of sports, the opportunities were at best shallow. For African American men who had dreams of playing basketball, the journey began and ended with Abe Saperstein's Harlem Globetrotters. Early Globetrotters play was the basketball equivalent of the minstrel shows so popular in vaudeville and on the big screen. But it was also the only way African Americans could make a living playing basketball until after World War II. As Nelson George wrote, "It's no accident that the Trotters' antics found favor with white fans at a time America's favorite Black movie star was Lincoln Theodore Monroe Andrew Perry, also known as Stepin Fetchit."[14]

But the 1920s were not just a time of minstrel basketball and Klan growth. It was the period of the Harlem Renaissance, when African Americans seized popular art in all its forms—poetry, literature, dance, music—and irrevocably altered its course. Through the Negro Leagues, they also changed how baseball was perceived and played.

No One's Sad Sister

The Negro Leagues in the 1920s are often discussed as the sad sister of segregation. Certainly players with tremendous talent were paid less and received a fraction of the fanfare of their white counterparts. "It was rough barnstorming," recalled the legendary player Cool Papa Bell.

> We traveled by bus, you see. You'd be surprised at the conditions we played under. We would frequently play two and three games a day. We'd play a twilight game, ride 40 miles, and play another game under the lights. . . . Every night they'd have to find us places to stay if we weren't in a big city up North. We went into a lot of small towns where they'd never seen a colored person in some of those places we couldn't find anyplace to sleep so we slept on the bus. If we had to, we could convert the seats into beds. We'd just pull over to the side of the road, in a cornfield or someplace and sleep until the break of day, and then we'd go on into the

next town, hoping we'd find a restaurant that would be willing to serve colored people. All those things we experienced, today people wouldn't believe it.[15]

But hardship was only part of the story. There is another reading of the Negro Leagues at this time: an independent locus of power and a source of pride and support, much like the historically black colleges. The Negro Leagues were welcomed by African Americans, especially given their treatment as spectators in other sports venues. Major league stadiums that seated blacks were routinely segregated, with African Americans in the outfield seats. African American photographer Ernest Withers remembered sitting up there "and hearing the white folks chant, 'Hit it in the coal pile'! That's where all the 'niggers' were."[16] At Negro League games blacks often shared bleachers with white folks, though there was still a dividing line. As Cool Papa Bell later recalled, "In the Negro Leagues the audience was mixed but mostly colored. Even down South there were some white people at the games. When we played the Birmingham Black Barons in their park, there were always lots of whites in the crowd, but they were separated by a rope. You could be sitting right next to a white man, but that rope was always there."[17]

But the white press never reported on the Negro Leagues. The black press also didn't cover it. As Withers remembered, "They didn't get no Sunday-to Sunday pictures of ball games. That wasn't part of their journalists workings." Casey Jones, the catcher for the Memphis Red Sox, said, "Nobody really knew about us. Oh the black people around the country and in the South knew about us but nobody else."[18] The Communist Party's newspaper, the *Daily Worker*, printed the scores when it started its sports section, but that wasn't until the 1930s. The success of the early Negro Leagues, in particular the Negro National League, was due to the influence of Rube Foster, known as the "father of black baseball."

Foster was a fine baseball player himself. He was also intelligent, prideful, and deeply competitive. Other men in the Negro Leagues fit this description as well. In 1903, when Foster played for the Philadelphia Giants, his first baseman, who could punch better than he could field, was Jack Johnson. But Foster's great accomplishments would come not on the field but in the owner's box.[19]

Under Foster's stewardship, the Negro Leagues became perhaps the largest and certainly the most geographically diverse black-owned business in the United States. That meant—and this is rarely explored in discussions of the Negro Leagues—it was an employer of not only marginalized black ballplayers but also African American accountants, bookkeepers, trainers, and all sorts of skilled and unskilled labor that otherwise would have struggled to find work.[20]

Foster had a vision of his Negro National League as an entity that could sit across the table from major league baseball and negotiate desegregation on equal terms. As Foster himself wrote with great optimism of the Negro National Leagues in 1906:

> Organization is its only hope. With the proper organization, patterned after the men who have made baseball a success, we will, in three years, be rated as other leagues are rated. We have the players and it could not be a failure, as the same territory is traveled now by all clubs, with no organization or money. It would give us a rating and standing in the daily papers which would create an interest and we could then let the best clubs in our organization play for the world's championship with other clubs, champions of their leagues.[21]

Certainly the major leagues gave Foster quiet respect. Managers would arrive unannounced at games Foster managed to take free lessons, and it was from Foster that the major leagues learned the bunt-and-run.[22]

Foster saw his approach as leading to a day when the color line would be eliminated through the wholesale integration of entire National Negro League teams into the major leagues. But it was a dream destroyed. Though he had a successful run, the pressure of this work ate away at Foster. He was an obsessive who believed—with some justification—that the league would fall apart without his constant stewardship. Once he hit a player across the head with his pipe for tripling after he was given the bunt sign. Deviations from order would mean chaos. Foster's family eventually had to commit him to a mental hospital. He was institutionalized until his death on December 9, 1930, at the age of fifty-one. The National Negro Leagues collapsed the year after he died. In 1981, he was finally inducted into the Baseball Hall of Fame.[23]

Women in the 1920s

The age of the whalebone corset was starting to give way. Women in sports were making a transition from passive and scorned to an active and accepted part of the public sporting life.

In 1922, a nineteen-year-old swimmer, Sybil Bauer, smacked down old perceptions when she broke the world (men's) record in the back-stroke. In 1926 Gertrude Ederle, a ten-Olympic-medal-winner from New York, gained international renown by becoming only the sixth person to swim the English Channel—two hours faster than the five men who preceded her.[24] In a 1927 *Chicago Defender* reader poll to name the city's most popular black athlete, women were five of the seventeen vote getters.

Athletics at women's colleges were in full swing. The Amateur Athletic Union (AAU), the chief organization of amateur athletics, which wore its social conservatism like a badge of honor, started to give way. In 1913 AAU president James Sullivan had declared that his all-important organization could never sanction women's athletics because he had "no desire to make girls public characters." As Susan Cahn writes, "Sullivan, like others, of his day, linked women's public athletic activity to the negative connotation of 'public women,' a term that re-ferred to prostitutes or disreputable women of the streets." In 1924, however, the AAU finally relented and offered a women's national track-and-field championship.[25]

For working-class women, factory teams in a variety of sports were sprouting around the country. Management saw this as a sound strategy for pulling women away from the radical movements that many were a part of in the previous decade. These leagues proved very popular, giving many women their first opportunity to play sports. They also provided a respite from the factory floor and a dose of fresh air.

The most famous female athlete of the first half of the twentieth century came out of the factory. Mildred Ella "Babe" Didrikson rose to fame as a multisport star, representing the Dallas-based Employers' Casualty Company team as an eighteen-year-old. She went on to win three medals in track and field in the 1932 Olympics. As she said later, "I could have won a medal in five events if they let me."[26] She also became the standard for all women golfers. Yet despite her towering athletic accomplishments, Didrikson was denounced as "mannish," "not quite female," and a "Muscle Moll" who could not "compete with other girls in the very ancient and time honored sport of mantrapping."[27]

Hearing that in addition to track and field she also played basketball, football, and numerous other sports, an astonished journalist asked Didrikson, "Is there anything at all you don't play?" She responded, "Yeah, dolls."[28]

In 1927 American tennis great Helen Wills won the first of her eight women's singles championships at England's prestigious Wimbledon tennis tournament. She dominated the sport for the next six years. But unlike her male counterparts, this was seen somehow as a deficit. Newspapermen who had once praised Wills's cool demeanor now described her as a "heartless crusher of lesser talents" and a "killer type of fighter" whose "austere and inexorable" style had "all the warmth and animation of a deceased codfish."[29]

Male sportswriters tended to vacillate, finding female athletic talent to be either threatening or titillating. Paul Gallico wrote, "There is no girl living who can manage to look anything but awful during the process of some strenuous game played on a hot day."[30]

In contrast, Grantland Rice had a different view of the sporting woman in his poem "The Baseball Girl":

> *The type of girl which keeps each head cavorting in a whirl,*
> *Is the nectarine of nature which we dub "The Baseball Girl."*
> *She's got "proper curves," you know, well rounded out and neat,*
> *She has the "speed"—nor do we refer to her feet.*

She always "makes a hit" to boot, and, what is very nice,
She's ready at the proper time to "make a sacrifice."[31]

Rice also wrote that the "alert and aggressive" American girl athlete "is not only getting a finely molded body . . . she is also getting the virility of will to battle against odds." The result was "a new type—a most attractive addition [who] can meet the male upon even terms."[32]

The AAU in 1932 set up a National Women's Sports Committee to investigate the charges that women's athletics were detrimental to women's physical health.

The committee surveyed 232 top athletes, reporting that nearly every one saw an overall health improvement and suffered no ill effects on menstruation due to competition. . . . Respondents firmly believed that the "competitive spirit" benefited rather than harmed female athletes. Popular media accounts made fewer references to political and maternal welfare, looking more often to the matter of sexual attractiveness to explain the value of women's sport. The announced benefits were double-sided: sport would enhance the sexual appeal of young women, at the same time heightening the viewing pleasure of audiences entranced by the attractive female competitors. Journalists likened athletes to chorus girls, movie stars, and beauty queens.[33]

But by 1932, sports had truly become a luxury, even for factory girls. In October 1929, the stock market crashed, plunging large sections of the country into dire poverty.

·4·

No Depression

In 1929, President Herbert Hoover assessed an American economy engorged on an ever-rising stock market and said, "We in America today are nearer to the final triumph over poverty than ever before in the history of any land."[1]

Missed it by that much. Instead, October 1929 saw the Super Bowl of economic crashes, beginning the Great Depression. More than five thousand banks and countless businesses shut their doors. Industrial production dropped 50 percent, and by 1933 as much as one-third of the country was unemployed. Starvation became a very real issue. For the first time in U.S. history, more people moved to the country from the cities than in the other direction, in the hope that subsistence farming could ward off malnutrition. Thousands of families lived in makeshift shantytowns known as Hoovervilles, named for the once optimistic president.[2]

The Great Depression destroyed people: their confidence, their sense of self, and their very identity. Studs Terkel wrote,

> It left upon them an "invisible scar." . . . The suddenly-idle hands blamed themselves, rather than society. True, there were hunger

marches and protestations to City Hall and Washington, but the millions experienced a private kind of shame when the pink slip came. No matter that others suffered the same fate, the inner voice whispered, "I'm a failure."

True there was a sharing among many of the dispossessed, but, at close quarters, frustration became, at times, violence, and violence turned inward. Thus, sons and fathers fell away, one from the other. And the mother, seeking work, said nothing. Outside forces, except to the more articulate and political rebels, were in some vague way responsible, but not really. It was a personal guilt.[3]

Phyllis Bryant recalled to *Michigan History* magazine her Depression-era childhood.

In 1929 I was six years old, but I remember quite a few things from that era, especially growing up and never having too much.

What sticks mostly in my mind was losing my money in the bank. I didn't quite understand why that bank had to close and take my money, which probably was only a few dollars. When they started paying off a few years later, my check was eleven cents. It helped when my brother gave me his, which was eighteen cents, and my older sister's, which was twenty-three cents. I was really in the money then.[4]

Rebellion became the sole option in many different cities. In 1934, Minneapolis, Toledo, and San Francisco were all shut down by general strikes. Three hundred twenty-five thousand textile workers struck across the South as well.[5]

The strikes changed people. Genora Dollinger said after the famed sit-down strikes of Flint, Michigan, "Following the strike, the auto worker became a different human being. The women that had participated actively became a different type of woman, a different type from any we had ever known anywhere in the labor movement and certainly not in the city of Flint. They carried themselves with a different walk, their heads were high, and they had confidence in themselves."[6]

Hysteria ruled the press: "The situation in San Francisco is not correctly described by the phrase 'general strike,' " wrote the *Los Angeles Times*. "What is actually in progress there is an insurrection, a Communist-inspired and led revolt against organized government. There is but one thing to be done—put down the revolt with any force necessary."[7]

But this decade of revolt encompassed more than just a few spectacular strikes. More than one million people passed through membership in the Communist Party over the course of the decade, although membership at any one time never exceeded one hundred thousand. Marches of the unemployed in New York drew half a million people; Unemployed Councils were set up in cities across the country. In Harlem, Communists became famous for moving people's furniture back into houses following evictions.[8]

Sports suffered a great deal over the course of the decade. The motors of the 1920s golden age—immigration, disposable income—were sputtering if not moribund. Teddy Roosevelt's ethos of Muscular Christianity had very little sway in a period where no one was feeling particularly muscular. In baseball, attendance drooped. Even Commissioner Landis took a 40 percent pay cut.[9]

And yet, as the decade wore on, if fewer people could afford to fill the coffers of sports teams, more actually were able to play and discuss sports. How did that happen? Part of Roosevelt's New Deal involved the Works Progress Administration, putting people to work on public building projects such as the construction of parks and gymnasiums. Couple the presence of these new facilities with high unemployment, and actual playing became more common. Also, the existence of the radio meant that people could be sports fans without having to buy tickets.

Chicago Counter-Olympics

As the social upheaval of the period continued, artists and others took the banner of revolt into different realms. Authors such as Richard Wright and John Steinbeck, photographers such as Dorothea Lange, and actors such as Charlie Chaplin used their craft and their fame as a platform for ideas. The Communist Party started what it called "John Reed Clubs" in thirty cities to foster political talent in the creative arts.[10]

In rather clumsy fashion, the Communist Party also attempted to enter the world of sports. In 1932, the party held the Chicago Counter-Olympics as a protest against the games being held in Los Angeles. They certainly had a political basis for attempting such a lofty venture: the Olympics were racially segregated and hypernationalistic. They also excluded the USSR. Furthermore, the Communist Party saw its event as a way to raise awareness around the case of imprisoned union activist Tom Mooney. Mooney was in the midst of a twenty-year prison sentence for throwing a bomb that had killed nine people in 1916, during a Preparedness Day parade in San Francisco. Mooney had always maintained his innocence, claiming to have been targeted for his union activity. By 1932, Mooney had been in a California prison for sixteen years and called for the Los Angeles boycott from his cell.[11]

The Communist Party's foray into sports was aided by the fact that one of its leaders was a former semipro baseball player named Clarence Hathaway. Hathaway embraced the idea of offering a sporting political alternative to the Los Angeles games. He saw the Counter-Olympics as being tactically in the same vein as the Communist Party writing clubs and defense committees: a way "to reach many thousands of workers not yet prepared for party membership."[12]

The Communists believed sports to be exclusively a tool to keep people distracted from their exploitation. There is no evidence that they saw anything redeeming in the act of play or anything positive in the way sports can bring people together. This brittle view of the games led to a Chicago Counter-Olympics that was an exercise in crude political messaging, despite their admirable goal of challenging Jim Crow in sports. Could this still have worked? They never really had the chance to find out. The AAU threatened a lifetime ban against any athlete who even competed in the preliminary heats. One thousand athletes were expected; somewhere between two hundred and four hundred showed up. Preparations were made for ten thousand fans, but the turnout was closer to twenty-five hundred. This doesn't mean the Counter-Olympics were without accomplishment. A third of the athletes who competed, roughly a hundred, were African American. In Los Angeles there were only four. In the final race, athletes wore signs on their shirts that said

"Free Tom Mooney" and "Free the Scottsboro Boys." But athletes with political slogans on their chests is in its way as condescending as the view that people are just sheep hypnotized by sports.[13]

Understanding the tension of how sports and politics can intersect would require a far more dynamic approach: an approach begun by Lester "Red" Rodney.

"Red" Rodney

Lester "Red" Rodney consciously used sports as a way to raise political issues. Rodney was the sports editor for the Communist Party's newspaper, the *Daily Worker*, from 1936 to 1958. Over the objections of many in the party itself, Rodney launched a political sports page that was light-years ahead of its time. His sports section vibrated with the intersection of sports and struggle. In the process he helped launch one of the first public campaigns to integrate baseball, became the first writer to scout a young second baseman named Jackie Robinson, and covered the famed 1938 boxing match between the "Brown Bomber," Joe Louis, and Hitler favorite Max Schmeling. Yet because of his background as a political radical, Rodney has remained a largely forgotten figure.

It was while he was taking night classes at New York University in the early 1930s that Rodney first met the radicals in the campus Communist Party. "People who weren't around during the 1930s can't fully grasp what it was like politically," he recalls. "In New York if you were on a college campus and you weren't some kind of radical, Communist, socialist, or Trotskyist, you were considered brain-dead, and you probably were! That's what all the conversation was about during the Depression. One day, on the way to class, I met someone selling a paper, the *Daily Worker*. This person said, 'Read this paper and see what you think.' I immediately connected with the tone of it, and I was ready to question capitalism at that time. But what caught my eye was that they also had a weekly column on sports."[14]

The radical in Rodney loved most of the newspaper, but the sports fan in him took a look at that sports column and "absolutely cringed." Rodney calls it "patronizing," and he is perhaps being too kind. Looking at archives of the *Daily Worker*, it seems that the only purpose of its early sports section was to tell its readership how stupid they were to like sports. Articles included lines such as "The purpose of baseball is nothing more than to distract workers from their miserable conditions" and "peddling dope and talking [about] boxing are one and the same."[15]

One time, a young reader wrote a letter of complaint about the tone of the sports page and received this response from the paper's editor: "I don't believe that Blondie Ryan [of the Giants], for example, is a conscious agent of the capitalist class seeking to dope the masses with his swell infielding. That would be the sheerest nonsense. But when a couple of dozen Blondie Ryans and Bill Terrys, with the aid of hundreds of sportswriters, rivet the attention of millions of workers upon themselves rather than upon unemployment, wage cuts and wars, then we can draw the conclusion that Ryans, et al, unconsciously serve the purposes of the ruling class."[16]

But the times were changing for this wooden view. As Rodney remembers:

> The party was beginning to change its demographic makeup. The ones who were pouring into the party were young people, born here in the States, and there were many trade unionists that played ball and were interested in sports. Ten years earlier, the party was probably 75 percent foreign born and they brought the prejudice of European immigrants about sports, seeing it as "grown people, wasting their time on children's games." They couldn't understand its appeal. When I met my wife's father for the first time, he said, "What do you do?" I said, "I write sports." He laughed uneasily and asked "But what do you really do?"
>
> Anyway, my feelings about the *Daily Worker* paper peaked enough that I sent a letter to them just mildly suggesting that, yes, they ought to speak about what's wrong with sports and so on, but realize that sports are also something that are meaningful to American workers and for good reasons. I didn't make some big argument that a collective effort of a team, the coming together, and finding satisfaction in getting the job well done, is some kind of revolutionary act. I didn't go into all that but I did say that the

paper ought to relax and cover sports and respect people who are interested in sports. They called me in and I was hired to head it up—even though at that point I hadn't even joined the party!

It was at this point that Rodney set about his real work: not just editing a broad sports page that covered games but covering sports with an eye to their social impact. Rodney used the sports page of the *Daily Worker* to launch the first sustained campaign to end the color line in major league baseball. The black press was part of this as well, but it was Rodney who gave it the feel of a social movement.

It was only a matter of time after I started when I said, "Look at this huge void here! No one is talking about this!" When Negro League teams came in, we highlighted who the good Negro players were and gave something of their background and history. That took investigative reporting. The other papers just said, "The Kansas City Monarchs will play the Baltimore Giants at such and such a time tomorrow" with no mention that any of them could have played big league baseball or even Minor League baseball and were banned from both. It's amazing. You go back and you read the great newspapers in the thirties, you'll find no editorials saying, "What's going on here? This is America, land of the free and people with the wrong pigmentation of skin can't play baseball?" Nothing like that. No challenges to the league, to the commissioner, to league presidents, no interviewing the managers, no talking about Satchel Paige and Josh Gibson, who were obviously of superstar caliber. . . . It was this tremendous vacuum waiting. Anybody who became sports editor of the *Daily Worker* would have gone into this. It was too obvious. After a while, some of the white comrades who had never paid attention to sports before began saying, "Is this an all-white sport?" People didn't think about it. It was the culture of the times and it was accepted. We also developed a relationship with the black press and printed each other's articles about the Negro League players and the color line which in those highly segregated times opened up new audiences for both of us.

Rodney stepped into this vacuum, taking the fight to integrate base-ball off the sports page and turning it into an activist campaign. It be-came a key part of the group's perspective on fighting racism in the 1930s.

> I spoke to the leaders of the YCL [Young Communist League]. They were enthusiastic about the sports page. We talked about cir-culating the paper. It just evolved as we talked about the color line and some kids in the YCL suggested, "Why don't we go to the ballparks—to Yankee Stadium, Ebbets Field, the Polo Grounds—with petitions?" They for the most part never encountered any hostility from fans. People would say, "Gee, I never thought of that." And then they'd say, 'Yeah, I think if they're good enough then they should have a chance." We wound up with at least a mil-lion and a half signatures that we delivered straight to the desk of Judge [baseball commissioner] Landis.

Rodney from that moment on seized every opportunity to raise the question of integration on the sports page.

> In 1937, we were in the dressing room at Yankee Stadium and somebody asked a young Joe DiMaggio, "Joe, who's the best pitcher you've faced?" And without hesitation, young Joe said, "Satchel Paige." He didn't say "Satchel Paige, who ought to be in the big leagues," he just said, "Satchel Paige." [DiMaggio had played Paige in an exhibition game on the West Coast.] So that was a huge headline in the next day's *Daily Worker* sports page, in the biggest type I had: "Paige best pitcher ever faced—DiMaggio." No other paper reported that, they didn't go into this. If the other reporters would hand that in, their editor would say, "Come on, you're not stirring this thing up." But I want to be clear that we didn't see it as a virtue that we were the only people re-porting on this. We wanted to broaden this thing and end the damned ban.

The campaign evolved step by step, and Rodney would put the question of integration to white ballplayers whenever he had the chance.

It was meaningful when players like Johnny Vander Meer or Bucky Walters said, "I don't see why they shouldn't play." That shot down the myth the owners would repeat that white players would never stand for it. From then on, every story we did had a purpose, and the *Daily Worker* was on the desk of every other newspaper. The *Daily Worker* had an influence far in excess of its circulation, partly because a lot of our readership was trade union people. When May Day came along, the Transport Workers Union, or Furriers, or District 65, would march with signs that said "End Jim Crow in Baseball!"

As Rodney fought to end the color ban, he also never stopped highlighting and covering the Negro League teams, giving them press at a time when they were at the margins of the sporting world. One of the players closest to Rodney personally was Negro League legend Satchel Paige.

Some people still say, "Well, maybe he wanted to stay with his own." I shot that down with an interview I did with him in which he challenged Major League Baseball to give him a tryout. He was twenty-nine at the time, and I told him, "Satch, Dazzy Vance is in the Hall of Fame and he didn't reach his peak until he was thirty-four." He said, "Okay, well I'll surely be in there by then." Thirteen more years went by and he was a forty-two-year-old rookie. America's gotten off the hook pretty lightly on this. Josh Gibson was the greatest catcher who ever put on a uniform. If you want to say Johnny Bench was the greatest catcher you ever saw, Gibson was at least as good as Bench defensively. And at bat he was nothing less than a right-handed hitting Babe Ruth. In any ballpark they played in they have places where Josh Gibson hit it out, and it measures 480 feet. That's how good he was. He became embittered and was over the hill and began drinking. It came too late for him. That kind of tragedy was for him more than Satchel because Satchel at least got a chance to make a cameo appearance and show the world how good he would have been.

Rodney remembers the Negro Leagues fondly, but the good times don't cover the truth of what it meant to play there.

Although these players were embittered, they had fun, they enjoyed it, and like any oppressed people they had their own spirit. That doesn't mean that they wanted to be playing in Podunk, and that they didn't want to be center stage of the national pastime and making that kind of money. I am highlighting Satchel Paige and Josh Gibson, but there were any number of players. [African-American sportswriter] Wendell Smith estimated that the Homestead Grays, the Black team in Pittsburgh [and later Washington, D.C.] around 1939, had six players in particular of potential all-star, big league quality.[17]

Owens and Louis

Rodney was a trailblazer in teasing out the connections between sports and politics. But the sharpest intersection of sports and politics in this era involved two men who themselves had little interest in politics but who, through their play, had the political concerns of the world thrust upon them. These two men were Jesse Owens and Joe Louis.

Outside the South, the white press trumpeted the success of Owens, Louis, and others to speak to the wondrous progress the United States had made in race matters. It was a celebration of paternalism. As the *Los Angeles Times* wrote in a 1935 editorial entitled "The Submerged Tenth,"

Jesse Owens, Negro college student, out-ran, out-hurdled, out-jumped the pick of white scholastic athletes of the country last week.

Joe Louis, 21-year-old Negro, out-boxed, out-generaled and

out-fought the former heavyweight white champion of the world
[Primo Carnera].

Paul Lawrence Dunbar, Negro, charmed the world with his
Mammy poems. George Garner is an outstanding tenor among
tenors of the country. The name of Booker T. Washington will live
as long as education. The best fighters in the Spanish War were
Negroes.

[Negroes] are among the most loyal of all Americans. Most of
them are quiet, unassuming, wholesome people. They have intelligence, stamina, and courage.

Uncle Sam can count on them.[18]

Owens and Louis were both born into abject poverty. But Owens was
a track star, which meant college. Louis was a boxer, which meant the
only schooling he got was in the ring. Sportswriters loved to contrast
these two, as if they came from different worlds. "If either were ever to
figure in the uplift of the race, then Owens would be that man," wrote
Washington Post columnist Shirley Povich. "Louis might capture the
imagination of the folks who laid great store by physical prowess and the
dynamite concentrated in a left hook, but Owens, an honor student at
Ohio State University, seemingly fitted the time-worn description—a
gentleman and a scholar."[19]

Povich may have been correct that Owens was a more presentable
presence of conventional "uplift," but he didn't consider the way boxing
has always been a sporting symbol of how African Americans fought
their way out of invisibility. As Ralph Wiley wrote years later, "Boxing
was on the one hand barbaric, unconscionable, out of place in modern
society. But then, so are war, racism, poverty, and pro football. Men died
boxing, yet there was nobility in defending oneself."[20]

Povich also missed Louis's unique place as well. Poet Maya Angelou
remembered Louis as "the one invincible Negro, the one who stood up
to the white man and beat him down with his fists. He in a sense carried
so many of our hopes, and maybe even our dreams of vengeance."[21]

Jesse Owens, more than Louis, was the most remarkable athlete of
his time. On September 12, 1913, James Cleveland Owens was born

into the sharecropping fields of Oakville, Alabama. Because of an absence of even basic health care, his early years saw him lose several siblings to early death, and a harrowing experience where his mother had to cut a fibrous tumor out of his chest with a kitchen knife.[22]

Owens lived to run. He wrote in his autobiography, "I always loved running—it was something you could do by yourself and under your own power. You could go any direction, fast or slow as you wanted, fighting the wind if you felt like it, seeking out new sights just on the strength of your own feet and courage of your lungs."[23] Owens's ascent is one of legend. He attended Ohio State on a scholarship, where he wrote and rewrote the record books with tremendous flair. The media lionized him with a distinctive awe seldom if ever bestowed on black athletes of the time.

Owens transcended mere athletic greatness when he won four gold medals at the 1936 Olympics, hosted in Adolf Hitler's Berlin. As political rebellion and resistance stalked the United States, fascism and the politics of Aryan dominance were on the march throughout Europe.

But Owens's famed Olympic feats almost never came to pass. A movement quickly sprouted in the states to keep the U.S. team out of Germany. The concern was that Hitler would use the Olympics as a pulpit for Nazism. Already Germany had produced posters, appearing throughout Europe, of Hitler with a faraway look in his eyes, with the slogan, "I summon the youth of the world."[24]

The extent of Hitler's crimes to that point hadn't surfaced, yet his politics of Aryan supremacy were well known and enough whispers had made their way across the pond about what Hitlerism would mean for the non-Aryans of Germany. This coalesced into the first Olympic boycott movement. As the boycott debate raged, some pointed out the hypocrisy of the United States taking this kind of moral stand against Germany. George S. Schuyler, who opposed the boycott, wrote to the *New York Times*,

> Where could the Olympic Games be held where liberty is not stamped into the mud and millions are not ruthlessly persecuted and exploited? Right now it probably would be impossible for the much-lauded Ralph Metcalfe, Jesse Owens, Eulace Peacock,

Cornelius Johnson, Al Threadgill, Archie Williams, Ed Gordon, Jimmy LuValle or any of the other sepia-tinted stars to get a decent meal or a room in any public hotel or café below the Mason-Dixon line (and but few above it), to say nothing of actually competing in a track meet with the Southerners. Why does the Fair Play Committee remain silent about this condition? Must we move our jim-crow areas to Germany before these gentlemen will break their silence?[25]

Walter White, the president of the NAACP, believed the boycott was necessary, Jim Crow or not. He wrote,

The United States has much to answer for in the matter of racial discrimination, especially against Negro athletes in the South. Instead, we ask the AAU to vote against participation on the ground that Germany has violated her pledges against racial discrimination, and for American athletes to participate would be to negate every principle upon which the Olympic games are based.

Refusal to participate will, we believe, do untold good in helping Germany and the world to realize that racial bigotry must be opposed in its every manifestation. To participate would be to place approval upon the German Government's deplorable persecution of racial and religious groups and would stultify the Amateur Athletic Union and all athletes who participate.[26]

White then wrote an open letter to the twenty-two-year-old Owens, asking him not to run.

I fully realize how great a sacrifice it will be for you to give up the trip to Europe and to forgo the acclaim, which your athletic prowess will unquestionably bring you. I realize equally how hypocritical it is for certain Americans to point the finger of scorn at any other country for racial or any other kind of bigotry.

. . . The issue of participation in the 1936 Olympics, if held in Germany under the present regime, transcends all other issues. Participation by American athletes, and especially those of our own race, which has suffered more than any other from American race hatred, would, I firmly believe, do irreplaceable harm. . . .

. . . I have written at greater length than I had intended at the outset. I hope, however, that you will not take offense at my writing you thus frankly with the hope that you will take the high stand that we should rise above personal benefit and help strike a blow at intolerance. I am sure that your stand will be applauded by many people in all parts of the world, as your participation under the present situation in Germany would alienate many high-minded people who are awakening to the dangers of intolerance wherever it raises its head.[27]

The *Amsterdam News* urged black athletes not to take part in the games. "Humanity demands that Hitlerism be crushed," an editorialist wrote, "and yours is the opportunity to strike a blow which may hasten the inevitable end."[28]

Owens early on in the process said publicly, "If there is racial discrimination against minorities in Germany, then we must withdraw from the Olympics." But neither he nor his coaches ever took boycotting the games seriously. This is not a hypocrisy that can be laid at the feet of Owens alone. The financial—and psychological—investment that goes into the training for these games makes a boycott a difficult if not impossible request to grant.[29]

But Owens was not the person who delivered the Olympics to Hitler. That was Avery Brundage. Brundage is the man who stands astride the history of the Olympics like no one before or since. Born, raised, and educated in material comfort in Illinois, the man who came to be called "Slavery Avery" was an athlete who competed in the pentathlon and decathlon at the 1912 Olympics in Stockholm. In 1935, Brundage was heading the United States Olympic Committee. He curtly rejected what he called the "politicization of sport" and believed the United States should compete proudly at the Berlin games. But the uproar would not subside, so he went to Germany himself to settle the question about whether Hitler was as bad as the boycotters said. He shared smiles and handshakes with the Führer for the cameras and returned to the States with tales of a new Germany that treated Jews and other national minorities with exceptional care.

Brundage's steadfast support of Hitler earned him the respect of the members of the International Olympic Committee. They voted to have him brought into their exclusive club, replacing the American representative, Ernest Lee Jahnke, who supported the Berlin boycott.[30]

Most famously, Brundage absolved himself of all moral responsibility when he said that organized amateur sport "cannot, with good grace or propriety, interfere in the internal, political, religious or racial affairs of any country or group." Of course, by bestowing approval on the Third Reich, he was doing just that. He claimed to believe that the "Olympic movement" should stand apart from politics, but it was really only a certain kind of politics.[31]

Brundage followed up his support of a Berlin Olympics with justifications backed by bigotry. "The fact that no Jews have been named so far to compete for Germany doesn't necessarily mean that they have been discriminated against on that score," Brundage said on July 26, 1935. "In forty years of Olympic history, I doubt if the number of Jewish athletes competing from all nations totaled one percent of those in the games. In fact, I believe one-half of one percent would be a high percentage."[32]

Frederick Rubien, the secretary of the United States Olympic Committee, backed Brundage up, saying, "The Jews are eliminated because they are not good enough as athletes. Why, there are not a dozen Jews in the world of Olympic caliber—and not one in our winter sports that I know of."[33] Actually, twenty-three Jewish athletes had won Olympic medals at the winter and summer games in 1932. The winner of the 100 meters in 1924 had been the British Jew Harold Abrahams, immortalized in the movie *Chariots of Fire*.[34]

As Red Smith said of Brundage, "Although Avery was frequently wrong-headed, he could also be arrogant and condescending."[35] None of his arrogance cautioned the Amateur Athletic Union, which voted by a narrow margin to participate in Berlin. Brundage's actions were no aberration. He was one of many prominent Nazi sympathizers in the United States. But unlike Henry Ford and Joseph Kennedy, Brundage— to his credit or damnation—never apologized for his Hitler leanings when the winds of the war turned. As late as 1941, he was praising the Third Reich at a Madison Square Garden "America First" rally. He was even expelled from the right-wing America First Committee because of his endless love of all things Hitler.[36]

But the games themselves at first seemed to justify every fear of the boycotters. To Hitler, the Berlin games were, as Jeremy Schaap writes in his book *Triumph*, "a fascist fantasy come true." Ceremonies were set up with the subtlety of a tank procession in Red Square, all aimed to shower further glory on the Nazis.[37]

Grantland Rice, covering the games, had a chilling description of what he saw:

> Just twenty-two years ago this day the world went to war. On the twenty-second anniversary of the outbreak of that great conflict I passed through more than 700,000 uniforms on my way to the Olympic Stadium—brown shirts, black guards, gray-green waves of regular army men and marines—seven massed military miles rivaling the mobilization of August 1, 1914. The opening ceremonies of the eleventh Olympiad, with mile upon mile, wave upon wave of a uniformed pageant, looked more like two world wars than the Olympic Games.[38]

Brundage's canard that politics and sport resided in separate worlds was betrayed by the Nazis' own publications. "Athletes and sport are the preparatory school of the political will in the service of the state," Kurt Münch wrote in a Nazi-sanctioned book titled *Knowledge About Germany*. "Non-political, so-called neutral sportsmen are unthinkable in Hitler's state."[39]

The Nazi pomp and circumstance launched the kind of over-the-top nationalism associated with the Olympics today. The Nazi Olympics also saw the birth of the kind of stark repression associated with the Olympics, as governments have attempted to cleanse cities for an international audience. On July 16, Berlin police had rounded up eight hundred Gypsies and put them in an internment camp. After the undesirables had been disappeared, Berlin was scrubbed down. Richard

Walther Darré, the German minister of food and agriculture, issued a decree that was sent to local authorities throughout Germany to enforce: "All anti-Semitic posters must be suppressed during the period in question. The fundamental attitude of the Government does not change, but Jews will be treated as correctly as Aryans at this time. . . . Houses on the main roads must be whitened, and even repainted if possible. Street lighting must be improved. Streets and squares must be cleaned. Agricultural workers in the fields must not take their meals near the roads, nor pass near the roads."[40]

But one thing Hitler and company did not count on was the dominance of not only Owens but several black Americans at the games. Black athletes starred at the Olympics, including 200 meter silver medalist Mack Robinson. Upon returning home, Mack was unable to find a job other than sweeping the Pasadena streets. Showing the defiant streak that would define his younger brother, Jackie, Mack would make it a point to sweep in his leather USA Olympic jacket, which caused local whites to call the police and charge him with being "provocative."[41]

But Owens was the star. He dominated his events, winning four gold medals: in the 100, the 200, the long jump, and the relay. No one had ever done that before, and only Carl Lewis in 1984 has done it since. "No European crowd had ever seen such a combination of blazing speed and effortless smoothness, like something blown in a gale," wrote Grantland Rice. "You could hear the chorus of gasps as he left all rivals far behind."[42]

This infuriated Hitler. He refused to be photographed with Owens or even acknowledge the existence of the man who stole the games. "The Americans ought to be ashamed of themselves for letting their medals be won by Negroes," he said. "I myself would never shake hands with one of them."[43]

Hitler wasn't the only world leader to give Owens the back of his hand. In 1940, Owens campaigned for Republican presidential nominee Alf Landon, saying in speeches, "Hitler didn't snub me—it was our president [Franklin Roosevelt] who snubbed me. The president didn't even send me a telegram."[44]

American sportswriters found a new appreciation for black athletes, now that the black was rimmed with gold. Westbrook Pegler wrote, "The American team will win, thanks to the Negro athletes, whose presence on the squad is proof of the democracy of sports in this country and the result necessarily will discredit dictatorial sportsmanship according to the values established by Adolf Hitler and Mussolini."[45]

"I can't help wondering," Bill Corum wrote from the press box shortly after Owens broke the tape, "if Herr Hitler was thinking about the racial superiority of pure Aryan strains as he saw the Midnight Express whip past. And Jesse, he doesn't even stop to whistle for the crossings."[46]

The black press had a no less appreciative view of Owens, although it was steeped in a consistent condemnation of Hitler and Nazi Germany. Dr. Clint Wilson wrote in the *Los Angeles Sentinel* upon Owens's death in 1980 that blacks "took pride in his achievements which offered solace during the Depression years amidst lingering Jim Crow practices and the legacy of 'separate but equal' policies. And while the world's eyes were on Berlin, capital of the Third Reich and Nazi propaganda, it couldn't help but see Jesse Owens—a Black man—expose the fallacies of racist ideology." In the same issue of the *Sentinel*, Brad Pye Jr. wrote, "Like Joe Louis' victories in the ring, Owens' four gold medal winning feats in the 1936 Olympic Games in Berlin gave Black America hope when there appeared to be nothing but despair, discrimination, degradation and defeat."[47]

But like Louis, upon his return Owens would soon meet with the reality of what it meant to be a black man in 1936 America. Opportunities were scarce, even for a college graduate with four gold medals. By December 1936, he was racing Julio McCaw, a five-year-old horse, in a sideshow spectacle.[48]

The Brown Bomber

The symbolic weight affixed to Owens in Berlin was shared by the first black heavyweight champion since the days of Jack Johnson: the "Brown Bomber," Joe Louis. Louis was born Joseph Louis Barrow in Lafayette, Alabama, the seventh of eight children. His father was committed to an insane asylum when Louis was two, and died two years later. Louis's mother remarried and moved to Detroit. It was here Louis honed his physique—a physique that would lead *Ring* magazine to call him "the greatest puncher of the twentieth century"—by lifting big blocks of ice up several flights of stairs. (This was also the after-school job for a young teenager named Henry Aaron, who also credited carrying the ice blocks for the strength in his wrists.)

Unlike the defiant Jack Johnson, Louis was a man of few words. He was handled very carefully by a management team that had a set of rules Louis had to follow, including to never be photographed with a white woman, never go to a club by himself, and never speak unless spoken to.[49] He was given instruction on hygiene and table manners. Sports reporter Russ Cowans gave him diction lessons, and advisors told him, "For God's sake, after you beat a white opponent, don't smile." He was part Jack Dempsey, part Eliza Doolittle.[50]

Louis may have been quiet outside the ring, but inside he was devastating, scoring sixty-nine victories in seventy-two professional fights—fifty-five of them by knockout. Louis often had to go for the knockout rather than risk a judge's decision, which might put more weight on his skin tone than on his punching prowess.[51]

Marcus Garvey was also a great supporter of Louis. He took pride in the Brown Bomber's ring triumphs, even disrupting the 1935 UNIA convention so that participants could listen to Louis's fight with Primo Carnera. As Garvey wrote,

> If in nothing else, in the realm of boxing, the Negro has raised the status of the black man. As a fact the black man is considered the only dangerous competitor of the white man in the ring and he has knocked him out so often as to leave the impression that he is safely the world's champion. The American Negro newspapers indulge in sports to a great extent. Sometimes more than fifty percent of their issues are devoted to sports news and activities. This may not be very constructive but it is very helpful.[52]

In other words, despite having an image (crafted by his handlers) of scraping and shuffling, Joe Louis and his dominance in the ring represented much more to poor blacks, and also to the radicalizing working class in the 1930s.

This played out most famously during Louis's two fights against German boxer Max Schmeling in 1936 and 1938. Hitler heavily promoted Schmeling as a living embodiment of "Aryan greatness." In their first bout, Schmeling scored a surprising knockout. Not only did Hitler and Nazi propagandist Joseph Goebbels have a field day, but the southern press in the United States gloated. One article in the New Orleans *Times-Picayune* wrote that the fight proved who really was the master race.

The Louis-Schmeling rematch in 1938 was a political maelstrom—a physical referendum on Hitler, the Jim Crow South, and the correctness of antiracism. The U.S. Communist Party organized radio listenings of the fight from Harlem to Birmingham that became mass meetings. Hitler closed down movie houses so people would be compelled to listen. It wasn't a wise move. Louis devastated Schmeling in one round.[53]

Richard Wright wrote about the Louis-Schmeling fight for the magazine *New Masses*. In his article, titled "High Tide in Harlem: Joe Louis as a Symbol of Freedom," he set the stage for that historic night:

> The Louis-Schmeling fight for the heavyweight championship of the world at the Yankee Stadium was one of the greatest dramas of make-believe ever witnessed in America, a drama which manipulated the common symbols and impulses in the minds and bodies of millions of people so effectively as to put to shame our professional playwrights, our O'Neills, our Lawsons, and our Caldwells. . . .
>
> Each of the seventy thousand who had so eagerly jammed his way into the bowl's steel tiers under the open sky had come already emotionally conditioned as to the values that would triumph if his puppet won. . . .
>
> But out beyond the walls of the stadium were twelve million Negroes to whom the black puppet symbolized the living refutation of the hatred spewed forth daily over radios, in newspapers, in movies, and in books about their lives. Day by day, since their al-

leged emancipation, they have watched a picture of themselves being painted as lazy, stupid, and diseased. In helpless horror they have suffered the attacks and exploitation which followed in the wake of their being branded as "inferiors." True, hundreds of thousands of these Negroes would have preferred that refutation could have been made in some form other than pugilism; but so effectively and completely have they been isolated and restricted in vocation that they rarely have had the opportunity to participate in the meaningful processes of America's national life. Jim Crowed in the army and navy, barred from many trades and professions, excluded from commerce and finance, relegated to menial positions in government, segregated residentially, denied the right of franchise for the most part; in short, forced to live a separate and impoverished life, they were glad for even the meager acceptance of their humanity implied in the championship of Joe Louis.[54]

Wright went on to describe Louis's physical domination of Schmeling:

At the beginning of the fight there was a wild shriek which gradually died as the seconds flew. What was happening was so stunning that even cheering was out of place. The black puppet, contrary to all Nazi racial laws, was punching the white puppet so rapidly that the eye could not follow the blows. It was not really a fight, it was an act of revenge, of dominance, of complete mastery. The black puppet glided from his corner and simply wiped his feet on the white puppet's face. The black puppet was contemptuous, swift; his victory was complete, unquestionable, decisive; his blows must have jarred the marrow not only in the white puppet's but in Hitler's own bones.

Then Wright famously described the reaction in Harlem:

In Harlem, that area of a few square blocks in upper Manhattan where a quarter of a million Negroes are forced to live through an elaborate connivance among landlords, merchants, and politicians, a hundred thousand black people surged out of taprooms, flats, restaurants, and filled the streets and sidewalks like the Mississippi River overflowing in flood time. With their faces to the night sky, they filled their lungs with air and let out a scream of joy that seemed would never end, and a scream that seemed to come from untold reserves of strength. They wanted to make a noise comparable to the happiness bubbling in their hearts, but they were poor and had nothing. So they went to the garbage pails and got tin cans; they went to their kitchens and got tin pots, pans, washboards, wooden boxes, and took possessions of the streets . . . ever seen in Harlem and marked the highest tide of popular political enthusiasm ever witnessed among American Negroes.

Negro voices called fraternally to Jewish-looking faces in passing autos:

"I bet all the Jews are happy tonight!"

The New York *Daily News* said more simply, "There was never a Harlem like the Harlem of last night. Take a dozen Christmases, a score of New Year's Eves, a bushel of July 4th's and maybe—yes maybe—you get a faint glimpse of the idea."[55]

Wright even wrote lyrics to a blues song, "King Joe (Joe Louis Blues)," put to music by Count Basie and sung by Paul Robeson, that went:

> *Old Joe wrestled Ford engines, Lord, it was a shame;*
> *Say Old Joe wrestled Ford engines, Lord, it was a shame;*
> *and he turned engine himself and went to the fighting game . . .*
> *Wonder what Joe Louis thinks when he's fighting a white man*
> *Bet he thinks what I'm thinking, cause he wears a deadpan.*[56]

The Brown Bomber held the heavyweight title for twelve years, the longest reign in history. He beat all comers, the overwhelming majority of them white, successfully defending his heavyweight title a record twenty-five times. In a society so violently racist, boxing became an outlet for people's anger—a morality play about the thwarted ability, the unrecognized talents, and the relentless fighting spirit that shaped the black experience in the United States.

Years after the fight, Martin Luther King Jr. wrote in *Why We Can't Wait*,

> More than twenty-five years ago, one of the southern states adopted a new method of capital punishment. Poison gas supplanted the gallows. In its earliest stages, a microphone was placed inside the sealed death chamber so that scientific observers might hear the words of the dying prisoner to judge how the victim reacted in this novel situation. The first victim was a young Negro. As the pellet dropped into the container, and gas curled upward, through the microphone came these words: 'Save me, Joe Louis. Save me, Joe Louis. Save me, Joe Louis. . . . ' "[57]

The Black Press

African American athletics were amplified by the success of Louis and Owens. But the unsung heroes of the African American press gave them political context. Sportswriters such as Chester L. Washington, Wendell Smith, Sam Lacy, and A.S. "Doc" Young had legions of loyal readers.[58]

Chester L. Washington, publisher of the *Los Angeles Sentinel*, celebrated Satchel Paige in a 1936 piece titled "Satchel's Back in Town," writing, "The satchel-like shape of his feet earned him the nickname that he bears today. . . . He's a natural showman as spectacular as a circus and as colorful as a rainbow." He also trumpeted a fact that the mainstream papers ignored. "Among Satchel's many achievements include the decisive defeat of several teams composed of major league stars, striking out 18 in one game and completely shutting out the Homestead Grays for the first time in their history."[59]

In 1931, after the death of Notre Dame coaching legend Knute Rockne, the African American press presented a radical counterargument, in the face of national mourning, that the world of black football didn't owe Rockne's memory an ounce of respect. In an editorial published in the black press from Chicago to Baltimore, editors wrote,

> When the great football teams of Tuskegee Institute and Wilberforce University locked horns last Saturday at Mills Stadium in Chicago, ten thousand or more members of the colored race stood bare-headed as the bugle sounded taps for the late, lamented Knute Rockne, great football coach at Notre Dame University. Now Rockne was a white man, no colored boys ever played upon his teams, in fact we know of no colored students even attending Notre Dame during Mr. Rockne's regime. Then why should ten thousand of us stand uncovered in tribute to him and why should colored boys sound taps? . . .
>
> We have listened to Rockne telling "darkey stories" over the radio and we have sensed the fact that colored people in general terms were "persona non grata" with him. It was stupid and silly for us to uncover and sound taps for him. We are a strange people who are not easily insulted, we are forgiving and long suffering but not withstanding these laudable virtues, we are guilty of some very asinine acts. This incident is a case in point.[60]

They also asked fundamental questions about sports and society as no mainstream papers did. Wendell Smith wrote in the *Pittsburgh Courier*:

> Why we continue to flock to major league ball parks, spending our hard earned dough, screaming and hollering, stamping our feet and clapping our hands, begging and pleading for some white batter to knock some white pitcher's ears off, almost having fits if the home team loses and crying for joy when they win, is a question that probably never will be answered satisfactorily. What in the world are we thinking about anyhow?
>
> The fact that major baseball refuses to admit Negro players within its folds makes the question just that much more perplex-

ing. . . . Major league baseball does not want us. It never has. Still, we continue to help support this institution that places a bold "Not Welcome" sign over its thriving portal and refuse to patronize the very place that has shown it is more than welcome to have us. We black folk are a strange tribe! . . .

. . . We keep on crawling, begging, and pleading for recognition just the same. We know that they don't want us, but still we keep giving them our money. Keep on going to their ball games and shouting till we are blue in the face. Oh, we're an optimistic, faithful, prideless lot—we pitiful black folk.

Yes sir—we black folk are a strange tribe.[61]

Harry Levette used verse for the *Minneapolis Twin Cities Herald* in a biting piece about sprinter Eddie Tolan titled "Eddie Tolan Is the Fastest Human—But":

He's a "nigger" right on
He can't run against white runners in Georgia
He can't eat with white runners in Alabama
He can't go to school with white runners in South Carolina
He can't ride the train with white runners in Texas
He can't sit beside a white runner in a street car in Florida
He can't pray in a church with white runners in Tennessee
He can't pose with white runners in Arkansas
Because he's just a "nigger."
Eddie's the "fastest human"—but
Mistreatment shall be his portion as long as life shall last
He's a "coon."
Who cares if he ain't got nothin' to eat?
He wants to be a doctor but money is scarce
Who cares?
Who'll give him a chance?
Filipino, Japanese, Chinese, Mexican, Indian—Opportunity
*   for All—*
But Eddie's a "nigger"

Dirty, different.
He can run like hell, but—he's a nigger right on.
He wins honors for American [sic], but nothing for himself
He must plot right on, passing up eating places while he's hungry
Begging for somebody to take his part so he can inch along.
The better he does the worse it hurts.
Like [Countee] Cullen, he can exclaim "I who have burned my
*   hands upon a star."*[62]

The black press of the 1930s also covered what the mainstream press would not: the way sports was starting to make inroads against Jim Crow. Roy Wilkins, writing for the New York *Amsterdam News* in 1936, before he became executive director of the NAACP, penned a piece called "That Ol' Southern Accent." It's an account of an all-white southern squad traveling north to face an opponent. What made this game different was that the northern team was integrated:

There were no boos and in my section of the stand I heard none of the familiar cries of "Kill the Negro!" So far, the University of North Carolina is still standing and none of the young men representing it on the gridiron appears to be any worse off for having spent an afternoon competing against a Negro player.

It is a fairly safe prediction that no white North Carolinian's daughter will marry a Negro as a result of Saturday's play, much to the chagrin of the peddlers of the bugaboo of social equality. . . .

The theory behind all these shenanigans has been that the prestige of a southern school suffers in some way if its sons compete in games with Negroes. Not only that, but the South and the white race generally were supposed to suffer something or other. Honor allegedly was involved. Sociology, anthropology and political science were dragged into the argument, the whole thing topped off by a rehash of the war of 1860–65.

There is no logic in this position, but prejudices are never logical. There is no sportsmanship in it either, but prejudices come first and sports second.[63]

This occurred in the press box as well. White reporters began to interact with their black counterparts and started to raise the issue of integration for the national pastime, major league baseball. Many a white journalist went public with their pleas for integration.

In April 1939, Povich wrote, "There's a couple of million dollars worth of baseball talent on the loose, ready for the big leagues yet unsigned by any major league clubs. . . . Only one thing is keeping them out of the big leagues—the pigmentation of their skin. . . . That's their crime in the eyes of the big league club owners. . . . It's a tight little boycott that the majors have set up against colored players."[64]

One of the major league team owners, Clark Griffith of the Washington Senators, gave a lengthy interview to *Baltimore Afro American* columnist Sam Lacy in 1938, and hinted at the possibility of integrated ball. He told Lacy, "Both the commissioner [Judge Landis] and I know that colored baseball is deserving of some recognition in the organized game. . . . However, I am not so sure that the time has arrived yet. . . . A lone Negro in the game will face rotten, caustic comments. He will be made the target of cruel, filthy epithets. . . . I would not want to have to be the one to have to take it."[65]

But someone would.

·5·

War and Its Discontents

With the bombing of Pearl Harbor on December 7, 1941, the United States officially entered World War II. Passed around the press box at Griffith Stadium in Washington, D.C., was the simple phrase "The Japanese have kicked off! War now!"[1]

Interestingly, the *Washington Post* sent its ace sports columnist, Shirley Povich, to the Marianas Islands to cover the war. In this way, the paper used the language of sports to sell the war. As Povich wrote in one story:

> Last July, the Japs were playing baseball on these islands when the word went out: Game called on account of Americans. That was the month the Marines landed on the beaches, chased the Nips into the hills, and proceeded to take over generally.
>
> Today I saw two teams of big leaguers play a ball game on the same diamond the Japs had carved out of the jungle . . .
>
> This was no USO troupe of baseball entertainers. The men on the field were former big leaguers who are in the Navy now.[2]

The global death toll from World War II is estimated at sixty million. From 1941 to 1945, eighteen million Americans served in the armed forces, with sixteen million deployed overseas. The people who came of age in the World War II era are described—and if you listen closely, you can hear Tom Brokaw cooing—as the "greatest generation." Implied is a unity and sense of self-sacrifice for a noble national goal: the defeat of the Axis powers. This history ignores the fact that it was a time in the United States that was anything but quiescent. The coming of the war meant that thousands of Japanese Americans were interned. War also meant war production. Factories had to operate without interruption. Blacks and women were needed for a war economy in a way that was without precedent. The Communist Party, which at the time had members in the leadership of many of the industrial unions, staunchly supported the "no-strike pledge" labor agreed to during the war. They also supported the internment of Japanese Americans, including members of their own party. Despite this, however, there were still fourteen thousand strikes, involving 6.77 million workers, more than in any comparable period in American history. In 1944, a million industrial workers were on strike.[3]

Sports in the Camps

On February 19, 1942, President Franklin Delano Roosevelt signed Executive Order 9066, which authorized the U.S. government to forcibly round up 120,000 people of Japanese descent into internment camps. But still there was resistance. The camps were the sites of strikes, mass meetings, refusal to sign loyalty oaths, and riots against camp authorities. Sports also became a way the interned made life liveable, as well as a way to build a sense of community. Ansel Adams took a famous series of photos of the interned playing baseball and football and doing calisthenics. At one camp in Gila River, Arizona, thirty-two teams competed in front of thousands of prisoners. "It was demeaning and humiliating to be incarcerated in your own country," remembered George Omachi to author Gary Otake. "Without baseball, camp life would have been miserable.' "[4]

One of the driving forces of baseball in the camps was the five-foot-tall, 105-pound catcher Kenichi Zenimura, known among Japanese Americans as the "Dean of the Diamond." After Executive Order 9066 was signed, Zenimura and his family were sent to multiple internment camps, but as his son, Howard, remembered, "Every time my dad went someplace, if there was no baseball park he'd make one." But it was at the Gila River, Arizona, camp, in the midst of the scorched desert, where Zenimura made history. The ground was sand, but alongside an army of fellow internees, Zenimura constructed a field that eventually served thirty-two teams in three divisions. Howard recalled that "we pulled up every other 4 x 6 wooden pole that anchored the barbed wire fence to build the backstop and grandstand." One internee who remembered Zenimura, family, and friends bringing baseball into the camp was Noriyuki "Pat" Morita, who would later earn an Oscar nomination for playing Mr. Miyagi in *The Karate Kid*: "I remember this little old man out there every day watering the infield," Morita said. "One of the great sounds of joy for me was the sound of baseball."[5]

Blacks During World War II

The same logic of racism that led to the internment of the Japanese was behind the wholesale segregation of the armed forces. A segregated army, with facilities both separate and unequal, was not the strongest way to win loyalty among African Americans. For blacks, fighting Hitler's white supremacy for ideals they didn't experience at home didn't gain the same kind of traction.

"The Negro . . . is angry, resentful, and utterly apathetic about the war," wrote black journalist Earl Brown in 1942. " 'Fight for what?' he is asking. 'This war doesn't mean a thing to me. If we win, I lose, so what.' "[6]

In September 1942, NAACP leader Walter White told the story of a young student at a historically black college saying to his professor, "The Army jim-crows us. The Navy lets us serve only as messmen. The Red Cross refuses our blood. Employers and labor unions shut us out. Lynchings continue. We are disenfranchised, jim-crowed, spat upon. What more could Hitler do than that?"[7]

In 1943, one black newspaper quoted what was called the "Draftee's Prayer":

Dear Lord, today
I go to war:
To fight, to die,
Tell me what for?
Dear Lord, I'll fight,
I do not fear,
Germans or Japs;
My fears are here.
America.[8]

At home it wasn't much better. During the war period, African American families began a migration to California, where promises of war-economy factory jobs and distance from segregation held strong appeal. At first these dreams were ruthlessly thwarted. A spokesman for one West Coast aviation plant said, "The Negro will be considered only as janitors and in other similar capacities. . . . Regardless of their training as aircraft workers, we will not employ them."[9]

But a combination of the needs of war and popular pressure changed the openings for blacks in the war. In 1941, union and civil rights leader A. Philip Randolph told President Roosevelt that he would march a hundred thousand people on Washington unless discriminatory labor practices came to an end. Roosevelt hurriedly issued Executive Order 8802, prohibiting discrimination in defense jobs or the government. And yet as the war wore on, opportunities to fight—and opportunities to work—opened up out of bare necessity. It started with a trickle: the War Department forming the Tuskegee Airmen in 1941 after pressure from the NAACP to have black troops do more than clerical work, cooking, and cleaning. By 1944, the Tuskegee Airmen flew alongside whites in European missions. General Eisenhower put two thousand black troops on the front lines as Hitler advanced in 1944's Battle of the Bulge.[10]

African American women nurses overcame whites' belief that it would be "inappropriate" for blacks to treat white soldiers. More than two million African Americans went to work for defense plants, and another two million joined the federal civil service. As these new opportunities drew more and more African Americans into cities, they opened the way for economic mobility, raised expectations, and created much broader support for the war in the African American community.[11]

Rosie the Pitcher

The overwhelming majority of those deployed were men. As the nation geared up for full war production, this meant that millions of women went to work in the factories. One symbol of this transformation was the iconic poster of Rosie the Riveter. Another symbol was the catapulting to prominence of women's professional baseball, perhaps best known from the movie *A League of Their Own*.

The All-American Girls Professional Baseball League, which lasted from 1943 to 1954, attempted to fill the void left when many major league baseball stars signed up for war duty. The AAGPBL was started as a nonprofit entity with such baseball kingpins as Philip K. Wrigley and Branch Rickey on the board. Teams played in and were supported by small working-class towns, finding homes in places such as Kenosha, Washington; Peoria, Illinois; South Bend, Indiana; and Battle Creek, Michigan.[12]

As Jeanie Des Combes Lesko, a pitcher for the Grand Rapids Chicks, remembered years later,

> In that time, it gave the local communities a place to go to have a good time, be with people and forget about the hard times; there was rationing of food, many people had to work in factories to make ends meet and replace the men in their families who were off at war. Many worked in defense plants making instruments of war just to be part of the fight for freedom for those who were being suppressed. People needed local heroes, like they do today, and we provided them with that.[13]

The women who participated in the league—all white, and overwhelmingly working-class—were required to attend charm school, where they were given a manual with advice such as:

Your ALL-AMERICAN GIRLS BASEBALL LEAGUE BEAUTY KIT Should always contain the following:

- Cleansing Cream
- Lipstick
- Rouge Medium
- Cream Deodorant
- Mild Astringent
- Face powder for Brunette
- Hand Lotion
- Hair Remover

. . . Remember the skin, the hair, the teeth and the eyes. It is most desirable in your own interests, that of your teammates and fellow players, as well as from the standpoint of the public relations of the league, that each girl be at all times presentable and attractive, whether on the playing field or at leisure. Study your own beauty culture possibilities and without overdoing your beauty treatment at the risk of attaining gaudiness, practice the little measure that will reflect well on your appearance and personality as a real All-American girl. . . .

Unwanted or superficial hair is often quite common and it is no problem to cope with in these days when so many beauty preparations are available. If your [sic] have such hair on arms or legs, there are a number of methods by which it can be easily removed. There is an odorless liquid cream which can be applied in a few moments, permitted to dry and then showered off.[14]

The "girls" were heavily chaperoned and monitored at all times. After World War II, the league proved that it was more than a sideshow, as teams would routinely attract 2,000 to 3,000 people per game. In 1948 the league peaked, with ten teams drawing more than 900,000 paid fans. However, attendance declined in the following years, and the league that gave more than six hundred women the chance to play baseball was no more by 1954.[15]

"If He's Good Enough for the Navy . . ."

The war also indirectly sparked the movement for civil rights in sports. Thousands of black vets came home from fighting what they were told was a battle against Nazi Germany's politics of racial supremacy. The expectations and hopes that were raised were transferred to the world of sports, fueling the fire to desegregate professional baseball. A prominent anti-racist slogan during World War II was "If he's good enough for the Navy, he's good enough for the majors."[16]

As the troops began to come home in 1945, the End Jim Crow in Baseball Committee was launched in New York City, with the support of Mayor Fiorello LaGuardia.[17]

Desegregating major league baseball had become a central goal not merely of radical sportswriters but of the civil rights community as a whole. Through it all, Commissioner Landis insisted that there was no "color line"—and indeed nothing was written, but everyone knew the score. One day in 1945, Hall of Fame pitcher Walter "Big Train" Johnson was idly marveling about the greatness of Negro League great Josh Gibson and said, "There is a catcher that any big league club would like to buy for $200,000. His name is Gibson. They call him 'Hoot' Gibson, and he can do everything. He hits that ball a mile. And he catches the ball so easy he might just as well be in a rocking chair. Throws like a rifle. . . . Too bad this Gibson is a colored fellow."[18]

This recalls the line from August Wilson's Pulitzer Prize–winning play *Fences*, in which the embittered former Negro League player Troy Maxson says, "Ain't got a pot to piss in or a window to throw it out of. . . . Now you take that fellow . . . what's that fellow they had playing right field for the Yankees back then? . . . Selkirk! That's it. Man batting .269, understand! .269. What kind of sense that make? I was hitting .432 with thirty-seven home runs! Man batting .269 and playing right field for the Yankees! I saw Josh Gibson's daughter yesterday. She walking around with raggedy shoes on her feet. Now I bet you Selkirk's daughter ain't walking around with raggedy shoes on her feet! I bet you that!"[19]

A serious step toward desegregation came in 1944 with the death of Kenesaw Mountain Landis. His successor, Happy Chandler, said in

1946, "If [blacks] can fight and die in Okinawa, Guadalcanal, in the South Pacific, they can play baseball in America. And when I give my word, you can count on it."[20]

Jack Roosevelt Robinson

Given how the war raised the expectations of blacks in America, it shouldn't be too surprising that the man who smashed the color line was a vet. One of those ten million U.S. citizens fighting overseas was Jack Roosevelt "Jackie" Robinson. Robinson was born in rural Georgia and raised in Pasadena, California. He attended nearby UCLA, where he achieved national recognition for his skills in both baseball and football. He was always combative, never someone to calmly absorb slights and jibes, racial or otherwise. He brought this approach to the segregated armed forces. Jackie was court-martialed on charges relating to his refusal to give up his seat on a bus (buses on military bases were nonsegregated at that time, unlike civilian buses in the South), though he was eventually acquitted. Another time, he heard a white superior officer call a black private a "stupid nigger son of a bitch." Jackie calmly stepped in and said, "You shouldn't speak to a soldier in those terms." He was then told, "Oh fuck you too nigger!" In a flash, according to one witness, "Jackie almost killed the guy." Only the intervention of heavyweight boxing champion Joe Louis, an admirer of Jackie's college exploits, prevented another court-martial. Without his athletic background, Jackie Robinson could have spent years in a military prison.[21]

After the war, Jackie, alongside his wife, Rachel, aimed to settle down, with dreams of becoming a gym teacher. But first he joined the Negro Leagues as a twenty-six-year old rookie. In 1946, Robinson caught the eye of Brooklyn Dodgers general manager and part owner Branch Rickey. Rickey thought Robinson could be the person to finally break through the color line that garrotted major league baseball. "I was thrilled scared and excited. Most of all I was speechless," remembered Jackie. The choice of Robinson was a shock to almost all baseball observers. Some thought the first player championed should be an aging Negro League legend such as Satchel Paige or Josh Gibson.

Others thought Robinson was a good but not great player and that he would fail. But Branch Rickey was looking for a "type" as much as a ballplayer. He believed that breaking the color line wouldn't be just about skill, but also about the ability to endure the harassment, threats, and daily pressure to perform. In the articulate college graduate and army veteran, Rickey had the man to take on what would be a mighty and official resistance to change. That previous winter, in a vote among major league owners, the count had been fifteen to one against integration, with Rickey the lone dissenter.[22]

Rickey was someone who acted from both the heart and the wallet. His heart had him telling a story of coaching the University of Michigan team and having an African American player, Charles Thomas, denied lodging on a road trip to South Bend, Indiana, for a game against Notre Dame. Rickey would recount to audiences of convincing the hotel manager to let Thomas stay in his room. Rickey found Thomas later, tugging at his hands, saying, "Black skin . . . if I could only make 'em white."[23]

But Rickey's idealism coexisted with his hard-headed assessment that, in the wake of World War II, integration was an inevitability, and he wanted to get in on the ground floor. "The Negroes will make us winners for years to come," Rickey said. "And for that I will happily bear being called a bleeding heart and a do-gooder and all that humanitarian rot."[24] "Regardless of the motives," pioneering African American ballplayer Monte Irvin said years later, "Rickey had the conviction to pursue and to follow through."[25]

William Bramham, the president of the minor leagues, had choice words from his North Carolina office for Rickey's "noble experiment." First he opined to a newspaper that the "Rickey Temple" was surely being built in Harlem. Then, in words that recall the resistance to Reconstruction nearly a century earlier, he said, "It is those of the carpetbagger stripe of the white race, under the guise of helping, but in truth using the Negro for their own selfish purposes, who retard the race. . . . And whenever I hear a white man, whether he be from the North, South, East, or West, broadcasting what a Moses he is to the Negro race, then I know the Negro needs a bodyguard."[26]

Robinson probably did need a bodyguard to protect him from Rickey, but for a different reason from what was stirring in the mind of William Bramham. In their first meeting, Rickey asked his new second baseman, "I know you have the skills. But do you have the guts?" This meant, in effect, did he have the guts to take torrents of abuse and not respond? A decade before the rise of Dr. Martin Luther King Jr. and his movement of nonviolent resistance, Rickey was asking Robinson, a player with a hair-trigger temper, to turn the other cheek. Robinson of course agreed to the challenge, but he couldn't have known what he would face.[27]

Robinson's first minor league manager, with the Montreal Royals, was Clay Hopper. Hopper was a southerner and complained immediately to Rickey about Robinson. His lips a-quiver, he asked his boss, "Mr. Rickey, do you really think a nigger's a human being?"

Montreal's every game was followed with zeal from Harlem to Watts, every at bat a test of whether African Americans had the "necessities" to achieve success in baseball. Sam Lacy wrote, "I felt a lump in my throat each time a ball was hit in his direction. . . . I was constantly in fear of his muffing an easy roller under the stress of things. And I uttered a silent prayer of thanks as, with closed eyes, I heard the solid whack of Robinson's bat against the ball."[28]

In the minors, Robinson got a sneak preview of what he would face in the major leagues: calls never going his way, black cats thrown onto the field during his at bats, and death threats that shadowed him and his family. As Robinson remembered, "The toll these incidents took were greater than I realized. I was overestimating my stamina and underestimating the beating I was taking. I couldn't sleep or eat." Yet his relentless competitiveness and stoicism in the face of racism won over his critics. Even his Montreal manager, Clay Hopper, in what would be a familiar transformation, said upon Robinson's call-up to the majors, "You're a great player and a fine gentleman and it's been wonderful having you on the team."[29]

He also was afforded a view of the incredible affection he would engender in black America. When the Royals met the Louisville Colonels in Kentucky, thousands of African Americans were turned away from the game because only a thousand tickets were available for those with black skin. Some climbed to rooftops nearby or attempted to watch from trees.[30]

As the day of his major league debut drew near, Branch Rickey, alongside NAACP president Walter White, went on the offensive against those they feared might destroy their dreams of integration: overexuberant African Americans. Rickey gave lectures to African American audiences that they must temper their pleasure for the good of the "noble experiment."

"The one enemy most likely to ruin [Robinson's] success—is the Negro people themselves," Rickey roared to one audience. "You'll hold Jackie Robinson days . . . and Jackie Robinson nights. You'll get drunk. You'll fight. You'll be arrested. You'll wine and dine the player until he is fat and futile. You'll symbolize his importance into a national comedy . . . and an ultimate tragedy—yes, tragedy."[31]

White endorsed Rickey's comments, writing:

Base runners with sharpened spikes rising high to break up double plays or lunging back to the bag to avoid being picked off are a normal part of professional baseball. A man's livelihood causes him to do lots of things he wouldn't ordinarily do, especially when players remember that the next season's contract and salary depend on batting averages, runs scored and batted in, bases stolen and all-around aggressiveness.

. . . Most of the big league players will treat him like any other player and in fact, probably go out of their way to avoid hurting Robinson for fear they may be accused wrongly.[32]

He then quite remarkably wrote, "Clay Hopper, Jackie's manager at Montreal, did everything he possibly could to help him make the big leagues." And White chided African American fans for booing Robinson's racist teammate Dixie Walker:

Jackie was cheered as lustily when he slapped into a double play as though he had hit a homes with the bases loaded. That was bad enough but not the worst example of bad manners. Whenever Dixie Walker came to bat he was lustily and even profanely booed for allegedly having said he would not play on the same team as a Negro.[33]

Rickey's and White's words ignored the harsh reality of what Robinson was facing. Before he played a single game, teammates such as Walker and others petitioned to get him off the squad. Other clubs threw at his head or spiked his legs. Respected baseball all-star and fellow veteran Bob Feller said at the end of the 1946 season that he didn't see one black player who was a legitimate major leaguer. "I have seen none who combine the qualities of a big league ball player. Not even Jackie Robinson."[34] Not only could Robinson not respond, no one came to his defense. He was a twenty-seven-year-old rookie who, as sportswriter Jimmy Cannon wrote, "is the loneliest man I have ever seen."[35]

The baseball of Robinson's day was provincial. The St. Louis teams, the Cardinals and Browns, were as far west as the league went, and the team of the South was located in that city of southern efficiency and northern charm, Washington, D.C. A typical player made $5,000 a year. Only the Yankees sent their broadcaster, Mel Allen, on the road.[36] But that was starting to change. The Brooklyn Dodgers drew only 482,000 in 1937, but in 1946 more than 1.7 million fans paid their way into Ebbets Field. After World War II, there was more disposable income, more diversity in the stands, and more support for Jackie Robinson.[37]

On April 22, 1947, Philadelphia Phillies manager Ben Chapman organized his team to chant "nigger"—and worse—at Robinson throughout the game. First Robinson ignored them, and his teammates did nothing. As Robinson remembered:

I felt tortured and I tried to just play ball and ignore the insults. But it was really getting to me. . . .

For one wild and rage-crazed moment I thought, "To hell with Mr. Rickey's 'noble experiment.' " . . . To hell with the image of the patient black freak I was supposed to create. I could throw down my bat, stride over to that Phillies dugout, grab one of those white sons of bitches, and smash his teeth in with my despised black fist. Then I could walk away from it all.

Finally, Robinson's teammates couldn't take it any more. Dodger leader Eddie Stanky yelled into the Phillies dugout, "Listen, you yellow-bellied cowards, why don't you yell at someone who can answer back?" The Dodgers then picked up bats and edged forward until the Phillies and Chapman backed down. As Rickey remembered, "Chapman did more than anybody to unite the Dodgers."[38]

The crowds that were coming to the ballparks to see Robinson also may have shifted the atmosphere. Large African American crowds, no matter what the city, would show up to root for the Dodgers, making every road game almost a home game, or at least deeply divided. As black novelist John A. Williams remembered, "Many of us who went to the park to see Jackie did so to protect him, to defend him from harm, if necessary, as well as to cheer him on."[39]

Yet even if the baseball fraternity was not ready to accept the new reality Robinson represented, his place on the field was a clear harbinger of things to come in sports and beyond. On July 5, 1947, Larry Doby of the Cleveland Indians integrated the American League. By the year's end, Robinson had won the first-ever Rookie of the Year Award and led the league in stolen bases. He became an instant legend in black America, and his "patient" demeanor made him a hero for large swaths of an emergent liberal white America. In a national poll, he ranked as the second most admired American, ahead of President Harry S. Truman and General Dwight D. Eisenhower and behind only Bing Crosby. As sportswriter Roger Kahn put it, "By applauding Robinson, a man did not feel that he was taking a stand on school integration, or on open housing. But . . . to disregard color, even for an instant, is to step away from the old prejudices."[40] This is surely correct. But it also led to a degree of irrational exuberance, with the *Sporting News* proclaiming that the issue of race in organized baseball "no longer exists."[41]

Racism in fact continued to rage. As Sam Lacy of the *Baltimore Afro American* wrote:

If the reports emanating from this quarter are so glowing as to give the impression everything in baseball's integration experiment is now honey and whipped cream, let me assure you that is far from the truth.

The blame for such a misconception—if one be alive—perhaps rests with me. It is very probably due to the rose-colored glasses I so frequently don when this type of assignment comes my way.

Regardless of any impressions you may have gotten to the contrary, the South has not accepted inter-racialism in baseball. It is merely tolerating it.

Jackie Robinson, Roy Campanella, Don Newcombe and Dan Bankhead are recognized in Dixie as Brooklyn Dodger baseball players, sure. But they are also recognized as colored men.[42]

This reality made Robinson seethe. The image of the quiet, subservient, soft-spoken gentleman was a ruse. Robinson's true personality, as seen in his army days, was angry, combative, and confrontational. For him, real progress occurred in 1948, when Rickey gave him more leeway to argue with umpires and even spike players back if they got him first.

As the 1949 season began, Robinson gained more confidence to speak, and he threw down a warning to umpires: "I am not going to be anyone's sitting duck. I know what's going on out there." He also was winning the undying friendship of white teammates, including shortstop Pee Wee Reese. Before one game in Cincinnati, when the local white supremacist group threatened to assassinate Robinson on the field, Reese laughed to reporters and said, "I think we will all wear 42 [Robinson's number] and then they will have a shooting gallery."[43]

"Four hundred fifty five years after Columbus eagerly discovered America," Shirley Povich wrote in a biting *Washington Post* piece, "Major League Baseball reluctantly discovered the American Negro; discovered that he could play ball as well, sometimes better, than the white boys and men to whom the national game supposedly belonged by right of pigmentation. The Negro ball player, in turn, made a discovery of his own once the Color Curtain was lifted. . . . The Negro player found that there is more democracy in the locker room than in baseball's front offices or even in the street."[44]

The Negro Leagues Are Picked Apart

Robinson's success, historic as it was, also heralded the Negro Leagues' eventual demise. Once Rickey got the go-ahead, he was merciless in strip-mining the Negro Leagues. As Rickey put it soon after Robinson entered the majors, "There is no Negro League as such as far as I'm concerned." Rickey insisted that Negro Leagues "are not leagues and have no right to expect organized baseball to respect them."[45]

What Rube Foster had feared, that the Negro Leagues would be "picked apart like a carcass by so many buzzards," was coming to pass. Robinson's victory, therefore, was not as universally cheered by black America as we are sometimes led to believe. There are far more shades of gray in this story of black and white. Gerald Early writes today:

> Robinson's achievement was fraught from the beginning with ambivalence, both his own and that of the blacks for whom he was a hero. And that ambivalence is characteristic of black assimilation into many arenas of American life. . . .
>
> Arising out of the insult and stigma of segregation, the Negro leagues were never meant to be an end in themselves. But because, through the leagues, blacks developed a more elaborate and enduring institutional relationship with baseball than with any other sport, baseball became not only a means to assimilate but also a black cultural and commercial venture. Black baseball demonstrated black independence as much as it showed whites that blacks were able, competitive, and desired very much to play baseball with them.
>
> By expressing the desire for freedom and respect, even esteem, through entrepreneurship and enterprise, as well as demonstrating the nationalistic urge of blacks to act independently of whites, the leagues—like black colleges, black churches, and other "shadow" institutions that blacks developed—became an end in

themselves, took on a compelling racial mission. Robinson's heroism, as a contradictory form of liberation, cannot be understood
outside this conundrum, one that explains a great deal about the
ambivalence that African Americans feel about integration as a political and social goal. . . .

What did integration cost? I have never heard a black person
mention Jackie Robinson without noting that he died a physical
wreck, at the age of 52—a fact attributed to the stress of his years
as a major-league player. And it is undeniable that once the Negro
leagues died, once baseball ceased to have an institutional presence in black life, blacks generally lost interest in professional
baseball as spectators and fans.[46]

Negro League owners who believed in integration as a political goal
found that one should be careful what you wish for. Effa Manley was a
case in point. Manley was the owner of the Newark Eagles from 1935 to
1948. She carried a stellar reputation as an advocate for her players and
the community in Newark. She was the first Negro League owner to
purchase an air-conditioned bus for her players. She was also a treasurer
of the Newark chapter of the National Association for the Advancement
of Colored People (NAACP) and held "Anti-Lynching Days" at the stadium. "We must never lose sight of the fact that the origin of Negro
baseball as it presently constituted was born of discrimination," Manley
said. "We would never have had all-Negro teams, or even all-Negro audiences if it had not been for the Jim Crow practices all of us have
sought to eliminate."[47]

After Robinson integrated major league baseball, Manley wanted to
sit across from major league club owners and do business. She even
was able to sell the contract of her star player Larry Doby to the Indians'
progressive owner Bill Veeck. But that was the exception. The talent was
raided, and the leagues crumbled seemingly overnight. Manley described "being squeezed between intransigent racial considerations on
one hand and cold business reasoning on the other."[48]

But she also highlighted the importance of the institution, saying, "If
we fail to support our Negro leagues in this crucial period we may be

hastening the day when no Negroes will be playing in the majors. The boys cannot make the jump from sandlot baseball into the big leagues without going through a period of development such as they are given in the Negro leagues."[49]

Football Ahead of Its Time

Using the political thrust of World War II to push for desegregation was not limited to baseball. On December 7, 1946, three members of the Miami University faculty resigned to protest the school's refusal to play football against integrated Penn State. The Dade County Civil Rights Council wrote the university president, "Negro and white soldiers fought together during World War II, and many of them died together. They certainly should be good enough to play football together anywhere in these United States."[50]

The University of Nevada and Pennsylvania State College refused to leave black players at home when their teams played at southern colleges. Fresno left black players behind even though students and athletes protested against the measure. In Rick Hurt's "Sports Train" column in the *Washington Afro American* he wrote, "Signs of progress are many. Nevada, Penn State, and Duquesne cancelled games rather than bench Negro players. Wyoming is to be barred from New York, because coach Irv Shelton shouted racial epithets on the Garden floor. Robinson set to join Dodgers. Buddy Young and Paul Patterson played in the Rose Bowl. Negroes are playing in both professional football leagues. New York has a Negro boxing commissioner, judge, referee, and announcer."[51]

Professional football, still a decidedly second-tier sport at the time, also saw the thrust toward integration. This was an easier leap than in baseball. The first black professional was Charles Follis back near the turn of the century, but the first black American Professional Football Association member was none other than Frederick "Fritz" Pollard, the former Brown University running back who signed to play for the Akron Indians in 1920. Pollard was one of thirteen blacks who played from 1920 to 1933 in the APFA and its successor, the NFL. He carried so much respect that when his team was denied service at a whites-only

hotel in Dayton, Ohio, his teammates, who included a number of southerners, all walked out as one. Other players in the early years of the game
included Henry McDonald and Paul Robeson. From 1934 through
1945, though, there was a color line. The color line was in step with the
times, and was thought to be the result of behind-the-scenes pressure
applied by Washington Redskins owner, George Preston Marshall, an
arch-segregationist.[52]

African American writer William Brower in 1940 made a plea for removing the color line. There is certainly an undercurrent of anger, but
the thrust of his piece is a call for some noblesse oblige from the game's
owners. He even generously calls Marshall a man of "estimable character."[53] As he wrote:

> There are no arresting or rational excuses for professional football
> to follow the dubious precedent set by professional baseball. Be-
> fore pro football was elevated to its present position of prominence
> and affluence on the national sporting panorama, Negroes were
> identified with it in playing capacity without displeasure. . . .
>
> You realize it is difficult to entertain any particular grievance
> against Tim Mara, George Halas, George Preston Marshall, Art
> Rooney and others of the NPFL officialdom. These are gentlemen
> of estimable character. They purged their game of all the poison
> with which it was formerly rife. It was their promotional ingenuity,
> generous and patient investment, courageous perseverance and
> commendable foresight which proved to be the optimum for the
> prevalent salutary status of the game. Their combined efforts
> lifted pro football from a floundering business in the ruck into an
> aura of respectability as an established enterprise of sports.
>
> But the evidence of double-jointed action towards the Negro
> somewhere along the line is transparent. The professional game of
> football has flourished with amazing celerity. One hopes that its
> guardians will not let its prestige continue to be retarded and tar-
> nished by discrimination because of color—the most truculent
> tentacle of Prejudice.[54]

Baseball and boxing were the kings of sports in the United States. Football, particularly professional football, was somewhat of a sideshow. It therefore escaped much notice when in 1946 a competitor league rose to challenge the NFL. The All-American Football League (AAFL) was largely taken over by the NFL in 1950, but in 1946 it took two steps that demonstrated it was ahead of its time. In that year the Cleveland Browns signed African American players Marion Motley and Bill Willis, ending the color line in the pro game. The AAFL leadership also located franchises in Los Angeles and San Francisco, on the economically thriving West Coast.[55]

Paul "Dr. Z" Zimmerman, the senior football writer for *Sports Illustrated*, calls Motley the greatest player in the history of the sport. In 1968 Motley became the first African American elected into the Pro Football Hall of Fame.[56]

Motley played on both sides of the line of scrimmage. He was a Hall of Fame quality linebacker but gained his reputation as a running back, averaging a galactic 5.7 yards per carry. He was six foot one, 238 pounds, which made him fifty pounds heavier than many linebackers. Dick "Night Train" Lane, a Los Angeles Rams defensive back, described what it was like trying to tackle Motley: 'He looked like a big tank rolling down on me. But you've got to take him on. I hit him with my head in his knees and he came down. I saw a few stars, but I felt good because I tackled Marion Motley."[57]

Motley, from a working-class community in Ohio, saw football as his best shot at class mobility. "I knew this was the one big chance in my life to rise above the steel mill existence and I really wanted to take it."[58] But despite his myriad accomplishments, Motley didn't earn much more than what a union job in a steel mill paid. He made $4,500 in 1946, with his salary never exceeding $15,000. He also received the flak that Jackie Robinson felt, without the glory. "My hands were always bloody," Motley said. "But if either Willis or myself had been hotheads and gotten into fights and things like that, it would have put things back 10 years. Sometimes I wanted to just kill some of those guys, and the officials would just stand right there. They'd see those guys stepping on us and heard them saying things and just turn their backs. That kind of crap went on for two or three years until they found out what kind of players we were. They found out that while they were call[ing] us, 'niggers,' I was running for touchdowns and Willis was knocking the [crap] out of them."[59] Later in life, Motley still felt the sting. When he asked a Browns executive about a job after his retirement, the reply was, "Have you ever tried the steel mills?" "I knew the game," he told a *New York Times* reporter in 1982, "but they never asked me to be a coach."[60]

African American Women

For African American women, opportunities to be athletic began to emerge. The year 1948 saw the first African American woman win an Olympic gold medal when Alice Coachman won in the high jump. Named to five All-American teams and eight halls of fame, Coachman was the dominant athlete of the 1940s, despite missing the 1940 and 1944 Olympics due to their cancellation as a result of the war. After retirement, Coachman formed the Alice Coachman Track and Field Foundation, "a nonprofit organization that provides assistance to young athletes and helps former Olympic athletes adjust to life after the games."[61]

A two-sport star at Tuskegee, Coachman was just one of many superb African American women athletes to come out of the historically black colleges and universities. "The most outstanding women's track and field athletes in the entire nation came from historically black state universities," wrote historians David Wiggins and Patrick Miller. "Joining Tuskegee, such schools as Florida A&M, Alcorn A&M, Prairie View A&M, Alabama State, Fort Valley State, and Tennessee State fielded great teams that captured various relay titles and championships at the local, regional, and national levels of competition. In contrast to the campus culture at the liberal arts colleges and black universities of the South, such as Fisk and Howard and their white counterparts, many African American communities displayed a more expansive notion of womanhood and supported athletic competition in demanding sports."[62]

Yet despite their achievement, as William Rhoden put it, "the most striking feature of the historical record on black women athletes is neglect."[63]

Start Your Engines

Today NASCAR carries television ratings second only to the National Football League. When it comes to attendance, seventeen of the top twenty sporting events in the United States in 2005 were NASCAR. While it still has a reputation as a regional sport, it is broadcast in more than 150 countries and claims 75 million fans, who support more than $2 billion in annual sales of licensed products. One only has to look at the cars to see how many Fortune 500 companies have embraced the sport. But its beginnings in 1946 were much more humble. The creation of NASCAR was an effort to tame something that had been going on since the days of prohibition. The roots of NASCAR lie in the outlaw culture of the South. Bootleggers running moonshine would soup up their engines to be able to outrun the law—or outrun the Klan. As they were more and more successful, their jacked-up machines became top-flight cars. The bootleggers began to race each other, the tradition being they would race Sunday afternoon and run liquor Sunday night. When the Volstead Act was finally repealed, the racing continued. NASCAR was the first effort to give it an actual organizational footing.[64]

But more than the engines were beginning to roar. The gears of the nation were revving toward the 1950s. Both the sports world and the real world were stricken by expansion fever.

· 6 ·

Have We Gone Soft?

If I wanted to destroy a nation, I would give it too much and
I would have it on its knees, miserable, greedy and sick. . . .
On all levels, American society is rigged.

—John Steinbeck[1]

The 1950s saw the greatest uninterrupted economic expansion in U.S. history. The abundance of disposable income, the creation of suburban tract housing, and the raised hopes of a generation all had a profound effect on the world of sports. *Fortune* magazine called the 1950s "a time of abundance," with 1.1 million families joining the middle class every year. *Fortune* said the United States was a "world of optimistic philoprogenetive [i.e., having a lot of babies] high spending, debt-happy, bargain-conscious, upgrading, American consumers." This extra wealth meant the spread of new technology in a way that was unprecedented. In 1950, 10 percent of American homes had television sets. By 1959, it was almost 90 percent.[2]

Athletes such as Mickey Mantle and Johnny Unitas were exemplars of the greatness that came with being a team player. In particular, Unitas, the star Colts quarterback with the flattop haircut and hard-scrabble background, was an icon of the time. But before the country could be primed for wealth, creature comforts, and flattop haircuts, the upheaval that accompanied both the Depression and the war economy had to be squelched. The 1940s had seen the greatest strike wave in U.S. history. The first task of the government was the destruction of this tradition—a process often referred to as McCarthyism, although it both predates and endured beyond the heyday of the Senator Joseph McCarthy.[3]

McCarthyism began in earnest in 1947, when Democratic president Harry Truman put in place a regulation that forced eight million government workers to sign anticommunist loyalty oaths to keep their jobs and allowed the FBI to investigate more than two million federal workers. Under the McCarran Act, signed by Truman in 1950, offenders could be deported. Meanwhile, thousands of people were grilled at hearings of the House Un-American Activities Committee about any kind of leftist or communist connection.

> It was the most widespread and longest lasting wave of political repression in American history. In order to eliminate the alleged threat of domestic Communism, a broad coalition of politicians, bureaucrats, and other anticommunist activists hounded an entire generation of radicals and their associates, destroying lives, careers, and all the institutions that offered a left-wing alternative to mainstream politics and culture. That anticommunist crusade . . . used all the power of the state to turn dissent into disloyalty and, in the process, drastically narrowed the spectrum of acceptable political debate.[4]

This was backed up culturally by an entire cottage industry of movies and books with titles such as *I Married a Communist* and *Communist Weapon of Allure*. During the 1950s, Mickey Spillane's salty noir Mike Hammer books, which sold millions of paperback copies, shifted from taking on the mob to taking on communists without missing a beat. "They were Commies. . . . They were real sons of bitches who should have died long ago. . . . They never thought there were people like me in this country."⁵ Even Robert Oppenheimer, one of the designers of the atomic bomb, was put under the microscope. Oppenheimer opposed the massive funding and development of the hydrogen bomb and therefore was said not to be "on the team."⁶

This hysteria saw its apex in the execution of Ethel and Julius Rosenberg, the son and daughter of Jewish immigrants, who grew up in working-class families in New York City. The Rosenbergs were the parents of two young boys, a fact that was given a lot of play in the media—not out of sympathy, but to send a message: if this couple could be atomic spies, then your neighbor could be a spy too.

Despite demonstrations held around the world, involving figures ranging from Albert Einsten to Dashiell Hammett, the fate of the Rosenbergs was sealed.

"We are not martyrs or heroes, nor do we wish to be. We do not want to die. We are young, too young, for death," Ethel wrote in the couple's last appeal to the president. "We long to see our two young sons, Michael and Robert, grown to full manhood. . . . We desire some day to be restored to a society where we can contribute our energies toward building a world where all shall have peace, bread and roses. Yes, we wish to live, but in the simple dignity that clothes only those who have been honest with themselves and their fellow men."⁷

Julius Rosenberg wrote in a letter to their lawyer Manny Bloch:

This death sentence is not surprising. It had to be. There had to be a Rosenberg case because there had to be an intensification of the hysteria in America to make the Korean War acceptable to the American people. There had to be hysteria and a fear sent through America in order to get increased war budgets. And there had to be a dagger thrust in the heart of the left to tell them that you are no longer gonna give five years for a Smith Act prosecution or one year for Contempt of Court, but we're gonna kill ya!⁸

Terror

Miriam Zahler, whose parents were Communists in Detroit, remembered:

> My worst nightmare when I was seven and eight was that my mother would be taken away . . . as the Rosenbergs had been from [their children]. Ethel and Julius were at the very center of my terror. . . . I asked my mother why the Rosenbergs were in jail. For passing out some leaflets, she said; I concluded that if the Rosenbergs were in jail because they passed out leaflets, my mother, who also passed out leaflets, might be arrested too. . . .
>
> I was overcome with fear that my mother would not return from the June 14 [1953] demonstration [for the Rosenbergs]. I went into her bedroom closet and stood among her clothes and cried. . . . My father tried to persuade me to come out, but I stood in the closet and wailed that I wanted my mother back—as if she had gone to meet the fate of the Rosenbergs, who were, in fact, electrocuted within the week.[9]

McCarthyism became a part of the sports world when Paul Robeson, possibly the most famous black American at the time, said in 1949, "Blacks would never pick up arms against the Soviet Union." The House Un-American Activities Committee (HUAC) saw its chance to strike at Robeson. To legitimize its attack, HUAC called on Jackie Robinson to testify. NAACP lawyers offered to defend Robinson's right not to speak, but he refused their aid. Rickey wanted him to testify, and Robinson, who was anticommunist yet understood the importance of Robeson to the black community, thought he could use the HUAC hearing to speak out for racial justice and let Robeson off with a mild chiding. He was wrong.

Robinson, in prepared statements, said, "Negroes were stirred up long before there was a Communist party and they'll stay stirred up long after the party has disappeared—unless Jim Crow has disappeared as well."[10] Robinson noted that out of four hundred major league players, there were only seven African Americans and out of sixteen teams only three had been integrated.

These were courageous statements, but it was Robinson's next statement that stood the test of time, devastating Robeson and his supporters.

"I can't speak for any 15 million people any more than any other one person can, but I know that I've got too much invested for my wife and child and myself in the future of this country, and I and other Americans of many races and faiths have too much invested in our country's welfare, for any of us to throw it away because of a siren song sung in bass."

With those words he had done the bidding of HUAC—giving it license and cover to attack and persecute Robeson. Robeson's passport was revoked and he was hounded into exile. Robinson later spoke of this testimony as one of the great regrets of his life.

In his 1972 autobiography, *I Never Had it Made*, Robinson said of Robeson,

> In those days I had much more faith in the ultimate justice of the American white man than I have today. I would reject such an invitation if offered now. . . .
>
> I have grown wiser and closer to the painful truths about America's destructiveness. And I do have an increased respect for Paul Robeson who, over the span of that twenty years, sacrificed himself, his career, and the wealth and comfort he once enjoyed because, I believe, he was sincerely trying to help his people.[11]

Robinson and Robeson weren't the only casualties in the athletic world. The Olympics became Cold War morality plays, with all the attendant pressure placed on the shoulders of amateur athletes. In the Eastern bloc, this meant a doping regimen that physically damaged tens of thousands of athletes.[12]

Stateside, the hypernationalism of the Cold War used sports as a hammer to pound in obedience and anticommunist readiness as well as the values of the private market. Sociologist David Riesman said that in the context of corporate life in America, "the road to the board room leads through the locker room."[13] Little League baseball expanded robustly in America as suburban housing developed on the outskirts of cities. The youth baseball federation began in 1939, and in 1946 all of its teams were still in Pennsylvania. But by 1948, with the war squarely in the country's rearview mirror, Little League was starting to attract corporate sponsors. By 1953, it was being broadcast on television, hosted by a young Jim McKay, who would for more than a quarter century host ABC's *Wide World of Sports*.

In the 1950s, Little League became more than a money machine. It was seen as a bulwark of Americanism in a time of both rampant insecurity and prosperity. Before the season, players had to take the Little League oath: "I trust in God, I love my country and will respect its laws. I will play fair and strive to win, but win or lose I will always do my best." Its oath can't be separated from the need to steel the country against godless communism.[14]

McCarthyism Strands Robinson

The McCarthy era was also disastrous in stalling the momentum for civil rights seen after World War II. As Manning Marable writes convincingly in *Race, Reform, and Rebellion*, McCarthyism is the only way to explain the seven-year gap between Truman's desegregation of the army and the *Brown vs. Board of Eduction* decision, the Montgomery bus boycotts, and the beginnings of the civil rights movement.[15]

It is no exaggeration to say that during this period, both white America's fear of civil rights and black America's aspirations were thrust upon the shoulders of professional athletes, particularly Jackie Robinson. Years later Martin Luther King Jr. called Robinson "a pilgrim walking the lonesome byways toward the high road of Freedom. He was a sit-inner before sit-ins, a freedom rider before freedom rides."[16]

Affection for Robinson in white America—outside of Brooklyn— began to wane. Robinson's speaking out against racism earned him the scorn of even previously friendly sportswriters such as Jimmy Cannon. "The range of Jackie Robinson's hostility appears to have no frontiers," Cannon wrote after Robinson sounded off to the press. "He is a juggler of a sort, flashily keeping feuds in motion like Indian clubs," offending "even Brooklyn partisans with his undisciplined protests." [17]

But Robinson was more eager than ever to speak out against Jim Crow and racism. In these dark years of McCarthyism, before the light of the Montgomery bus boycotts, "only Jackie Robinson," as his biographer Arnold Rampersad wrote, "insisted day in and day out on challenging America on the matter of race and justice." [18]

Goodbye Rosie

Part of McCarthyism's shock therapy involved getting Rosie the Riveter out of the factory, back in the kitchen, and once again making babies. Two months after the war, 800,000 women had been fired; within two years after the war's end, that number was 2 million. Eighty-two percent of the country disapproved of a woman being in the labor force if she had a hardworking husband. Twenty-six of forty-eight states had laws against hiring married women. While the 1940s presented the formidable Rosie as a feminine ideal, the 1950s saw Marilyn Monroe, June Cleaver, and Donna Reed take center stage. Unless you could do housework and raise kids while wearing pearls, you were something less than a woman. [19]

This backlash was seen in women's baseball. Before the league was finally shut down for good, new rules were instituted in 1951 to make the game more ladylike. Dress guidelines included: "Always appear in feminine attire. This precludes the use of any wearing attire of masculine nature. Masculine hair styling? Shoes? Coats? Shirts? Socks, t-shirts are barred at all times." Players who challenged these rules were jettisoned. Others perceived as masculine got the boot. One player, Josephine D'Angelo, was cut for her "butch haircut"—but in reality, her firing was due to suspicions of lesbianism. [20]

More to the press's liking was African American female track star Wilma Rudolph, nicknamed the "Black Gazelle." Another woman who uncomfortably tried to fit the mold was Babe Didrikson. She was now known as Babe Didrikson Zaharias, having married George Zaharias, a mark in her favor. She also now played the more acceptably feminine sport of golf. It says something about Babe's bottomless athletic talent that she was able to thoroughly master a sport she didn't take up until adulthood. She was asked how "a girl" could hit a golf ball so far. She answered, "Just take off your girdle and swing."[21]

Babe was incredible, winning a ridiculous twenty-one straight golf tournaments. In 1947–48, with Rosie not yet out of the factories, and women still on the baseball diamond, Babe applied to play in the men's draw of the 1948 U.S. Open. When one considers the stink caused in recent years when Michelle Wie and Annika Sorenstam have tried to enter the men's tour, one can imagine the response. Babe demurely withdrew from the 1948 Open after the rules were hastily rewritten to say that this was a "male" event.[22]

When Babe Didrikson Zaharias died of cancer in 1956, Shirley Povich wrote, "The opponent that licked her, it must be noted, was the same deliverer of the sneak body-attack that also cut down those other champions, Jim Thorpe and Babe Ruth. It was not a stand up foe to be out-gamed or out-performed, else Babe Zaharias would have won this one, too, her admirers are sure."[23]

Bowling as Community

With suburban living came dislocation and isolation. Sports attempted to fill the void, particularly bowling, which was inexpensive and social. The number of bowling alleys and leagues exploded. A PR campaign was launched to cement bowling's appeal with the new middle class. The fancy shoe company Capezio introduced a line of bowling shoes with display ads showing aristocratic matrons and debs at the lane. The invention of the automatic pin-setting machine also made the game easier to play. Television brought the sport into people's homes. Shows such as *Championship Bowling*, *Make That Spare*, *Celebrity Bowling*, and *Bowling for Dollars* became staples in many living rooms.[24]

The Growth of the Civil Rights Movement

The oxygen around Robinson began to increase in 1954 and 1955 when *Brown v. Board of Education* came before the Supreme Court. The Court ruled that the separation of schoolchildren by race "generates a feeling of inferiority . . . that may affect their hearts and minds in a way unlikely ever to be undone." In the field of public education, it said, "the doctrine of 'separate but equal' has no place." The Court did not insist on immediate change; after the 1954 decision the Court heard arguments about how fast the decision should be implemented and eventually ruled that segregated facilities should be integrated "with all deliberate speed." Throughout the 1950s, as major league baseball touted its integration project, black children played at decayed inadequate facilities and competed in segregated leagues.[25]

In 1955, the Montgomery bus boycotts began, exposing the nation to a twenty-six-year-old preacher named Martin Luther King Jr. As King said,

> We have known humiliation, we have known abusive language, we have been plunged into the abyss of oppression. And we decided to raise up only with the weapon of protest. It is one of the greatest glories of America that we have the right to protest. If we are arrested every day, if we are exploited every day, if we are trampled over every day, don't ever let anyone pull you so low as to hate them.[26]

But 1955 was also the year of the first backlash to the emerging trend toward an embrace of civil rights. This was the year of fourteen-year-old Emmett Till's brutal murder. The White Citizens' Council had swelled to 300,000 members. More than a hundred congressmen signed a document pledging to uphold segregation.

By this time in the world of baseball, a new generation of African American players had established themselves as stars. Only three teams now didn't have a black player in their farm system. Future Hall of Famers such as Willie Mays, Henry Aaron, Ernie Banks, and Roy Campanella wowed multiracial crowds across the country. It was a significant and special time in baseball history—and exposed white fans to the idea of cheering for black talent.

Pete Hamill, remembering his youth in Brooklyn, wrote,

How full of marvels was the world! One of the marvels is that I got to see Roy Campanella coming to the plate, a bat in hand and men on base. I saw Jack Roosevelt Robinson rounding third, heading for home. I saw Willie Mays. And I saw them in the company of thousands of roaring human beings, glad people in a glad place in a glad time, all of them members of my tribe, the New York tribe. Nobody can ever tell me that such moments were trivial, mere examples of mindless entertainment and diversion, part of the bread and circuses devised by those who rule us. Such moments were possible only among people who ruled themselves.[27]

Althea Gibson

One of the women who changed perceptions was tennis star Althea Gibson. Many of the African American athletic successes had come from the South and the historically black colleges. They had also seen their success come almost exclusively in track and field. Gibson was different. First and foremost, she was from Harlem, the mecca of black cultural life in the United States. Second, her sport was tennis, the most country-club and lily-white of sports. Third, unlike most tennis players, she grew up poor. Gibson was a sharecropper's daughter raised on welfare. But what really set Gibson apart was that she was no "black gazelle," quiet and graceful. She was tough as steak from an old bull. She said, "People thought I was ruthless, which I was. I didn't give a darn who was on the other side of the net. I'd knock you down if you got in the way." She also said, "Being a champ is all well and good, but you can't eat a crown."[28] In 1957, Gibson won both Wimbledon and the U.S. Open on her way to becoming the first African American woman to be named Associated Press Female Athlete of the Year, an honor she repeated the following year.

"I always wanted to be somebody," she said. "If I made it, it's half because I was game enough to take a lot of punishment along the way and half because there were a lot of people who cared enough to help me." The people who helped Gibson most were those who demanded she receive the place in the game her abilities demanded. As journalist Alice

Marble, herself a former tennis champ, wrote in a 1950 issue of *American Lawn Tennis* magazine:

> The entrance of Negroes into national tennis is as inevitable as it has proven in baseball, in football, or in boxing; there is no denying so much talent. The committee at Forest Hills has the power to stifle the efforts of one Althea Gibson, who may or may not be succeeded by others of her race who have equal or superior ability. They will knock at the door as she has done. Eventually the tennis world will rise up en masse to protest the injustices perpetrated by our policymakers. Eventually—why not now?[29]

Robinson Agonistes

While players such as Mays and Aaron, silent and symbolic, were largely embraced, Robinson, silent no longer, found himself in the doghouse with many white fans. The more progressive *Sport Magazine* called him "the most savagely booed, ruthlessly libeled player in the game, his every appearance greeted by a storm of cat calls and name calling." At least in his professional life Robinson had the last laugh, leading the Dodgers to victory in the 1955 World Series. He retired in 1956 after learning that he had been unceremoniously traded to the rival Giants. Robinson then became a spokesman for the NAACP and quickly became the group's most requested speaker (number two was Martin Luther King Jr.). He would end speeches by saying, "If I had to choose between baseball's Hall of Fame and first-class citizenship I would say first-class citizenship to all of my people." In 1958, he was the marshal and lead organizer of the Youth March for Integrated Schools, which attempted to get one thousand black and white students to march on the Lincoln Memorial. They got ten thousand.[30]

In April 1959, he started writing a column on the sports page of the *New York Post* (then—believe it or not—a liberal paper) on a variety of topics that ranged from sports to civil rights. Critics, both black and white, said that as an athlete, Robinson didn't have the right to speak out on politics, but such comments never slowed him down.

Walter O'Malley, the Red Scare, and Chavez Ravine

Over a ten-martini lunch, famed scribes Pete Hamill and Jack Newfield, the legend goes, decided to write down on napkins a list of the ten most evil people of the twentieth century. For the first three, they wrote the same names in identical order: Hitler, Stalin, and Walter O'Malley. As anyone raised in postwar Brooklyn will attest, O'Malley's 1958 move of the Dodgers to Los Angeles ranks as something beyond the diabolical. In his defense, O'Malley saw the writing on the wall: a massive migration west was already under way. The exploding Cold War defense industry had taken root on the left coast, and LA had become a place of profound promise. Moving baseball out there was just business, not personal. But you couldn't tell that to the people of Brooklyn. As Hamill wrote, "After 1957, it seemed like we would never laugh again. Of course, we did. It's just that we were never young again."[31]

But Brooklyn wasn't the only place gutted by O'Malley's far-seeing avarice. There was another community out west, seen by O'Malley and major league baseball as merely the future site of Dodger Stadium. This was Chavez Ravine, called by its residents "a poor man's Shangri-la." It had been home to generations of Mexican Americans looking to live in a tight-knit valley community in the shadow of the big city. The people of Chavez Ravine ran their own schools and churches and even grew their own food. It was at the center of the Zoot Suit Riots, the epic 1943 battles between white sailors and the pachucos in their styling threads.[32]

In 1949, Chavez Ravine residents were informed that their community was going to be leveled for public housing. Some left willingly, receiving meager compensation. The ones who stayed had their homes bulldozed and received nothing, with the city claiming eminent domain. A protest movement arose to defend the area, but resistance was difficult to generate in the era of anticommunist crusades.

Here is where the story starts to twist in that pulpy left coast way. LA's big business interests accused the public housing proponents of being communists, particularly Frank Wilkinson, the assistant director of the Los Angeles City Housing Authority. These business interests organized themselves in a group called Citizens Against Socialist Housing, or

CASH. They wanted the Chavez Ravine land for development. Wilkinson was brought before HUAC for leading this "communist plot" of federal housing. He was fired from his job and sentenced to one year in jail.[33]

By 1952, the entire area had been flattened, but nothing had been built on top of it. This thriving community, this cradle of Chicano culture, had become a ghost town. As Wilkinson said years later, "It's the tragedy of my life, absolutely. I was responsible for uprooting I don't know how many hundreds of people from their own little valley and having the whole thing destroyed."[34]

This is what set the stage for O'Malley to swoop in and grab the land for little more than peanuts and Cracker Jack. As Wilkinson said, "We'd spent millions of dollars getting ready for [public housing], and the Dodgers picked it up for just a fraction of that. It was just a tragedy for the people, and from the city it was the most hypocritical thing that could possibly happen."[35]

Yet another protest movement, the first anti-stadium movement, arose over O'Malley's shady shenanigans. Debates flared up across the city. An actor and professional anticommunist making a transition to politics, Ronald Reagan, stepped in to call opponents of the stadium plan "baseball haters." He might as well have argued that they were breaking black bread and sipping borscht with Khrushchev. A public referendum was forced on the issue, and stadium proponents won with 51.5 percent of the vote, allowing O'Malley to move forward. (Of course, many of the refugees from Chavez Ravine were immigrants and could not vote.) On April 10, 1962, the 56,000-seat Dodger Stadium officially opened, but the period 1951–61 is still known among many Angelenos as "the Battle of Chavez Ravine."[36]

Corruption of College Athletics

This period also saw a flood of money swamp the college game. It had always been there, as we have seen, but in the postwar era, with the expansion of higher education, it became pervasive. Jim Aiken, head football coach at the University of Oregon from 1947 to 1950, put it bluntly: "If you have to choose between breaking the rules and losing games, wouldn't it be better to break the rules? If you lose your games you're certain to be fired. If you break the rules, you have to get caught to be fired." University of Southern California football coach Jeff Cravath said the game "reduced players to perjurers, scalpers and football gigolos. The alumni demand winning football teams. To get winning teams, colleges must violate the rules they themselves have made."[37]

Nowhere was the corruption more visible than at the City College of New York. City College was the preeminent basketball power in the country, having won both the NCAA and NIT championships in 1950. It was found that the team had been involved in an extensive point-shaving scandal. In February 1951 three players were arrested on bribery charges. That was just for starters. By the end of March, seventeen New York City college basketball players had been arrested. Eventually, district attorney Frank Hogan arrested thirty-two players from seven colleges who fixed eighty-six games between 1947 and 1950.[38]

As sportswriter Maury Allen said, "That was the last time I really believed in pure idealism. For these guys to sell out their schools and themselves and their careers for $800 was just such an emotional blow. You never really recover from something like that. It is a wound to your psyche for the rest of your life."[39]

In Allen's words we see the dominant view of the scandal: the players were sellouts. They had sold out their school and their sport. And they were bought cheap, as journalist Stanley Cohen described:

> They were poor, most of them, they needed the money. But that is a reason, not an explanation. It explains only why they were ready to dump for relatively small sums. . . . None of the players had about him the mood of a criminal. If they had not been college basketball players, it is not likely they would have ended up in the courts. They would not have stolen the money. They would not have robbed banks or knocked over gas stations or rolled drunks in Central Park. The likelihood is that most of them had committed the one crime for profit of which they were capable.
>
> They had, of course, functioned in an environment in which it might have been more difficult to play it straight than it was to ac-

cept a bribe. For point shaving was as much a part of college basketball in the forties and fifties as the two-hand set shot.[40]

Cohen was dead right. This was a far more pervasive issue, one that
went beyond just City College or New York City. Adolph Rupp, the Kentucky coach, blamed it on New York City gamblers. "They couldn't
touch my boys with a 10-foot pole," he said. He was wrong. Three players from the Wildcats' 1949 championship team were found to be involved, and Kentucky had to suspend its basketball program for a year.
While the players took the fall, something more rotten was revealed.
Most of the City College team, consisting mostly of African American
and Jewish players, came from working-class backgrounds. The players
were soaked by the bookies, as Allen indicates, for very small sums. The
NCAA put the weight of the responsibility on the players. This really set
the tone for how the NCAA would deal with these kinds of gambling or
payola scandals for the next fifty years. Never would the NCAA look at
the system with the critical perspective evident in Aiken's and Cravath's
remarks. Never has the NCAA taken a step back and noticed that it was
making billions off unpaid labor, and that perhaps this was the root of
the problem.[41] It continues to be a narrative that catches minnows while
whales swim free.

Pro Football's Ascendancy

The 1958 championship game between the Baltimore Colts and New
York Giants delivered in one day the modern era of pro football, pro-
pelling it on a journey that would make it the most popular sport in the
country. The game was a 23–17 thriller that ended in overtime with a
plunge over the goal line by Alan "the Horse" Ameche. As Shirley Povich
wrote, "As art form, it had an aspect of Greek tragedy with sudden death
the inexorable ticket of one of the antagonists. And it launched a million
debates." Pro football, a fringe sport for decades, was tailor-made for
television like nothing else on the landscape.[42]

With popularity, however, came scrutiny. When Marion Motley and
Bill Willis broke football's color line in 1946, few noticed. But now the
fact that the majority of teams were all white could no longer escape

notice. One of the most notorious segregationists was the patriarch of the Washington Redskins, George Preston Marshall. Marshall's Skins were the last team to integrate in the entire NFL. Povich once wrote famously that the Redskins' colors were "burgundy, gold and Caucasian." Marshall finally integrated the team in 1962 only when the Kennedy administration's interior secretary, Stewart Udall, issued an ultimatum: sign an African American player or be denied use of the new government-financed 54,000-seat D.C. Stadium. Marshall responded by making Ernie Davis, Syracuse's all-American running back, his number one draft choice. One problem: Davis's response was a forthright "I won't play for that S.O.B." Davis was traded to Cleveland for African American all-pro Bobby Mitchell.[43]

Marshall's racism was more than just a set of ideas. It was the material foundation upon which the Redskins empire was built. He had brought his football team to Washington with a plan to make them "the South's team." He signed TV contracts with stations in southern cities, and he drafted players mostly from southern colleges. The team, once again to quote Povich, "became the Confederates of the NFL." In fact, in the original version of the fight song "Hail to the Redskins," the line "Fight for old D.C." was "Fight for old Dixie."[44]

While the Redskins were the last team to integrate in the NFL, that "honor" in major league baseball went to the Boston Red Sox, who in 1959 brought up a marginal utility player, Pumpsie Green. But it didn't have to be Pumpsie. In April 1945 the Red Sox held a tryout at Fenway Park for Robinson himself. With only management in the stands, someone yelled, "Get those niggers off the field," and the door was shut. In 1949, the Red Sox laughed off the chance to sign the legendary Willie Mays, who would go on to hit 660 career home runs and awe crowds with his speed and defense. That decision killed the possibility that Mays and Ted Williams might have played in the same outfield.[45]

In the 1950s, as teams immeasurably strengthened themselves by signing players such as Mays, Aaron, Ernie Banks, Don Newcombe, Roy Campanella, Elston Howard, and others, the Red Sox stood pat with an all-white hand. Though Boston fans for decades complained about the "curse of the Bambino," the curse of racism in fact had a far worse effect.

As the civil rights movement blossomed, New England's black baseball fans would root for integrated clubs over their own home team. Unlike in other cities, such as New York and Chicago, where rooting for an integrated team actually helped advance people's consciousness and challenge racist ideas, the Red Sox were proudly planting themselves on the wrong side of history.

· 7 ·

Sports on the Edge of Panic

John Kennedy loved sports, or so he told us. The man with the dazzling smile and slender physique delighted in giving the country a vision of a president with boundless energy, athletic passion, and a penchant for touch football games. In *Sports Illustrated*, the youngest elected president in U.S. history made a plea—not unlike Teddy Roosevelt and others—against the "soft American."[1] In reality, Kennedy was plagued by crippling back pain, Addison's disease, spastic colitis, and a need for painkillers in order to be able to function.[2] This gap between image and reality—touch football for the cameras and debilitating medical problems behind closed doors—matches a decade that started with aspirations of a new frontier and ended with, as Howard Zinn put it, "a series of explosive rebellions in every area of American life, which showed that all the system's estimates of security and success were wrong."[3]

As 1960 began, sports were still viewed as bedrock for the America of people's dreams: a place where the best of muscled white male America came together to act as an exemplar for the rest of us in how not to be "soft." But a new day was dawning that would turn these notions on their head. The leading edge of struggle in both the world of sports and in the streets was found in the arena of civil rights. Perhaps fittingly, one of the most prominent athletes of that year was an African American woman, Wilma Rudolph, who soared to superstardom after becoming the first woman to win three gold track-and-field medals in a single Olympics.

By 1960, the civil rights movement had reached an impasse. But on February 1, 1960, that changed when four black college students in Greensboro, North Carolina, sat at the whites-only Woolworth's lunch counter. They were refused service, but rather than leave, they remained planted in their chairs. The owners shut the lunch counter down, but in the days that followed, the students returned repeatedly. Lit cigarettes were put in their faces. They were cursed, beaten, and threatened. But they had resolve, and thanks to a national media, their efforts were seen around the country.

"The students in that picture had a certain look on their faces, sort of sullen, angry, determined," said an observer named Bob Moses, who would soon be a central participant in the civil rights movement "Before, the Negro in the South had always looked on the defensive, cringing. This time they were taking the initiative. They were kids my age, and I knew this had something to do with my own life."[4]

In the next year, more than 50,000 people, mostly black, some white, participated in demonstrations of one kind or another in one hundred cities, and more than 3,600 people were put in jail. You didn't have to be a sports star to prove that you were no longer a "soft American." You could be the kind of person who faced a terror most football players couldn't comprehend. And you could win. By the end of 1960, lunch counters were open for business to those of African descent in Greensboro, not to mention many other places. A growing group of young people discovered that protest worked. People believed that what they did actually mattered. The glacial realities of "all deliberate speed" would no longer carry the day.[5]

This spirit of change affected every aspect of American life, including the citadel of sports. Athletes actually had to defend their right not to be political. Willie Mays was criticized for not being vocal enough about racial discrimination. His response is fascinating: "I don't picket in the streets of Birmingham. I'm not mad at people who do. Maybe they shouldn't be mad at the people who don't."[6]

Sepia magazine gave a full-throated defense of athletes' right to not take a stand:

The basic question—should Negro athletes be civil rights fighters?—goes deeper than selected incidents or personalities. It now involves, in many cases, the situation or problem or case of "Black Nationalism" and the widespread intolerance, on the part of publicized civil rights demonstrators, of all Negroes who aren't walking picket lines or laying their bodies down in front of trucks, or sitting in or wading in or getting "in" in some other way. . . .

Long before protest demonstrations became a national entity, Joe Louis was changing anti-Negro attitudes to pro-Negro attitudes. No American civil rights fighter has yet reached the 300 million (or more) people as Willie Mays does, around the world, in a World Series. Two years prior to the Supreme Court's momentous school integration decision, Negroes starred in Southern baseball and three years prior to the Supreme Court decision, Southern baseball was integrated. Integrated baseball was seen and accepted in such states as Louisiana, Tennessee, Georgia, Florida, and Virginia long before local authorities got around to serious consideration of overall democracy. Baseball fought segregated housing, eating facilities, segregation in other areas in the South.[7]

In 1959, one of the NBA's stunning new black players, Elgin Baylor of the Minneapolis Lakers, attracted national attention to the issue of segregation of public accommodations when he refused to play in a regular conference game scheduled in Charleston, West Virginia. He sat stoically on the team bench in street clothes to protest the refusal of a local hotel to permit him to register with his teammates.[8]

It was a time of flux, including for Jackie Robinson. Robinson was a proud northeastern Republican, never more so when he was a guest at the 1960 Democratic National Convention and saw nominee John Kennedy sitting side by side with Orval Faubus, the Democratic governor of Arkansas and an arch segregationist. This confirmed his suspicions that there was nothing really new in Kennedy's New Frontier. But Robinson would be disappointed time and again by Republicans' "commitment" to civil rights. When Martin Luther King Jr. was sentenced to four months on a Georgia work gang, Robinson asked his friend Richard Milhous Nixon to intervene and was ignored.[9]

Though disillusioned with both political parties, Jackie never stopped going to the front lines of the civil rights battles and encouraging African Americans to vote. On a speaking tour to raise money for the SNCC sit-ins, Robinson said in Tennessee, "We are going to get our share of this country—we are going to fight for it. We must take it step by step and support the youngsters in their stand-ins and sit-ins."[10]

As the black freedom struggle grew and a revolutionary wing developed, Robinson, in spite of his actions, was viewed as a "white man's Negro" due to his abiding faith in electoral politics and belief in integration. He was an icon of "the old way of doing things in the eyes of many." He was especially a target of scorn because of his verbal feud with Malcolm X. Robinson was tough, never backing down in the face of Malcolm's withering scorn. He wrote in his *New York Post* column, "Malcolm is very militant on Harlem street corners where militancy is not that dangerous. I don't see him in Birmingham. . . . He is terribly militant on soapboxes and street corners yet he has not faced the police dogs or gone to jail for freedom."[11]

Robinson could not have known that he was touching on the pressure point of Malcolm's pain and frustration with the political abstention of the Nation of Islam. Yet although they were political opponents, Robinson and Malcolm shared something in common: their ideas shifted in the struggles of the 1960s. Yet neither could have been prepared for the man who was about to impact both of their lives—not to mention the lives of everyone else.[12]

Shaking Up the World

Muhammad Ali's identity was forged in the 1950s and 1960s, as the black freedom struggle heated up and boiled over. He was born Cassius

Marcellus Clay Jr. in Louisville, Kentucky, in 1942. His father, a frustrated artist, made his living as a house painter. His mother, like Jackie Robinson's mother, was a domestic worker. The Louisville of 1942 was a segregated horse-breeding community where being black meant being seen in service-oriented jobs and rarely heard. But the young Clay could do two things that set him apart: he could box and he could talk. His mouth was like that on other no fighter or athlete or any public black figure anyone had ever heard. Joe Louis used to say, "My manager does my talking for me. I do my talking in the ring." Clay talked, inside the ring and out. The press called him the "Louisville Lip," "Cash the Brash," "Mighty Mouth," and "Gaseous Cassius." He used to say he talked so much because he admired the style of a pro wrestler named Gorgeous George. But in an unguarded moment he once said, "Where do you think I'd be next week if I didn't know how to shout and holler and make the public take notice? I'd be poor and I'd probably be down in my hometown, washing windows or running an elevator and saying 'yassuh' and 'nawsuh' and knowing my place."[13]

Ali, of course, could back up the talk. His boxing skills won him the gold medal in the 1960 Olympics at age eighteen. When he returned from Rome—and this was the first step in his political arc—the young Clay held a press conference at the airport, his gold medal swinging from his neck, and said:

> To make America the greatest is my goal
> So I beat the Russian, and I beat the Pole
> And for the USA won the Medal of Gold.
> Italians said "You're greater than the Cassius of old."[14]

Clay loved his gold medal. Fellow Olympian Wilma Rudolph remembered, "He slept with it, he went to the cafeteria with it. He never took it off." The week after returning home from the Olympics, Clay went to eat a cheeseburger with his medal swinging around his neck in a Louisville restaurant—and was denied service. As he later said, that medal found a home "at the bottom of the Ohio River."[15]

The young Clay actively looked for political answers and began finding them when he heard Malcolm X speak at a meeting of the Nation of Islam. He heard Malcolm say, "You might see these Negroes who believe in nonviolence and mistake us for one of them and put your hands on us thinking that we are going to turn the other cheek—and we'll put you to death just like that." Malcolm X was an attractive figure. His impatience, his militancy, his rejection of nonviolence, and his stony-eyed critiques of Democratic politicians and middle-of-the-road civil rights leaders gave him a following far beyond his organization.[16]

As Malcolm X said in 1964,

> You'll get freedom by letting your enemy know that you'll do anything to get your freedom; then you'll get it. It's the only way you'll get it. When you get that kind of attitude, they'll label you as a "crazy Negro," or they'll call you a "crazy nigger"—they don't say Negro. Or they'll call you an extremist or a subversive, or seditious, or a red or a radical. But when you stay radical long enough and get enough people to be like you, you'll get your freedom.[17]

The young fighter and Malcolm X became both political allies and fast friends. Malcolm stayed with Clay as he trained for his fight against the "Big Ugly Bear," the champion Sonny Liston.

Before he had signed to fight Clay, Liston had been portrayed in the press as eight steps beyond evil. He had an arrest record that could fill a file cabinet and had been in the past employed by the mob as a strike-breaker and enforcer. Radical poet Amiri Baraka (then LeRoi Jones) called Liston "the big black Negro in every white man's hallway, waiting to do him in, deal him under for all the hurts white men, through their arbitrary order, have been able to inflict on the world."[18]

Before Liston's championship fight when he won the title against Floyd Patterson, President Kennedy took the time to call Patterson and express that it would not be in "the Negroes' best interest" if Liston won. As one writer noted dryly, "The fight definitely was not in Patterson's best interest." Liston destroyed Patterson, setting the stage for his fight against Clay.[19]

The writer James Baldwin was sent to cover Liston before the fight.

He wrote, "[Liston] is far from stupid; is not, in fact, stupid at all. And, while there is a great deal of violence in him, I sensed no cruelty at all. On the contrary, he reminded me of big, black men I have know who acquired the reputation of being tough in order to conceal the fact that they weren't hard. Anyone who cared to could turn them into taffy."[20]

But by this point, most of the press were paying far more attention to Clay, little of it positive. With Malcolm around, rumors flew that Clay was going to join the Nation of Islam, and the press hounded him, wanting to know. At one point he said, "I might if you keep asking me."

While everyone was predicting an easy knockout for Liston, Malcolm said that Clay would win. He "is the finest Negro athlete I have ever known, the man who will mean more to his people than Jackie Robinson, because Robinson is the white man's hero." Malcolm also pointed out, "Not many people know the quality of mind he has in there. One forgets that though a clown never imitates a wise man, the wise man can imitate the clown."[21] Although the verdict was out on whether he was wise or a clown, no one gave him a chance against Liston. But Clay—quicker, stronger, and bolder than anyone knew—shocked the nation and beat Liston. He then shouted to the heavens, over a reporter's questions, "I'm king of the world!"

When Clay said he was the greatest, it wasn't far from the truth. The day after he beat Liston, he announced publicly that he was a member of the Nation of Islam, causing a firestorm. The fact was that the heavyweight champion of the world was joining the organization of Malcolm X. The Olympic gold medalist had linked arms with a group that called white people "devils" and stood unapologetically for self-defense and racial separation. Not surprisingly, the power brokers of the conservative, mobbed-up, corrupt fight world lost their minds. Jimmy Cannon, the most famous sportswriter in America, apparently forgetting the entire career of Jack Johnson, wrote that this was the first time that boxing had ever "been turned into an instrument of mass hate. . . . Clay is using it as a weapon of wickedness."[22]

Clay was attacked not only by Cannon and his ilk but also by the respectable wing of the civil rights movement. "Cassius may not know it, but he is now an honorary member of the White Citizens' Councils," said Roy Wilkins. Clay's response at this point was very defensive. He repeatedly said that his wasn't a political stand but purely a religious conversion. His defense reflected the conservative perspective of the Nation of Islam: "I'm not going to get killed trying to force myself on people who don't want me. . . . Integration is wrong. The white people don't want integration, and the Muslims don't believe in it. So what's wrong with the Muslims?" At another point he said, "I have never been to jail. I have never been in court. I don't join any integration marches. . . . I don't carry signs."[23]

But much like Malcolm X, who at the time was engineering a political break from the Nation, Clay—much to the anger of Elijah Muhammad—found it impossible to explain his religious worldview without speaking to the mass black freedom struggle exploding outside the boxing ring. He was his own worst enemy—claiming that his was a religious transformation and had nothing to do with politics, but then in the next breath saying, "I ain't no Christian. I can't be when I see all the colored people fighting for forced integration get blowed up. They get hit by stones and chewed by dogs and they blow up a Negro church." Unrepentantly Clay said, "People are always telling me what a good example I could be if I just wasn't a Muslim. I've heard it over and over, how come I couldn't be like Joe Louis and Sugar Ray. Well, they've gone now, and the black man's condition is just the same, ain't it? We're still catching hell."[24]

If the establishment press was outraged, the new generation of activists was electrified. "I remember when Ali joined the Nation," remembered civil rights leader Julian Bond. "The act of joining was not something many of us particularly liked. But the notion that he would do it, that he'd jump out there, join this group that was so despised by mainstream America and be proud of it, sent a little thrill through you. . . . He was able to tell white folks for us to go to hell; that I'm going to do it my way."[25]

For a time he was known briefly as Cassius X, but Elijah Muhammad gave Clay the name Muhammad Ali—a tremendous honor and a way to ensure that Ali would side with Elijah Muhammad in his split from Malcolm X. Ali proceeded to commit what he would later describe as his greatest mistake—turning his back on Malcolm. But the internal politics of the Nation were not what the powers that be and the media noticed. To them the Islamic name change—something that had never occurred before in sports—was a sharp slap in the face.

Almost overnight, whether an individual called the champ Ali or Clay indicated where that person stood on civil rights, black power, and eventually the war in Vietnam. The *New York Times* insisted on calling him Clay as editorial policy for years thereafter.

This all took place against the backdrop of a black freedom struggle rolling from the South to the North. During the summer of 1964, there were a thousand arrests of civil rights activists, thirty buildings bombed, and thirty-six churches burned by the Ku Klux Klan and their sympathizers. In 1964, the first of the urban uprisings and riots in the northern ghettoes took place in Harlem. The politics of black power was starting to emerge, and Muhammad Ali became the critical symbol in this transformation. As news anchor Bryant Gumbel said, "One of the reasons the civil rights movement went forward was that Black people were able to overcome their fear. And I honestly believe that for many Black Americans, that came from watching Muhammad Ali. He simply refused to be afraid. And being that way, he gave other people courage."[26]

A concrete sign of Ali's early influence was seen in 1965 when Student Non-violent Coordinating Committee (SNCC) volunteers in Lowndes County, Alabama, launched an independent political party. Their new group was the first to use the symbol of a black panther. Their bumper stickers and T-shirts were of a black silhouette of a panther and their slogan was straight from the champ: "We Are the Greatest."[27] It's this broader context that allows us to understand why Ali's post-name-change fights—like the Louis-Schmeling fight years before—became incredible political dramas of the black revolution versus the people who opposed it. Floyd Patterson, who wrapped himself tightly in the American flag, challenged Ali and said, "This fight is a crusade to reclaim the title from the Black Muslims. As a Catholic I am fighting Clay as a patriotic duty. I am going to return the crown to America."[28]

In the fight itself, Ali brutalized Patterson for the entire twelve rounds, dragging it out and yelling, "Come on America! Come on white

America!" Future Black Panther Party leader Eldridge Cleaver wrote in his 1968 autobiography *Soul on Ice*, "If the Bay of Pigs can be seen as a straight right hand to the psychological jaw of white America, then [Ali/Patterson] was a perfect left hook to the gut."[29]

Vietnam

During 1965, more than 200,000 American soldiers were implanted in South Vietnam. In 1966 200,000 more were sent. The U.S. Air Force was in the process of dropping more bombs on the country than were used in all of World War II.[30] To this point, however, sports had been little touched by the controversy over the war.

One exception was Billy Mills, an Oglala Sioux raised on the Pine Ridge reservation in South Dakota. Pine Ridge was and remains one of the poorest areas in the United States, a place where sneakers were a luxury. Mills was an orphan who earned a track scholarship at the University of Kansas, where he was an all-American in 1959 and 1960. He left running to join the Marines but came back and despite remarkable odds won the 1964 gold medal in a mammoth upset in the 10,000 meters at the Tokyo Olympics. Yet by 1965, Mills was done with running: "I felt I could not participate in a sport when people were being killed in Vietnam."[31] The 1983 film about his life, *Running Brave*, starring Robby Benson, ends after Mills's Olympic triumph, and his former Kansas coach apologizing for his prejudice, preserving the ideal of the redemptive powers of sports.

As the hippie and black power cultures began to flower, sports became more than a symbolic weight against an era of sex, drugs, and resistance. They became a very overt political opposition to the new. Coaches such as Notre Dame's Ara Parseghian called hippies "scum." In 1966, the American Football League proscribed all facial hair save mustaches.[32]

On the day Martin Luther King Jr was assassinated in 1968, Larry James, a track star at the University of Tennessee, heard that news of King's death started a standing ovation in the student center. He was pondering this while jogging to an on-campus meet when, as, James recalled, "a VW passed and I heard, 'run, nigger, run!' I immediately started to walk. And I began to internalize things."[33]

At Penn in 1965, jocks "taunted, grabbed, and hit some students and faculty members who happened to be carrying signs of protest [though] most were content to chant 'Hit 'em again, harder, harder' . . . or to sing the national anthem." Michigan State football player Phil Hoag said simply that demonstrators were "just losers, going nowhere, doing nothing. There was no question that anytime you could punch one, you punched them."[34]

Often, the 1960s radicals analyzed sports in a way similar to the pre–Lester Rodney communists: an opiate, a distraction, a negative good for little more than manufacturing consent. It was called "the worst kind of indulgence in the American cult of the rugged, unique, superior individualist."[35]

And yet, in the most individualistic, rugged, and violent sport of them all, an athlete who finished at the bottom of his high school class went down as the most famous draft resister since Thoreau.

In early 1966, the army came calling for Ali and he was classified 1-A, eligible to be drafted. Ali heard this news surrounded by reporters, and he blurted out one of the most famous phrases of the decade: "Man, I ain't got no quarrel with them Vietcong." This was an astounding statement.

"What I saw that afternoon wasn't particularly religious or political," New York Times reporter Robert Lipsyte recalled. "That was a patina that came later. I saw a twenty-four-year-old scared of being drafted. It was, 'How can they do this to me? I don't want my career ruined.' He thought he'd put the draft behind, and now his life was about to be turned upside down. Someone had just told him he was going to Vietnam. Then the telephone started ringing. . . . Finally after the tenth call—'What do you think about the Vietcong?'—Ali exploded. 'Man, I ain't got no quarrel with them Vietcong.' And bang. There it was. That was the headline. That was what the media wanted."[36]

There was little opposition to the war at the time. The antiwar movement was in its infancy and most of the country still stood behind the war. *Life* magazine's cover read, "Vietnam the War Is Worth Winning," the song "Ballad of the Green Berets" was climbing the charts, and standing against this seemingly insurmountable tide was Ali. As Mike Margusee wrote, Ali's response "was a major boost to the anti-war movement. This was not an academic or a clergyman, not a beatnik or a bohemian or a clergyman . . . [he] could not be dismissed as 'unmanly' or 'cowardly.' "[37]

It is worth noting though that Ali did not create antiwar sentiment among blacks. That was already beginning to bubble. In 1965, a black student in the South who lost a close friend in Vietnam passed out leaflets on his campus reading, "No Mississippi Negroes should be fighting in Vietnam for the White Man's freedom, until all the Negro People are free in Mississippi. Negro Boys should not honor the draft here in Mississippi. Mothers should encourage their sons not to go. . . . No one has a right to ask us to risk our lives and kill other Colored People in Santo Domingo and Vietnam, so that the White American can get richer."[38]

But Ali was the heavyweight champion. The reaction was therefore immediate, hostile, ferocious, and at times hysterical. Jimmy Cannon wrote,

> He fits in with the famous singers no one can hear and the punks riding motorcycles with iron crosses pinned to their leather jackets and Batman and the boys with their long dirty hair and the girls with the unwashed look and the college kids dancing naked at secret proms held in apartments and the revolt of students who get a check from dad every first of the month and the painters who copy the labels off soup cans and surf bums who refuse to work and the whole pampered style-making cult of the bored young."[39]

And the two most famous sportswriters in the United States weighed in strongly against Ali. Red Smith declared, "Cassius makes himself as sorry a spectacle as those unwashed punks who picket and demonstrate against the war." In the *Los Angeles Times*, Jim Murray called the champ "the white man's burden."[40]

Jack Olsen wrote years later in *Sports Illustrated*, "The noise became a din, the drumbeats of a holy war. TV and radio commentators, little old ladies . . . bookmakers, and parish priests, military strategists at the Pentagon and brave dog feet wading across the ricefields of Vietnam, all joined in a get-Cassius clamor."[41]

Ali was given every opportunity to recant, to apologize, to sign up on some cushy USO gig boxing for the troops and the cameras, just like most athletes of his era. At one point in 1966, only 2 of 960 pro athletes were serving in the military. Many local National Guard boards would have whole regiments made up of athletes from particular teams.[42]

But Ali refused an easier way out. Once again, the man who told the world how pretty he was would turn conventional notions of manliness inside out. As Ali explained to the Louisville draft board,

> Sir, I said earlier and I'd like to again make that plain, it would be no trouble for me to go into the Armed Services, boxing exhibitions in Vietnam or traveling the country at the expense of the Government or living the easy life and not having to get out in the mud and fight and shoot. If it wasn't against my conscience to do it, I would easily do it. I wouldn't raise all this court stuff and I wouldn't go through all of this and lose the millions that I gave up and my image with the American public that I would say is completely dead and ruined because of us in here now. I wouldn't jeopardize my life walking the streets of the South and all of America with no bodyguard if I wasn't sincere in every bit of what the Holy Qur'an and the teachings of the honorable Elijah Muhammad tell us and it is that we are not to participate in wars on the side of non-believers, and this is a Christian country and this is not a Muslim country. We are not, according to the Holy Qur'an, to even as much as aid in passing a cup of water to the wounded. I mean, this is the Holy Qur'an, and as I said earlier, this is not me talking to get the draft board or to dodge nothing. This is there before I was born and it will be there when I'm dead and we believe in not only part of it, but all of it.[43]

His refusal was gargantuan because of what was taking place in U.S. society. There was the black revolution over here and the draft resistance and antiwar struggle over there. And the heavyweight champ had one foot planted in both. Howard Cosell captured this dynamic when he said, "Look at what was happening then: . . . riots in the streets, an ugly unwanted war, assassinations. . . . That time period was incredible, and Ali understood it; he was at the heart of violent, turbulent, almost indecipherable time in America, and Ali was in all of those fires at once; he helped shape it."[44]

An incredible groundswell of support built up for Ali. That is why, despite the harassment and the media attacks and the prospect of a prolonged stay in a federal prison, he stood firm. At one press conference later that year, he was expected to apologize. Instead he stood up and said, "Keep asking me, no matter how long / On the war in Vietnam, I sing this song / I ain't got no quarrel with the Vietcong."[45]

"It's hard now to relay the emotion of that time," remembered the poet Sonia Sanchez. "This was still a time when hardly any well-known people were resisting the draft. It was a war that was disproportionately killing young black brothers, and here was this beautiful, funny, poetical young man standing up and saying no! Imagine it for a moment! The heavyweight champion, a magical man, taking his fight out of the ring and into the arena of politics, and standing firm. The message that sent!"[46]

But Sanchez's was still a minority view. No less a force than army veteran and sports trailblazer Jackie Robinson said, "He's hurting the morale of a lot of young Negro soldiers over in Vietnam. And the tragedy to me is, Cassius has made millions of dollars off of the American public, and now he's not willing to show his appreciation to a country that's giving him, in my view, a fantastic opportunity. That hurts a great number of people."[47]

Jerry Izenberg, at the time another young writer more willing to identify and listen to Ali, remembered, "I can't tell you what I went through for defending him. All the cancellations of my newspaper column, the smashed car windows, the bomb threats; the thousands of letters from

Army war veterans talking about Jews like me and concentration camps."[48]

Ali had to go to Canada to fight because promoters were more and more concerned that the despised heavyweight champ couldn't draw a crowd in the States. Starting in March 1966, he defended his title seven times, four of them outside the United States.

Bob Arum, a leading fight promoter, called Ali a "dead piece of merchandise." But by becoming such a polarizing political figure, he became someone everyone, love him or hate him, had to see. As Ali said years later:

> All kinds of people came to see me. Women came because I was saying, "I'm so pretty," and they wanted to look at me. Some white people, they got tired of my bragging. They thought I was arrogant and talked too much, so they came to see someone give the nigger a whuppin'. Longhaired hippies came to my fights because I wouldn't go to Vietnam. And black people, the ones with sense, they were saying, "Right on, brother; show them honkies." Everyone in the whole country was talking about me.[49]

In 1967, Ali fought Ernie Terrell. Before the fight, Ali was his typical self, seemingly immune to the "drumbeat of a holy war." At the airport he uncorked a classic poem saying, "I predict that Terrell will catch hell at the sound of the bell. He is going around saying he's a championship fighter but when he meets me he'll fall 20 pounds lighter. He thinks he's a champ but after I'm finished he'll just be a tramp. Now I'm not saying this just to be funny. But I'm fighting Ernie because he needs the money."[50]

But the fight itself was anything but fun and games. "I had a question for him when we met to sign," Ali said two days before the fight. "It was only three words—'What's my name?' And Terrell said, 'Cassius Clay,' using my slave name. That made it a personal thing, so I'm gonna whup him until he addresses me by my proper name. I'm gonna give him a whupping and a spanking, and a humiliation." Terrell called Ali "Clay" in the lead-up, which led to Ali hitting him mercilessly, shouting, "I'll keep on hitting him, and I'll keep talking. Here's what I'll say. 'Don't you fall, Ernie.' Wham! 'What's my name.' Wham! I'll just keep doing that until he calls me Muhammad Ali. I want to torture him. A clean knockout is too good for him."[51]

This is exactly what happened. Ali was at the height of his powers, overmatching, taunting, and beating Terrell. Some would say this is exactly what boxing is, the art of brutalizing an opponent, but Ali was not praised for his skill; instead, he was torn apart for it. The New York *Daily News* called the fight "a disgusting exhibition of calculating cruelty, an open defiance of decency, sportsmanship and all the tenets of right versus wrong." Jimmy Cannon called it "a kind of lynching."[52] It was as if the entire history of boxing was a gentleman's sport that Ali was sullying because he was a political figure. The coverage served to further deepen animosity to Ali on Main Street USA.

In 1967, in another huge step for the antiwar movement, Martin Luther King Jr. came out against the war. In a press conference where King proclaimed his opposition he said, "As Muhammad Ali has said, we are all victims of the same system of oppression."[53]

Ali and King, to the anger of the Nation of Islam, struck up a private friendship that we know about thanks to the good people at the FBI. Here is a synopsis of one wiretapped conversation between King and Ali in which Ali is referred to as "C":

> MLK spoke to Cassius, they exchanged greetings. . . . C invited MLK to be his guest at the next championship fight, MLK said he would like to attend. C said he is keeping up with MLK, that MLK is his brother, and he's with him 100% but can't take any chances, and that MLK should take care of himself . . . and should watch out for them whities.[54]

The only other time these private friends came together in public was later that year, when Ali joined King in Louisville, where a bitter and violent struggle was being waged for fair housing. Ali spoke to the protesters, saying,

In your struggle for freedom, justice and equality, I am with you. I came to Louisville because I could not remain silent while my own people—many of whom I grew up with, went to school with, and some of whom are my blood relatives—were being beaten, stomped and kicked in the streets simply because they want freedom, justice and equality in housing.

Later that same day he cemented his position as a lightning rod between the freedom struggle and the antiwar struggle when he said:

Why should they ask me to put on a uniform and go ten thousand miles from home and drop bombs and bullets on brown people in Vietnam while so-called Negro people in Louisville are treated like dogs and denied simple human rights? No, I am not going ten thousand miles from home to help murder and burn another poor nation simply to continue the domination of white slavemasters of the darker people the world over. This is the day when such evils must come to an end. I have been warned that to take such a stand would put my prestige in jeopardy and could cause me to lose millions of dollars. But I have said it once and I will say it again. The real enemy of my people is right here. I will not disgrace my religion, my people or myself by becoming a tool to enslave those who are fighting for their own justice, freedom and equality. . . . If I thought the war was going to bring freedom and equality to twenty-two million of my people, they wouldn't have to draft me, I'd join tomorrow. . . . I have nothing to lose by standing up for my beliefs. So I'll go to jail. We've been in jail for four hundred years.[55]

When it came time for Ali to go to the induction center in Texas, it was still up in the air whether he would take that step forward when his name was called. Outside the building, twenty demonstrators walked in a circle, carrying placards reading, "Draft Beer—Not Ali." When the induction officer said the name "Cassius Clay," Ali did not move. Ali was informed that he was risking fine and imprisonment by refusing induction. He said he understood.[56]

Afterward in a statement, he made clear just how much he understood. "I am proud of the title 'World Heavyweight Champion'. . . . The holder of it should at all times have the courage of his convictions and carry out those convictions, not only in the ring but through all phases of life. It is in light of my own personal convictions that I take my stand in rejecting the call to be inducted into the armed services. I do so with full realization of its implications and possible consequences."[57]

Years later, upon reflection, Ali said he had no regrets. "Some people thought I was a hero. Some people said that what I did was wrong. But everything I did was according to my conscience. I wasn't trying to be a leader. I just wanted to be free. And I made a stand all people, not just black people, should have thought about making, because it wasn't just black people being drafted. The government had a system where the rich man's son went to college, and the poor man's son went to war. Then, after the rich man's son got out of college, he did other things to keep him out of the Army until he was too old to be drafted."[58]

Said Julian Bond, "When Ali refused to take that symbolic step forward everyone knew about it moments later. You could hear people talking about it on street corners. It was on everybody's lips. People who had never thought about the war—black and white—began to think it through because of Ali."[59]

One hour after Ali refused induction—before he'd been charged with any crime, let alone convicted—the New York State Athletic Commission suspended his boxing license and withdrew recognition of him as champion. Soon all other jurisdictions in the United States followed suit, and the title Ali had worked for throughout his life was gone. It was the beginning of his three-and-a-half-year exile from the ring.

Ali's refusal to cross the line was front-page news not only in America but also around the world.

In Guyana, Cheddi Jagan led a picket of the U.S. embassy. In Karachi, a young Pakistani fasted outside the U.S. consulate. There was a demonstration in Cairo. An editorial in the *Ghana Pioneer* deplored what it called the "concerted efforts" to strip Ali of his championship. During the first major British demonstration against the war in April 1967, among the host of leaflets handed out in Grosvenor Square was one reading, "LBJ Don't Send Muhammad Ali to War." Bertrand Russell congratulated Ali on his courage and assured him, "The air will change. I sense it." An Irish boxing fan named Paddy Monaghan picketed the U.S. embassy in London and collected twenty thousand signatures over the course of three years.[60]

Manthia Diawara, presently chair of the Africana Studies Department at New York University, said:

> You see, for me then [in Mali], and for many of my friends, to be liberated was to be exposed to more R&B songs and to be au courant of the latest exploits of Muhammad Ali, George Jackson, Angela Davis, Malcolm X, and Martin Luther King, Jr. These were becoming an alternative cultural capital for the African youth— imparting to us new structures of feeling and enabling us to subvert the hegemony of *francité* after independence.[61]

Ali at this point saw himself as someone who had a responsibility to an international base that saw him as something beyond his sport. "Boxing is nothing, just satisfying to some bloodthirsty people. I'm no longer a Cassius Clay, a Negro from Kentucky. I belong to the world, the black world. I'll always have a home in Pakistan, in Algeria, in Ethiopia. This is more than money."[62]

Support also began to come from unlikely sources at home. Floyd Patterson, who was himself being shaped by the movements around him, said, "What bothers me about Cassius Clay's situation is that he is being made to pay too stiff a penalty for saying and doing what is right. The prizefighter in America is not supposed to shoot off his mouth about politics, particularly if his views oppose the government's and might influence many among the working classes who follow boxing."[63]

This view that Ali was being made to pay too high a price gained greater currency when he received a five-year sentence for his refusal to fight. The day of Ali's conviction, the U.S. Congress voted 337–29 to extend the draft four more years. It also voted 385–19 to make it a federal crime to desecrate the flag. At this time, a thousand Vietnamese non-combatants were being killed each week by U.S. forces. One hundred U.S. soldiers were dying every day, the war cost $2 billion a month, and the movement against the war was growing.

Kwame Toure, who then was known as Stokely Carmichael, said:

Muhammad Ali had everything. Fame, glory, money, women, good looks, champion of the world. So when Muhammad would call me—we'd speak back and forth on the telephone—and he'd tell me, "I ain't going," I'd say, "Yeah; right on!" But I always wondered, when that final moment comes and he actually has to take that step, how will it come out? Because, no question, the FBI viewed Ali as more of a threat than H. Rap Brown and myself. Muhammad Ali had a broader base than we had. The government recognized that Muhammad Ali could cause a lot more trouble than all of us. That's why we understood that the weight of the blow would be hardest against Muhammad Ali. They were going to take his championship crown; no doubt about it. They were going to prosecute him; no doubt about it. They were going to do everything possible to bring him to his knees. And of all the people who opposed the war in Vietnam, I think that Muhammad Ali risked the most. Lots of people refused to go. Some went to jail. But no one risked as much from their decision not to go to war in Vietnam as much as Muhammad Ali. And his real greatness can be seen in the fact that, despite all that was done to him, he became even greater and more humane."[64]

On June 23, 1968, Ali appeared at his first and only antiwar demonstration. Lyndon Johnson was scheduled to speak at a $500-a-plate fund-raising dinner at the Century Plaza Hotel in Los Angeles. In response, local antiwar activists organized a rally at the Cheviot Hill Playground. Twenty thousand turned out for the largest antiwar gathering yet held in southern California. The speakers included Benjamin Spock and Rap Brown. Ali arrived in a Rolls-Royce and mounted a garbage can to address the crowd. "Anything designed for peace and to stop the killing I'm for one hundred percent," he told them. "I'm not a leader. I'm not here to advise you. But I encourage you to express yourself." Then he began his familiar refrain: "Who's the champion of the world?" The *Los Angeles Times* reported that marchers replied with "Clay's Black Muslim name."[65]

In 1968, Ali was accumulating tremendous financial debt. He attempted to stop the flow by giving a series of speeches, two hundred by his count, at college campuses around the country. In the late 1960s, when *Esquire* magazine gave Ali five pages to do with what he would, he crafted a political manifesto. He wrote that black athletes should "take all this fame the white man gave to us because we fought for his entertainment, and we can turn it around. Instead of beating up each other . . . we will use our fame for freedom." Arguing for reparations long before the term ever entered the parlance of our times, he proposed using $25 billion allocated for the Vietnam War and use it to construct houses in the South. "Each black man who needs it is going to be given a home," he wrote. "Now, black people, we're not repaying you. We ain't giving you nothing. We're guilty. We owe it to you." Later, in a 1970 interview in *Black Scholar*, it was clear Ali had been radicalized. "I was determined to be one nigger that the white man didn't get," he said. "Go on and join something. If it isn't the Muslims, at least join the Black Panthers. Join something bad."[66]

Ali got his first taste of jail in December, serving ten days for driving without a license. "He got sentenced for being Cassius Clay," Ali's lawyer told reporters after Ali was sentenced. "Everyone is caught up in the hate Clay hysteria."[67]

Yet Ali's isolation would reach new depths in April 1969, when Elijah Muhammad and the Nation of Islam officially distanced themselves from Ali. On the front page of *Muhammad Speaks*, the Nation of Islam's newspaper, was this statement:

We tell the world we're not with Muhammad Ali. Mr. Muhammad Ali plainly acted the fool. Any man or woman who comes to Allah and then puts his hopes and trust in the enemy of Allah for survival is underestimating the power of Allah to help them. Mr. Muhammad Ali has sporting blood. Mr. Muhammad Ali desires to do that which the Holy Qur'an teaches him against. Mr. Muhammad Ali wants a place in this sport world. He loves it. Mr. Muhammad Ali shall not be recognized with us under the holy name Muhammad Ali. We will call him Cassius Clay.[68]

Why would the Nation of Islam so disavow someone who had sacrificed so much? The most obvious answer is that the Nation was a very conservative organization. It did not believe in the kind of active resistance being practiced by Ali, who was too incendiary even for them. But still Ali did not waver. Perhaps the late actor Richard Harris said it best when he commented, "All boxers would sell their soul to become heavyweight champion of the world. He regained his soul by giving it up."[69]

Yet the Ali saga was far from over. Elimination bouts were held to fill the vacant title. Protesters appeared outside of the venues with placards reading "Hell No We Ain't Goin' " and "Fight Racism, Free Muhammad Ali." The promoters didn't care, but Ali warned with the voice of truth: "Everybody knows I'm the champion. My ghost will haunt all the arenas. I'll be there, wearing a sheet and whispering, 'Ali-e-e-e! Ali-e-e-e!' "[70]

Bill Russell Goes Up

Those at the absolute zenith of the sports world were disproving the old saw that politics and sports don't mix: that off-field "distractions" would undermine the ultimate goal of victory. There was Ali in the world of boxing—an individual sport, of course—and then the most successful athlete in the history of team sports: the Boston Celtics' Bill Russell. The Celtics won eleven championships in thirteen seasons. The mainstay of that team was Russell, a player of immense skill, unselfishness, and leadership. Russell won five MVPs to go with his eleven rings. In 1967 he became the first African American coach of a pro team. In 1974 he was elected to the Basketball Hall of Fame, and in 1980 the country's basketball sportswriters voted him the greatest player in the history of the NBA.

Russell also felt a duty to resist racism. Once in Marion, Indiana, he had been given the key to the city only to be refused service that evening in his hotel's dining room.[71]

His fierce pride (which the media called a "bad attitude") did not exactly mix well with the Boston fans of the day. The result was that the greatest player in Boston team sports history was the target of a constant campaign of racial harassment. When Russell tried to move from his home in the Boston suburb of Reading to a new home across town, neighbors filed a petition trying to block the move. When that failed, others in the community banded together to try to purchase the home that Russell wanted to buy, remembered Tom Heinsohn, a close friend of Russell's who played with him from 1956 to 1964. Once, vandals broke into Russell's home and defecated on his bed.[72]

Russell's achievements during his days in Boston, from 1956 to 1969, drew national acclaim but never won local fans' hearts the way later Boston sports heroes did, from hockey player Bobby Orr to baseball player Carl Yastrzemski to basketball player Larry Bird. Despite all the championships, the Boston Garden averaged 8,406 fans during Russell's playing career, thousands short of a sellout. "We always sold out on the road, but rarely when we played at home," said Satch Sanders, who played with the Celtics from 1960 to 1973. By contrast, the Celtics teams led by Larry Bird in the 1980s sold out the 14,890-seat Garden for 662 straight games, from 1980 to 1995. "I didn't play for Boston," Russell once said, "I played for the Celtics." Another time he called Boston a "Flea Market of Racism."[73]

Russell did more than confront the racism that planted itself in his face. He also took part in the 1963 March on Washington and launched an integrated sports training camp in the South. Russell also organized investments in Liberian rubber plantations as a way to aid the West African country's ailing economy. In 1966, he wrote a groundbreaking autobiography, *Go Up for Glory*, in which he would echo the late Malcolm X's words and make the case that "civil rights today has become too tranquil, too filled with compromise."[74]

The Miners of Texas Western

No one would confuse Don Haskins at first glance with a civil rights pioneer. The man who would coach the 1966 Texas Western Miners to a national championship took the job in 1961 after taking a pay cut from coaching high school. What made Haskins different was his desire to coach the best possible players he could get to come to the borderlands of El Paso. Hardly a revolutionary idea, but then again neither is wanting to use a public water fountain nor asking for a cup of coffee at the local luncheonette.[75]

The 1966 Miners were the first African American starting five to win the NCAA championship game. Their legend was burnished further by vanquishing Kentucky, led by fabled coach and arch-segregationist Adolph Rupp. The contest's symbolic magnitude, occurring in the eye of the black freedom struggle, has transformed it into far more than just a game. Over time, the contest's aura has only grown. Texas Western versus Kentucky is now the athletic equivalent of the Selma Bridge or a Greensboro lunch counter. It has the feel of a bygone era, aided both by the fact that Texas Western no longer exists by that name (it is now the University of Texas at El Paso) and that in those days the finals, far from the billion-dollar spectacle they are now, were shown on tape delay with the grainy production values of a hostage video.

The Miners of Texas Western have been grossly misrepresented over the years. The story has been that by using "urban" black players, Texas Western's "athleticism" overwhelmed the "fundamentally sound and intelligent" Kentucky farm boys. This idea, of course, has very racist roots. "Hot Rod" Hundley, the former West Virginia and Lakers star, said of Texas Western at the time, "They can do everything with the basketball but sign it.' " James H. Jackson of the *Baltimore Sun* wrote, "The Miners, who don't worry much about defense but try to pour the ball through the hoop as much as possible, will present quite a challenge to Kentucky, The running, gunning Texas quintet can do more things with a basketball than a monkey on a 50-foot jungle wire."[76]

Yet, as columnist Frank Fitzpatrick analyzed in his brilliant breakdown of old game footage, the Miners were far from flashy. They more accurately fit their moniker, playing a lunch-pail-style ball that stressed defense and rebounding. The Miners gave up a scant 62 points a game and, in the pre-shot-clock era, didn't so much walk as trudge the ball up the court. "We played the most intelligent, the most boring, the most disciplined game of them all," said Texas Western guard Willie Worsley. This approach put shackles on a Kentucky team that tried to turn the game into a track meet.[77] Yet one place where legend does intersect with reality was the psychological importance of the contest for the emerging civil rights struggles sweeping the South.

Before the game, Rupp allegedly vowed that "five Negroes" would never beat his team. Whether Rupp said it or not, Haskins told his team of Rupp's promise. This was not something to say in 1966 when blacks in a quest for civil rights were being stoned and beaten across the South. The Texas Western players made their own locker-room vow that Rupp would eat his words.

On the Miners' second possession, Miners center David "Big Daddy" Lattin slammed a forceful dunk over Kentucky's Pat Riley, then said, "Take that you white honky." As Riley—a future Hall of Fame NBA coach—recalled, "It was a violent game. I don't mean there were any fights—but they were desperate and they were committed and they were more motivated than we were." In the end, Rupp choked on the loss, leaving the runner-up trophy in the locker room. Rupp clung to his all-white policy until 1971.[78] This was a proper capstone for a man who can be likened without exaggeration to George Wallace with a clipboard. When school president John Oswald ordered Rupp to desegregate, he reportedly let out the plaintive whine, "That son of a bitch is ordering me to get some niggers in here. What am I going to do?"[79]

Unlike other legendary southern coaches, such as Alabama's Bear Bryant, who recanted any role they may have played in buttressing the system of Jim Crow, Rupp was unrepentant, and the bitterness of that 1966 loss ate him alive. "[He] carried the memory of that game to his grave," wrote Russell Rice, biographer.[80]

"No one will remember him without remembering us," said Texas Western's Harry Flournoy. "And I guess there is a certain justice to that."[81]

Revolt of the Black Athlete

Russell, Ali, and the success of Texas Western were canaries in the coal mines, signaling what was about to explode onto the sports landscape. Arriving was what Dr. Harry Edwards would label "the revolt of the black athlete." As Edwards wrote, "It was inevitable that this revolt of the black athlete should develop. With struggles being waged by black people in the areas of education, housing, employment and many others, it was only a matter of time before Afro-American athletes shed their fantasies and delusions and asserted their manhood and faced the facts of their existence. . . . The roots spring from the same seed that produced the sit-ins, the freedom rides and the rebellions in Watts, Detroit and Newark."[82]

In 1965, the twenty-one African American players involved in the American Football Conference's all-star game forced Commissioner Joe Foss to move the game to Houston from New Orleans because of the Crescent City's politics of segregation. The *New York Times* called the rebellion "a boycott without precedent in professional sports by 21 Negro athletes."[83] In 1968, black athletes at the University of California at Berkeley football team boycotted athletic activities to support suspended black basketball player Bob Presley. John Erby was soon named as the first black assistant coach at Berkeley to appease the newly restless athletes.[84]

Doc Young wrote in 1968, "The black players—about 35 Negro athletes on the campus—then organized a protest, demanding that three coaches be dismissed on the grounds of 'general incompetence,' lodging various charges of racial discrimination and demanding that the school administration hire 'five or six' Negro coaches. . . . It is absolutely stupid for a white coach or general manager to indulge himself in bigotry and then expect a Negro athlete to play his best. Sports need Negro athletes, and sports had better believe it."[85]

The next year, players at Michigan State delivered a list of demands, drafted by black professor Robert Green, to coach Biggie Munn.[86]

Calvin Hill, now known best as the father of NBA star Grant Hill but a top football player in his day, remembered in a 1988 interview his shock at how quickly things had politicized for black athletes, even at his alma mater, prestigious Yale University.

> Now a change occurred between my freshman year and sopho-more year: the thrust became more cultural. In my sophomore year (1966–67), guys came back with Afros and dashikis and those kinds of things. When I was shifted from quarterback there were some black students on campus who approached me and asked me if I wanted to make an issue of the fact that as a black I had been shifted. I remember meeting an upperclassman, had lunch with him, I guess my second week there, and he asked me: "How would you feel about us picketing the offices because they shifted you from quarterback?" I'd been there four or five days. The last thing I wanted to do was to cause any controversy, you know? I mean I was trying to figure out what the hell was happening at Yale.[87]

NBA star Chet Walker described in the book *Long Time Coming: A Black Athlete's Coming of Age in America* the specific conditions that spurred the black athletes' revolt. He wrote about his experience at Bradley University.

> Bradley's first road trip in 1960 began in St. Louis. Before the game that night, the St. Louis University marched out playing "Dixie," and we came out on the court surrounded by a sea of wav-ing Confederate flags, which almost made me sick to my stomach; to me, going onto that court was like running headlong into a mili-tary rally.
>   . . . During warm-ups for the Houston game, fans threw lit cig-arette butts on the floor at us and screamed, "Nigger!" I was in a state of great confusion and frustration, and scored only one point in the first half, wondering why I was subjecting myself to such abuse. At halftime, Coach Orsborn had a different take on the

game. He berated me, yelling, "Don't quit on me, Chet. Just don't quit on me!" With a final sneer he concluded more softly, "All-American, my ass!"

. . . My fleeting sense of equality was gone. Heaven help me if I permanently lost the ability to play basketball. . . .

Sometimes I feel [Branch] Rickey should have given Jackie permission to punch somebody's lights out. The incident might have resulted in a race riot, the end of the "great experiment." But suppose not? Suppose that Robinson's courage had validated an outward expression of just anger? Suppose it was acknowledged that Jackie had a right to express that anger instead of being lionized for withholding it? Because Jackie had the great strength to endure, he set a precedent. All black athletes since have had to live up to his powerful dignity and forbearance. But my soul died a little each time a nightmare like that southern trip had to be lived through."[88]

Walker also wrote about what it was like to feel like chattel on the campus.

I became desperate enough to consider flunking out. If I couldn't play for another school, I would just fail and go home. Of course, my lack of self-confidence had taken over. Like countless black kids before and after me, I'd been placed in a white society that seemed unnavigable. I had no support systems. I was lonely. My options were zero. I remember taking a music appreciation course that spring. For the final exam we listened to recorded selections and then identified the composer, such as Mozart or Bach. I scrawled across the top of my exam, "The only music I can appreciate is the Blues," and then left the rest of the paper blank. The professor gave me a C and wrote on the exam that I showed "great vision." So I was caught. . . . Bradley had me as its employee; they had me as a commodity for as long as I was of use. If I publicly expressed my anger or desire to leave, they would destroy me.

. . . One minute I was an All-American basketball player as full of myself as a powerful young man could be. But the next minute, I was reduced to the nigger in the doorway. No amount of sports heroism in America could change that. Early on I understood this doubleness and that it would never truly change for me.[89]

The successful basketball coach at Kansas State University during the 1960s, Tex Winter, said: "We're getting ourselves into a situation where outstanding Negroes with talent are being exploited."[90]

No Turning Back: 1968

Already in 1968 the world had seen the Tet offensive in Vietnam, proving that the U.S. military was vulnerable to defeat; the Prague Spring, where Czech students challenged the Stalinist tanks; the assassination of Martin Luther King Jr. and the mass revolts that followed; the growth of the Black Panther Party in the United States; and the largest general strike in world history in France. In 1968, this ferment spread to the world of athletics.

In March, all-American guard and future hall of famer Calvin Murphy slammed the admissions policy of his school, Niagara, which had resulted in only two black players on the team and six on campus.[91]

In April, after the assassination of King, Pirates star outfielder Roberto Clemente, who idolized King because of the latter's positions against the war in Vietnam and structural poverty in the United States, led a charge to prevent the Pirates and Astros from opening their season on April 8, the day before King's burial. Opening day was moved to April 10. Roberto Clemente had put sports in its proper perspective in a way that no one could miss.[92]

Arthur Ashe emerged in the lily-white world of tennis. He won both the U.S. Open and the U.S. Amateur Open in 1968. Years later, he was described by journalist Mike Towle as "a statesman, author, activist, husband, father, teacher, politician, barrier breaker, traveler, student, champion, board director, television commentator, trusted friend, protestor. And that's not a complete list." But in 1968, he was just a great tennis player. He told the *Washington Afro American*, "Athletes have an obligation to the civil rights cause."[93]

The campuses were at the forefront of Ashe's call to ideological arms. University of Washington athletes pushed for a study of racism in the athletic department after accusing the football trainer of making racial slurs and providing inadequate treatment for injuries. The university's athletic director, Jim Owens, admitted to the presence of racism within the department and announced, in the words of the *Afro American*, "Colored athletes agree to play in exchange for a search for a colored coach; colored professor to serve as a link between athletes and staff; a student-athlete advisory committee will be formed."[94]

The jocks, whom administrators had been counting on to keep the hippie freaks in line, were starting their own journey away from unquestioned obedience. Now athletes, the people who were supposed to be examples of how to succeed through following the rules, were coming up with their own demands. In May, athletes and coaches at Howard University threatened to quit unless their concerns were addressed. Removing athletic director Samuel Barnes topped their list of demands. They also wanted "better food, more medical attention, streamlined means of transportation, more equipment, better living conditions and a fulltime sports information director." Student assembly president Ewart Brown Jr. (today the premier of Bermuda), a member of the track team, burned his Howard varsity sweatshirt. As it went up in ashes, football player Harold Orr said, "This is what we think of the athletic program. [We need a] cremation of the old system."[95]

The student athletes issued a statement reading:

> We the athletes of Howard University in order to create a more cohesive atmosphere in the athletic program here, are addressing ourselves to the token and modicum benefits that we as athletes are receiving. We, as athletes, would like to see a furbished upheaval of the paternalistic attitudes that are embedded in Howard's fibers of administrative rule which have diffused into the athletic charade. The athletes have seen the archetype of hypocrisy in both society and athletics, and are at odds with all forms of authority that sham; be it captain, coach, department head or administrator. We, as athletes, who believe sincerely that we are the chosen few

and are aloof, would like to know conclusively who in athletic hierarchy is committed and his degree of commitment to needs of athletes and athletic program here at Howard.[96]

Not all athletes were moving in this direction. Also in 1968, college football players were called upon to break up campus protest rallies, most infamously at Columbia, where the football team formed a ring around the buildings occupied by antiwar students to keep out efforts to get them food and water. Campus activist James Kunen described the situation as one where "every so often I get hit with eggs, which a small group of jocks are having good clean fun throwing. Since they have no arguments and no support for their arguments (of which they have none) they have no recourse but to assault us like this and sing fight songs—that's right, fight songs. They are standing there—I beg you to believe this—throwing eggs and singing 'Roar Lion Roar' all the while."[97]

Actions like this were applauded. Representative Gerald Ford said, "Personally I'm glad that thousands of fine Americans can spend this Saturday afternoon 'knocking each other down' in a spirit of clean sportsmanship and keen competition instead of assaulting Pentagon soldiers or policemen with 'peace' placards and filthy words." Spiro Agnew made a career of speeches extolling the "manhood" and "character building" of athletics, in contrast to the un-American unwashed protesters. But now the line between those out on a Saturday afternoon and the people with the peace placards wasn't so clear-cut.

The Utterly Explosive 1968 Olympics

It has been forty years since Tommie Smith and John Carlos took the medal stand at the 1968 Olympics and created what is arguably the most enduring image in sports history, their black-gloved fists extended to the sky. Smith and Carlos's stunning gesture of revolt and resistance was not the result of some spontaneous urge to get face time on the evening news, but rather the result of several years of organizing.

In the fall of 1967, amateur black athletes formed the Olympic Project for Human Rights (OPHR) to organize an African American boycott of the 1968 Olympics in Mexico City. OPHR, its lead organizer, Dr.

Harry Edwards, and its primary athletic spokespeople, 200-meter star Tommie Smith and 400-meter sprinter Lee Evans, were very influenced by the black freedom struggle. Their goal was nothing less than to expose how the United States used black athletes to project a lie, both at home and internationally. But it started on much humbler terms. As Lee Evans said to me, "I didn't speak out until the fall of 1967, when no one would rent us housing close to the university. At that time, the only black males on the campus were athletes: basketball, football, or track. Harry Edwards was working on his doctorate and he was around. He got wind about our complaints and called a meeting. This is how it started. We started the Olympic Project for Human Rights. And all this came out of us not finding housing close enough to the university."[98]

For Smith, it started through what he was learning in his classes at San Jose State. "It really started last semester," he said in 1968. "I took a class in black leadership. It started me to thinking. What the hell is going on in the U.S.? I'm a human. What kind of rights do I have? What kind of rights don't I have? Why can't I get these rights?"[99]

In the founding statement of OPHR, they wrote,

> We must no longer allow this country to *use* . . . a few "Negroes" to point out to the world how much progress she has made in solving her racial problems when the oppression of Afro-Americans is greater than it ever was. . . . We must no longer allow the Sports World to pat itself on the back as a citadel of racial justice when the racial injustices of the sports industry are infamously legendary . . . any black person who allows himself to be used in the above matter is . . . a traitor . . . because he allows racist whites the luxury of resting assured that those black people in the ghettos are there because that is where they belong or want to be.[100]

The roots of the boycott had started to develop in 1964, when black activist/comedian Dick Gregory (also once upon a time a fine college athlete in his own right) called for an international boycott of the 1964 games alongside Olympic veteran Mal Whitfield, who said in a 1963

Ebony magazine article, "It is time for American Negro athletes to join the civil rights fight—a fight that is far from won.' "[101]

Roots of Kareem

One of the first to get on board with OPHR was Lew Alcindor. Later known as Kareem Abdul-Jabbar, Alcindor was at the time the most prominent college athlete in the United States. Alcindor dominated the basketball world as the center for John Wooden's dynastic UCLA Bruins teams. Alcindor talked to *Sports Illustrated* about why he was joining the revolt:

> I got more and more lonely and more and more hurt by all the prejudice and finally I made a decision: . . . I pushed to the back of my mind all the normalcies of college life and dug down deep into my black studies and my religious studies. I withdrew to find myself. I made no attempt to integrate. I was consumed and obsessed by my interest in the black man, in Black Power, black pride, black courage. That, for me, would suffice. I was full of serious ideas. I could see the whole transition of the black man and his history. And I developed my first interest in Islam.[102]

At the founding conference for OPHR, the soft-spoken Alcindor made a speech that put the crowd on their feet.

> I'm the big basketball star, the weekend hero, everybody's All-American. Well, last summer I was almost killed by a racist cop shooting at a black cat in Harlem. He was shooting on the street—where masses of people were standing around or just taking a walk. But he didn't care. After all we were just niggers. I found out last summer that we don't catch hell because we aren't basketball stars or because we don't have money. We catch hell because we are black. Somewhere each of us have got to make a stand against this kind of thing. This is how I take my stand—using what I have. And I take my stand here.[103]

The struggle was on. OPHR had six central demands: (1) restore Muhammad Ali's title, (2) remove Avery Brundage as head of the United States Olympic Committee, (3) bar South Africa and Rhodesia from the Olympics and other athletic competitions, (4) boycott the New York Athletic Club, (5) hire more black coaches, and (6) the "complete desegregation" of the New York Athletic Club.[104] Tommie Smith took the boycott case public in a piece titled "Why Negroes Should Boycott" for the March 1968 issue of *Sport*. He wrote:

We learn through observation and education. I know more now than I did when I was a boy. I know now, for instance, that Negroes do not have equality in the United States and do not have all of the rights supposedly granted to them by the Constitution of the United States. What is right is right. What is wrong is wrong. I recognize wrongs and I am willing to fight for right. . . .

I am not a militant. I am an extremist only where a fight for my rights as a human being are concerned. I recognize that Negroes have had greater opportunities in sports in general and the Olympics in particular than they have in [any] other field. . . .

. . . To emphasize my point, I have said I would give up my right arm to win a gold medal in the Olympics, but I would not give up my personal dignity. . . .

I am not entirely sure of my actions. No one could be. But I have searched my conscience and I am acting as I believe I should act. I am concerned that I may have harmed my "image" and thus damaged the future I hope to make for my family. I would be a fool not to be concerned. But I would be less than a man if I did not act for what I believe.[105]

Gene Johnson, a world-class high jumper, concurred:

I would like to pose this as a question: what would be the fate of a Ralph Boston were he not a 27-foot broad jumper? Or of a Charlie Greene if he were not a 9.2 sprinter? They would be "faceless" black men caught in the same system of racial discrimination as many other black citizens. . . .

I am proud to see that those proposing the boycott have enough social awareness to realize that this struggle of the man in Fillmore, Watts and Harlem is their struggle also. The efforts of Negroes in athletics have benefited only the athlete involved. The Civil Rights Movement or struggle requires the aid and contributions of all black men regardless of station in life. Negro athletes should not be exempt, nor should they divorce themselves from this struggle. The fact that a great sacrifice is involved such as foregoing [sic] an opportunity to participate in the Olympics points to the urgency.[106]

The boycott became a national debate. California governor Ronald Reagan had harsh words for the plan: "I disapprove greatly of what Edwards is trying to accomplish. . . . Edwards is contributing nothing toward harmony between the races." (Reagan's statement was indirectly profoundly offensive to people such as Smith, Evans, and Alcindor, who resented being represented as Edwards's puppet.) Edwards responded to Reagan by calling him "a petrified pig, unfit to govern."[107]

It would be wrong though to think that resistance to the boycotters came only from the "petrified pig" section of the establishment. Just as Roy Wilkins and the 1950s civil rights activists had spoken against Muhammad Ali, there was a similar backlash against the boycotters. Black press sportswriting icon A.S. "Doc" Young wrote in the *Chicago Tribune*,

If Tommie Smith . . . believes "I'm nothing but a nigger" when he isn't performing on the track, then he is "nothing but a nigger." When one considers that millions of American Negroes have withstood the worst of Southern bigotry without ever being reduced to the acceptance of the state, what is Tommie Smith crying so much about? I have nothing but contempt for people who complain because we don't have enough heroes but who spend their time trying to destroy the showcases for which heroes are produced and displayed. The charge that "America is as racist as South Africa" is the most extravagant lie in our times."[108]

But their boycott received support from none other than Jackie Robinson, who said, "I do support the individuals who decided to make the sacrifice by giving up the chance to win an Olympic medal. I respect their courage. We need to understand the reason and frustration behind these protests . . . it was different in my day . . . perhaps we lacked courage."

It also received solidarity and support from Martin Luther King Jr. in the months before his death. His spokesman, Andrew Young, said, "Dr. King applauds this new sensitivity among Negro athletes and public figures and he feels that this should be encouraged. Dr. King told me this represents a new spirit of concern on the part of successful Negroes for those who remain impoverished. Negro athletes may be treated with adulation during their Olympic careers, but many will face later the same slights experienced by other Negroes."[109]

Later, speaking for himself alongside Edwards, King gave the boycott "absolute support. . . . This is a protest and a struggle against racism and injustice and that is what we are working to eliminate in our organization and in our total struggle. . . . No one looking at these demands can ignore the truth of them." He went on, "Freedom always demands sacrifice and . . . they have the courage to say 'We're going to be men and the United States of America have deprived us of our manhood, of our dignity and our native worth, and consequently we're going to stand up and make the sacrifices."[110]

Momentum built throughout the year. The assassination of King shook some of the stalwart antiboycott athletes. Ralph Boston, the most prominent track-and-field star, said, "For the first time since the talks about the boycott began, I feel that I really have a valid reason to boycott." He explained how he arrived at this conclusion:

I sat and thought about it and I see that if I go to Mexico City and represent the United States I would be representing people like the one that killed Dr. King. And there are more people like that going around. On the other hand, I feel if I don't go and someone else wins the medal and it goes to another country, I haven't accomplished anything either. It is disturbing when a guy cannot even talk to people and he is shot for that. It makes you think that Stokely Carmichael and Rap Brown are right. All my life I felt that violence wasn't the way to deal with the problem. How do you keep feeling this way when things like that keep coming? How?[111]

Throughout the year, more and more athletes began asking the same question. Historian Douglas Hartmann writes in his book *Race, Culture, and the Revolt of the Black Athlete*:

Nine track-and-field stars (including future gold medalist long jumper Bob Beamon) at the University of Texas at El Paso were kicked off the team by coach Wayne Vanderburge after they refused to compete in a meet with BYU in protest for the Mormon Church's treatment of blacks. . . . (Every edition of the *Track and Field News* that spring contained at least a couple of snippets regarding incidents of protest or discontent among top-flight black trackmen.) In July, twenty-three of the twenty-five black athletes at Iowa State announced their withdrawal from school effective August 1 because the athletic council rejected some of their eight demands—including one that called for the hiring of Negro coaches in all sports.[112]

A boycott looked like a possibility, but it was not to be. The wind went out of its sails for a myriad of reasons. Some felt threatened by Brundage's stern warning, "If these boys are serious, they're making a very bad mistake. If they're not serious and they're using the Olympic Games for publicity purposes, we don't like it." Others felt that just raising the issues was enough. But the most central problem was that athletes who had trained their whole lives for their Olympic moment quite understandably didn't want to give it up.[113]

Track legend Rafer Johnson, in his autobiography *The Best That I*

Can Be, reflected the conflicted feelings some black athletes had toward the boycott and the movement itself. It is a rather clear exposition of the double consciousness of black athletes, who carry both a taste of privilege and a taste of pain. "What you have to ask yourself is, 'What good is it going to do? Is it going to help housing? Is it going to help education? Is it going to help job opportunities?' I don't see how a boycott of the Olympics is relevant at all to these problems." He also wrote about the movement as a whole, "The militant tactics of Stokely Carmichael, H. Rap Brown, Angela Davis, and Malcolm X seemed divisive and sometimes destructive. Still, I was glad they were around. They dared to utter truths that others could not, and their fervor accelerated the process of social change. The larger society might have never awakened if those fierce, threatening voices had not been raised."[114]

John Carlos expressed to me years later his frustration about this mind-set. "A lot of the athletes thought that winning medals would supersede or protect them from racism. But even if you won the medal, it ain't going to save your momma. It ain't going to save your sister or children. It might give you fifteen minutes of fame, but what about the rest of your life?"[115]

But it accomplished its goal of raising a broader awareness. As Lee Evans said:

> Harry [Edwards] was media savvy. He said all year that we were going to take a vote at the Olympic trials and all year there was commentary in all the newspapers. Some editors made fools of themselves. They would write, "Look at these narrow, stupid Black guys. They don't know what they're doing." They just said things that exposed themselves to who they really were. The athletes, of course, voted down the boycott. I was hoping it was going to be voted down because I wanted to run in the Olympics. I knew that this would happen, that the proposal was a way for us to get leverage. Tom and I had talked about it, and I said, "Let's say we're going to boycott so we can get some things done," but we all knew that we were going to run in Mexico. Push comes to shove, we were going to be there.[116]

One person who was not there, it must be noted, was Lew Alcindor, who staged his own one-person boycott and stayed home.

Then on October 2, ten days before the Games opened, Mexican security forces massacred hundreds of students in Mexico City. Jean-Paul Sartre and Bertrand Russell issued a statement on Mexico and the Olympic Games:

> The Mexican government has behaved with a barbarity comparable only to the massacres carried out by occupying Nazi troops in Europe or by napalming American planes in Vietnam. Throughout the world people have been aroused to passionate anger and alarm. We express our profound solidarity with the heroic Mexican students. We ask people, organizations and nations to boycott the Olympic games. . . . Almost immediately after this ambush-massacre occurred, the Mexican Government met with the Olympic Committee and said: "The intervention of the forces of order have assured calm and there will be no trouble to prevent the Olympics from taking place." The same day the United States State Department declared: "The disturbances in Mexico City affected only a small part of the population and order is now restored." There is a clear complicity between the United States and Mexican Governments to meet popular resistance with massacre. If the Olympic Committee agrees to hold the games in Mexico, it stands guilty of complicity in this crime.[117]

Although you cannot compare the harassment and intimidation of the OPHR athletes to the massacre of the students and their supporters, the intention was the same: to stifle protest. The effort to silence the OPHR athletes came in different forms, even in the form of track legend Jesse Owens. Brundage sent Owens to discredit the Olympic rebels. As Douglas Hartmann wrote,

> In Owens's view, the boycott was nothing but "political aggrandizement," which he condemned on the grounds that "there is no place in the athletic world for politics." Instead, Owens claimed,

'The Olympics help bridge the gap of misunderstanding of people in this country," thus promoting the "way of American life." In a follow-up statement published under the title "Olympics a Bastion of Non-Discrimination," the legendary figure added that athletic scholarships help youngsters to attend the colleges of their choice.[118]

Owens wasn't the only black athletic legend to come down on OPHR. As the *Washington Afro American* reported, "Joe Louis says colored athletes should consider themselves Americans first and colored Americans second and disagrees with those pushing for a boycott. 'Whenever you have a chance to do something for your country you should do it,' Louis said."[119]

In Mexico City, Brundage sent Owens to talk to the track team to try to discourage them from any protest on the track. Brundage's ear was notoriously tin. He could not have picked a worse representative. As Lee Evans tells the story:

Jesse was confused as far as I'm concerned. The USOC [United States Olympic Committee] dogged him, and he knew they dogged him. . . . Treating him badly after his exploits in the [Berlin] Olympic games, when he ran [and won four gold medals]. He came back, didn't have a job, was racing horses for money. We were really annoyed with him because he knew what we were going through, yet he pretended that it didn't exist, and that just blew our minds when he called a meeting with us in Mexico City. I thought he called this meeting because Avery Brundage sent him there. Jesse Owens was sitting on the fifty-yard line with all the important people of the world, the royalties, the Avery Brundages. They have a special section where they sit in the games, right at the fifty-yard line, and Jesse—that's where he was sitting. He thought he was one of them. He had forgot that he was once an athlete struggling like we were. So he came and talked to us like he was Avery Brundage or the King of England or somebody, and really talking stupid to us, and we just shouted him out of the room.

. . . I still admire him to this day, that's why I say he was confused, coming to talk to us like that, because we knew that he was being victimized. He was a victim, and we felt sorry for him, actually.[120]

(After the events of 1968, Owens said to Smith and Carlos, "The black fist is a meaningless symbol. When you open it, you have nothing but fingers—weak, empty fingers. The only time the black fist has significance is when there's money inside. There's where the power lies.")

It was on the second day that Smith and Carlos took their stand. First Smith set a world record winning the gold and Carlos won the bronze. Smith then took out the black gloves. When the silver medalist, a runner from Australia named Peter Norman, saw what was happening, he affixed an OPHR button to his chest to show his solidarity on the medal stand.

As the U.S. flag began rising up the flagpole and the anthem played, Smith and Carlos bowed their heads and raised their fists in a black power salute. But there was more than the gloves. The two men also wore no shoes, to protest black poverty, and beads, to protest lynching. Within hours, Smith and Carlos were expelled from the Olympic Village and word spread that they had been stripped of their medals (although they were not). Avery Brundage justified this by saying, "They violated one of the basic principles of the Olympic games: that politics play no part whatsoever in them."[121]

Ironically, it was Brundage's reaction that really turned the spotlight on the protest. As Red Smith wrote, "By throwing a fit over the incident, suspending the young men and ordering them out of Mexico, the badgers multiplied the impact of the protest a hundred fold."[122]

In Brundage's unpublished autobiography he was still muttering about Smith and Carlos, writing, "Warped mentalities and cracked personalities seem to be everywhere and impossible to eliminate."[123]

But Brundage was not alone in his furious reaction. The *Los Angeles Times* accused Smith and Carlos of a "Nazi-like salute." *Time* magazine had the Olympic logo but instead of the motto "Faster, Higher, Stronger," it blared, "Angrier, Nastier, Uglier." The *Chicago Tribune* called the act "an embarrassment visited upon the country," an "act contemptuous of the United States," and "an insult to their countrymen." Smith and Carlos were "renegades" who would come home to be "greeted as heroes by fellow extremists."[124]

The coup de grâce was by a young reporter for the *Chicago American* named Brent Musberger, who wrote, "One gets a little tired of having the United States run down by athletes who are enjoying themselves at the expense of their country. Protesting and working constructively against racism in the United States is one thing, but airing one's dirty clothing before the entire world during a fun-and-games tournament was no more than a juvenile gesture by a couple of athletes who should have known better." He then described Smith and Carlos as "a pair of dark-skinned storm troopers."[125]

For Smith and Carlos, there were no regrets. Carlos was clear on why he had to act:

> I was with Dr. King ten days before he died. He told me he was sent a bullet in the mail with his name on it. I remember looking in his eyes to see if there was any fear, and there was none. He didn't have any fear. He had love and that in itself changed my life in terms of how I would go into battle. I would never have fear for my opponent, but love for the people I was fighting for. That's why if you look at the picture [Carlos and Smith with their raised fists] Tommie has his jacket zipped up, and [Australian silver medalist] Peter Norman has his jacket zipped up, but mine was open. I was representing shift workers, blue-collar people, the underdogs. That's why my shirt was open. Those are the people whose contributions to society are so important but don't get recognized.[126]

Upon their return home, there was support for Smith and Carlos in the black community, but not the entire black community.

> There was pride, but only from the less fortunate. What could they do but show their pride? But we had Black businessmen, we had Black political caucuses, and they never embraced Tommie Smith

or John Carlos. When my wife took her life in 1977 they never said, "Let me help."

Carlos believes to this day that the lack of support led to his wife's suicide.

We were under tremendous economic stress. I took any job I could find. I wasn't too proud. Menial jobs, security jobs, gardener, care-taker, whatever I could do to try to make ends meet. We had four children, and some nights I would have to chop up our furniture and make a fire in the middle of our room just to stay warm. . . . I was the bad guy, the two headed dragon—spitting fire. It meant we were alone.[127]

But if Smith and Carlos were being attacked from all corners, they received immediate solidarity from their track-and-field allies. As Lee Evans said, "I was very distraught. I wanted to go home. I said I wasn't going to run. But Tommie and John—they came to me and said I better run and I better win. They came to my room, and that freed my mind up to go run because I was confused, but when they told me that I should run that really freed me up." Evans made his own statement when he and his fellow medal winners wore black berets on the medal stand. When the media asked him why, he said sarcastically that it was because it was raining. The reality was quite different. As Evans recalled:

We knew that the black beret was a symbol of the Black Panther Party. . . . I thought they were pretty brave guys, but I wouldn't do what they were doing. They were having a shoot-out with the po-lice almost every day. So my job [protesting at the Olympics] was easy. This is one of the things I learned from Malcolm X and Mar-tin Luther King. Everybody can play a part, but everyone has to do something. I used to say to guys I was trying to get to come to meetings, I said, "It's going to be easy for us. We're just going to the Olympic games. I know some guys in Oakland shooting out with the police. So what we're doing is nothing compared to those guys.

We're not putting our life on the line." But, as it turned out, we did put our lives on the line because I had maybe twenty death threats on my life in Mexico City. You have mailboxes in the Olympics. I had the KKK, the NRA, saying "Yeah we're going to shoot you niggers." They even tell you what time they're going to shoot you.

But Evans also remembers criticism from people back home.

I had a tough time too because the Blacks thought that I didn't do enough, and the whites were just mad. I got it from both sides. The Black people thought I should have done nothing less than dynamite the victory stand. That's the only thing that would have satisfied them because, after Tommie and John, what else could I do?[128]

They also received support from unlikely sources. The Olympic crew team, all white and entirely from Harvard, issued the following statement: "We—as individuals—have been concerned about the place of the black man in American society in their struggle for equal rights. As members of the U.S. Olympic team, each of us has come to feel a moral commitment to support our black teammates in their efforts to dramatize the injustices and inequities which permeate our society."[129]

Not every athlete showed them love. Boxer George Foreman, in what was seen as a direct rebuke of Smith and Carlos, waved a small American flag to all four corners of the ring after winning heavyweight gold. This endeared him to the corporate media, but not to others. As Foreman said in 2003, "Most people thought it was great, but then something happened that caused me more pain than I had ever felt as an individual. I was a happy nineteen-year-old boy, and some people came up to me in the 5th ward and said, 'How can you do that when the brothers [Smith and Carlos] are trying to do their thing?' They thought I betrayed them. That people would think that caused great pain." (Foreman, unlike the track team, was given and accepted an invitation to the Nixon White House.)[130]

OPHR and the actions of Smith and Carlos were a terrific rebuke to the hypocrisy at the heart of the Olympics. However, present was one deep flaw that was mirrored in other aspects of the new left and black power movement: women were largely shut out. Many of OPHR's calls to action had statements about "reclaiming manhood," as if African American women weren't victims of racism or were incapable of being a strong voice. The foolishness of this move was quickly seen when many women athletes became major voices of solidarity after the fact. The anchor of the women's gold-medal-winning 4-by-100 team, Wyomia Tyus, said, "I'd like to say that we dedicate our relay win to John Carlos and Tommie Smith." Tyus commented years later, "It appalled me that the men simply took us for granted. They assumed we had no minds of our own and that we'd do whatever we were told."[131]

The critiques are valid, but Smith and Carlos's efforts are immortal as a moment when the privileges of athletic glory were proudly trashed for a greater goal. Jimmy Hines, the 100-meter gold medalist in Mexico City, said of the effect Smith and Carlos's protest had on the 1968 Olympics in people's minds, "I've done maybe a thousand speaking engagements and after each I've had the question: 'Were you the ones . . . ? The ones who . . . ?' I guess that's forever."[132]

The Revolt After Mexico

Despite the backlash, the struggle continued after the Mexico City games. As Douglas Hartmann writes, "Black students took to reenacting Smith and Carlos's clenched-fist salute in athletic contexts and arenas across the country. . . . Posters of the two athletes poised on the victory stand appeared within weeks . . . in 'head-shops, radical churches and student-movement headquarters' around the country."[133] The *Washington Afro-American* reported in January 1969 that posters of Carlos and Smith in full black-fisted glory were banned from the room of a student who was attending a Catholic Youth Organization meet.[134]

In February, African American players on Notre Dame's basketball team threatened to quit unless they receive a public apology from students for booing them at a game at Michigan State. Basketball players Bill Chamberlain and Charlie Scott spoke openly of "affiliating" with the black student movement at the University of North Carolina, and students at the University of Houston demanded that the school's new fieldhouse be named after basketball star Elvin Hayes instead of Roy Hofheinz, owner of the Houston Astros.[135]

Brigham Young University (BYU) became a particular lightning rod for controversy. BYU was affiliated with the Mormon Church, which denied leadership positions to African Americans, claiming that their dark skin was "the mark of the curse of Ham." Fourteen African American players were dismissed from the University of Wyoming football team on October 14 for wearing black armbands the evening before the team was scheduled to play BYU. They called themselves the Black 14 and with the support of the NAACP unsuccessfully sued for $1.1 million in damages. On October 25, in a game with San Jose State, the entire San Jose team wore black armbands to support the fourteen.[136]

In December, a headline in the black press read, "College Cager Dropped for Ignoring 'Anthem.'" The article was about Chris Wood, the co-captain of the Adelbert College basketball team. He was unceremoniously dumped from the team he led after refusing to stand during the national anthem. Jasper Wood, Chris's father, supported his son, saying, "We believe in the fellowship of man. We don't believe in nationalism."[137]

In November 1969, Stanford University president Kenneth Pitzer announced that Stanford would henceforth honor what he called an athlete's "right of conscience." This would allow the athlete to boycott a school or event that he or she deemed "personally repugnant." Though this was not heartily endorsed by other schools, it was nevertheless a breakthrough.[138]

This all led Oklahoma State and U.S. Olympic basketball coach Hank "Mo" Iba to tell Sports Illustrated in the summer of 1969. "We are facing the greatest crisis in sports history. In the next eight months we could see sports virtually destroyed. Nobody seems to realize how critical this situation is."[139]

Even the walled city of segregation known as professional golf gave way as Lee Elder and Charlie Sifford were granted entry to play in Grand Slam tournaments. In 1970, for the first time, blacks could tee off at the Masters. This was a huge crack in the system. Sifford would recount a story of a tournament in 1959: "I had a good chance to get in the Masters if I finished good. . . . Suddenly I was intercepted by five white men who started following me around the course. They threw their beer cans at me and called me 'nigger' and other names."[140]

The political situation was cutting so closely to the surface, it was even finding expression in professional football.

Dave Meggyesy: Out of Their League

David Meggyesy was an all-American linebacker at Syracuse University before playing for the National Football League's St. Louis (now Arizona) Cardinals from 1963 to 1969. He was active in the movements for civil rights and stood in opposition to the war in Vietnam. In 1970 he wrote his football autobiography, *Out of Their League*, which examined how big-time sports in the United States can dehumanize athletes and fans alike. As a player, he was part of something new.

> Coaches and teammates would see me reading various progressive books and magazines on the away game plane trips, and sometimes they would ask me what I was reading, but it wasn't any big deal. We didn't have sit-ins or study groups reading Karl Marx. I was going through a process of my own self-education. Through these various influences, I got involved in the Civil Rights movement. I was reluctant, at first, to tell my African-American teammates about it. My feelings were that it would be embarrassing for them to have this white guy being active and they maybe feeling like they should have been involved . . . but if I would be reading *Ramparts* magazine or an interview with Malcolm X, other players, including our star running back Johnny Roland, would give me a power fist salute as if to say, "We're with you."[141]

Toward the end of his career, Meggyesy began to look very critically at the relationship between sports and football and society.

> I began wondering why other countries don't play this game. I was coming to the understanding that big-time football was more than

a game, that it was a form of political expression and political theater. During that time there was this jingoistic, super patriotic use
of football, particularly during the Super Bowl, to sell the war in
Vietnam. Yet there were a tremendous number of people against
the war including myself. My response was to get more serious
and start organizing my teammates on the Cardinals. I started a
petition drive on the Cardinals, which would be sent to our con-
gressional delegation and senators, calling for an end to the war.
My teammate Rick Sortun and I put it together. Rick was a Goldwater Republican in 1964, and he was my roommate on the road.
We had many heated discussions. During the off season in 1967,
he went back to the University of Washington, and when he came
back for training camp in 1968, he had gone from Goldwater Republican to a member of the Young Socialist Alliance. I kid Rick
and tell him he was my first convert.

The times they were a-changing. The next petition Rick and I put
together, in 1969, we had thirty-seven teammates sign it. . . . The
next day Cardinals head coach Charlie Winner said to me, "I want
you to apologize to the team. This is a big distraction for the team,
and you owe the team an apology." I got up in front of the team and
said I was sorry the petition almost went public because I said it
would be kept private and that was all I was apologizing for. I told
them if they wanted to sign a new petition they could stop by my
locker after practice and do it. Charlie almost had a heart attack." [142]

Meggyesy felt the immediate pressure from management to cease
and desist all "radical" activities.

They tried to put the hammer on me to get me to stop my antiwar
activities. In 1968, I was taken outside by one of the coaches and
asked, "Do you want to play football? I have been told to tell you by
the ownership that if you continue to do what you're doing, you are
going to be thrown out of the League." A few days later, I wrote the
Cardinal management and told them if they continued to threaten
me this way, I would go public. I said in my letter that half the

country is against this war, and my antiwar work doesn't impact my playing, and it is my right as a citizen to protest the war. Nothing happened. Later in the season, NFL Commissioner Pete Rozelle sent an order down to the teams that when the national anthem is being played, we, the players, would have to hold our helmets under our left arm, look up, and salute the flag. I found it repulsive that anyone would be telling me and my teammates that we had to salute the flag and how to do so. So I did a low-key "Tommie Smith" and held my helmet in front of me and bowed my head. The next week, a sports columnist wrote about how reprehensible it was that anyone would refuse to salute the flag. The team didn't know what to do. They thought that if they would be cool, maybe it would go away. So at the start of our next game, some fans unfurled a big banner that said "The Big Red [the nickname of the Cardinals] thinks Pink." It was their way of saying that I was a "pinko" (a communist), and we were a "pinko" team.

Midway through the 1969 season, I got benched. That hurt as much as anything because the ultimate power management has over a player is whether you play or not. At the professional level, this is also your livelihood. When they benched me, I just couldn't believe it. Clearly, I was superior to my backup. On the plane ride back to St. Louis with Rick Sortun after our last game in Green Bay, we decided were going to quit. We were tired of being part of what we saw as an American war game and political theater that was supporting the Vietnam War. Personally, what really hurt was not being allowed to play. . . . When I was benched for "political reasons," all kinds of self-doubts began to creep into my mind. Because one of the core values in sports from the athlete's point of view is that it is a meritocracy: The best players play. An athlete has to believe this is true, or he can't play. When someone messes with that, it messes with everything that is great about sports.[143]

Women Roar

For women, the 1960s was a decade of evolution, as opposed to the revolution the 1970s would bring. It was the time when the groundwork for the revolution was laid. Roberta Gibb in 1966 was the first woman to run the full Boston Marathon. In 1968, Wyomia Tyus became the first woman to win golds in consecutive Olympics in the 100-meter dash. In 1969, Diane Crump became the first woman to ride in a parimutuel race in the United States, and in 1970 she became the first woman to ride in the Kentucky Derby. In 1969, a schedule of national championships for women's sports was announced that included gymnastics and track and field for the first time. In 1968, when the most prestigious tennis tournaments for women were officially open only to amateurs and under-the-table payments were offered to the top players to ensure they would play, a working-class tennis player (itself an oddity) named Billie Jean King began to make waves by insisting that prize money be paid to women openly at Wimbledon.

Rebellion even made it to the cheerleaders. In Oakland, an all–African American cheerleading squad chanted, "Ungawa! Black Power! Destroy White Boy, We said it! We meant it, We always represent it!!"[144]

In 1969, Dodgers owner Walter O'Malley—the lord of Chavez Ravine, a combination of Hitler and Stalin to the people of Brooklyn—looked ahead to the 1970s and said, "Is baseball on the spot? I would say yes. But then religion is on the spot, government is on the spot, the integrity of treaties is on the spot. These are times when people spit on the flag, when priests go over the fence. You have to understand the pattern of things today. There is rebellion against the establishment and baseball is linked to the establishment."[145]

· 8 ·

The Flood Gates

The early 1970s were defined by both anger and uncertainty, driven by the war in Vietnam and the movement that had risen up against it. And it was all brought to you live.

During the 1969–70 school year, the FBI recorded 1,785 student demonstrations, with 313 buildings occupied. In 1970 one million college students told pollsters they considered themselves "revolutionaries" and ten million believed they would see a revolution in the United States in their lifetime.[1]

In Vietnam the war was being lost within the ranks as soldiers began their own revolt. Underground newspapers sprang up at military bases across the country; by 1970 more than fifty were circulating. Among them were *About Face* in Los Angeles; *Fed Up!* in Tacoma, Washington; *Short Times* at Fort Jackson; *Vietnam GI* in Chicago; *Graffiti* in Heidelberg, Germany; *Bragg Briefs* in North Carolina; *Last Harass* at Fort Gordon, Georgia; and *Helping Hand* at Mountain Home Air Base, Idaho. A popular helmet logo was "UUUU," which meant "the unwilling, led by the unqualified, doing the unnecessary, for the ungrateful."[2]

The soldiers' revolt began with combat avoidance and made a shift to mutiny after the Tet offensive of January 1968. Tet was a clarion call to everyone, from respected news anchor Walter Cronkite to the grunts in "the shit," that this was not a war that would be won and Westmoreland's "light at the end of the tunnel" was an oncoming train.[3]

Not only did acts of mutiny escalate after the Tet, but so did fragging. Fragging is the murder of officers by their troops. One GI newspaper in 1970 had an article suggesting that troops not desert but instead go to Vietnam and kill their commanding officers. U.S. troops carried out an estimated eight hundred to one thousand acts of fragging attempts against their commanding officers. While U.S. soldiers were revolting against their commanding officers, they were also making peace with the Viet Cong. U.S. soldiers were refusing to attack the Viet Cong, as the two were not enemies but brothers in a war against a common oppressor. The U.S. soldiers and the Viet Cong established an agreement not to open hostilities on one another unless first fired upon. U.S. troops wore red bandanas and peace signs to illustrate that they would not harm the Viet Cong. After the 1970 invasion of Cambodia, the soldiers from Fire Base Washington led a sit-in. They told *Up Against the Bulkhead*, "We have no business there . . . we just sat down. Then they promised us we wouldn't have to go to Cambodia." Within a week, there were two additional mutinies, as men from the 4th and 8th Infantry refused to board helicopters to Cambodia. One infantry officer reported, "You can't give orders and expect them to be obeyed."[4]

Vietnam GI argued after the brutal expedition known as Hamburger Hill, "Brass are calling this a tremendous victory. We call it a goddam butcher shop. . . . If you want to die so some lifer can get a promotion, go right ahead. But if you think your life is worth something, you better get yourselves together. If you don't take care of the lifers, they might damn well take care of you."[5]

"In grade school we learned about the redcoats, the nasty British soldiers that tried to stifle our freedom and the tyranny of George III," said W.D. Ehrhart, Vietnam veteran and poet. "Subconsciously, but not very subconsciously, I began increasingly to have the feeling that I was a redcoat. I think it was one of the most staggering realizations of my life."[6]

Jan Barry, one of the founders of Vietnam Veterans Against the War, said, "Some of the special forces people would come back from their missions and say we should be supporting the other side, because these people have legitimate grievances and the other side is the only one . . . really trying to do something for these people. This was a rather startling thing to hear."[7]

Pete Zastrow, a former army captain, said, "My feeling was that most of the Vietnamese we were fighting against . . . didn't want to shoot us any more than we wanted to shoot them. They had their job, which was to carry supplies, and we had our job, which was to stop them. But if we stayed out of their way, they sure wouldn't come looking for us. So we stayed out of their way. . . . The military teaches you mission first, men second. But because I felt the mission was stupid . . . the men were much more important to me than the mission. We were doing nothing that I could see was worth anybody getting shot for. It's as simple as that."[8]

In 1971 Colonel Robert D. Heinl Jr. wrote in the *Armed Forces Journal*, "Our army that now remains in Vietnam is in a state approaching collapse, with individual units avoiding or having refused combat, murdering their officers and noncommissioned officers, drug-ridden, and dispirited where not near mutinous . . . conditions [exist] among American forces in Vietnam that have only been exceeded in this century by . . . the collapse of the Tsarist armies in 1916 and 1917."[9]

It is this collapse of the military—alongside the resistance in Vietnam and the protest movement at home—that ultimately forced the United States to pull out of Vietnam and put an end to the war. Black soldiers were a central part of this rebellion. In 1970, journalist Wallace Terry traveled to Vietnam to survey 392 African American and white soldiers. He compared his results with a similar survey taken in 1967 and saw a dramatic change. The heroes of black soldiers were Martin Luther King Jr., Stokely Carmichael, and Muhammad Ali—all because they were seen as symbols of opposition to the war in Vietnam.

Some of the other results of Terry's 1970 survey:

- 50% of African Americans said that they would use their weapons in the struggle for civil rights in the United States.
- 30% said they would join black power organizations.

- 83% believed that additional American race riots were inevitable and 45% of those said that they would participate in such riots.
- 45% would refuse orders to put down riots involving African Americans.
- 72% approved of Eldridge Cleaver.
- 70% approved of Malcolm X.
- 69% approved of Muhammad Ali.

As one analysis of Terry's findings expressed, "It is not surprising that the attitudes of veterans changed so dramatically when one considers some of the racial incidents described by Terry. . . . For instance, in April of 1968 when Martin Luther King, Jr. was assassinated, crosses were burned at Cam Ranh Bay and Confederate flags were flown in Danang."[10]

The army was disintegrating, and maverick sportswriter Leonard Schecter was willing to use sports as a way to explain the prolonged and painful end to the war. He wrote in his 1969 book *The Jocks*, "We play our games, or watch them contested, with the same tenacious ferocity with which we fight a war in Vietnam and with as little reason or sense. We are taught from the cradle that we have never lost a war and that winning is everything, tying is like kissing your sister and losing is nothing."[11]

Sports also worked its way into the explanation of U.S. withdrawal and the strategy the Nixon regime called "Vietnamization." Secretary of Defense Melvin Laird characterized the escalation of bombing and the mining of Haiphong Harbor as "an expansion ball club." The White House staff nicknamed it "operation linebacker," and Nixon's code name was "Quarterback."[12]

It was hard to pin down where pro football ended and the Nixon administration began. The NFL in an official release in praise of its own product called the sport "vicarious warfare nurtured by the technology that is this land's hallmark."[13]

Nixon also had a direct line to Washington Redskins coach George Allen (whose son is the former Republican senator George "Macaca" Allen, who used the epithet "macaca" to describe an American-born young man of Indian descent). Nixon would call in plays from the White House that Allen would immediately send into the game. They tended to not work particularly well. It pushed Redskins quarterback Billy Kilmer to say, "[Nixon's] really hurting us. He calls us all the time. . . . I think I'm going to ask George Allen to tell the president not to talk about the game until after we've played it."[14]

As Dave Meggyesy said, in a figurative flip of the bird at the entire football world, "The Mitchell-Agnew-Nixon mentality is what the game is all about. Politics and pro football are the most grotesque extremes in the theatric of a dying empire. It's no accident the most repressive regime in history is ruled by a football freak."[15]

Protest Comes to Husky Stadium

Nowhere was safe from protest. Seattle-based journalist Dean Paton relayed the following story:

> We don't usually think of major college football teams standing up against the American war machine. But it happened in Seattle, in 1972, at the University of Washington. The team's action was pulled off so exquisitely, so powerfully, that the players' protest trapped—and then stunned—a stadium full of conservative football zealots. Well, at least half a stadium.
>
> In the 1970s, spring football practice at the UW would culminate with a popular ritual called the Varsity-Alumni Game, a contest between the next fall's gridiron heroes and a motley team of former Husky football players. Though the varsity usually won, it was often a good game, because most of the grads were still fairly young and a few had gone on to play professionally.
>
> The 1972 game was scheduled for an uneventful Saturday, May 13. But on May 8, the Monday preceding the popular scrimmage, President Richard Nixon triggered yet another round of nationwide antiwar protests when he ordered U.S. naval ships to mine Haiphong harbor, the major seaport serving North Vietnam. Protests erupted in cities across the country. In Seattle, citizens slept on the downtown lawn of the United States Courthouse.

There were daily marches, the usual speeches—and of course the war continued.

I remember coming from one of the downtown rallies to my job—the perfect student job—at the Sports Information Office, just north of the football stadium. I shared an office with Jack Pfeifer, a graduate student and former *Seattle Times* sportswriter, and the two of us compiled press guides, edited football programs, worked with coaches, wrote press releases, and sometimes traveled with various teams to games or meets. It beat working at the campus photocopy shop.

On this particular Tuesday, Jack was at his desk talking with some of the football players—about the war. I heard only bits and pieces of their conversation, but when the players left Jack turned and said, "You're not going to believe this. The players want to protest Nixon's mining of the harbor. At the game on Saturday. And they want us to help." . . .

The players, led by quarterback Sonny Sixkiller and all-conference cornerback Calvin Jones (who went on to play with the Denver Broncos), worked with other players to craft a team statement. Spring practice intensified each day, as excitement about Saturday's game grew on campus and in the press. The players gave Jack a copy of their statement on Thursday. It was strong, unequivocal. I made a copy on the athletic department's Xerox machine and felt like I was committing espionage. . . .

The players' plan was to wait until just before the second half kickoff and then have the legendary announcer read their statement. I have no idea what transpired during the first half of play, or during halftime, but I do remember the fear I felt as the teams came out to play the second half. As they warmed up and the captains walked toward midfield to shake hands, I pulled the half sheet of paper from my notebook and walked into the public booth. I walked up behind Wendell and tapped him on the shoulder. He turned around and smiled.

"I've been asked by the players to give this to you," I said politely. "They would, uh, like you to read it now."

Wendell scanned the words and stopped smiling. "This?" he said derisively. "Uh, yes," I said, "just the first part," and I remember looking toward midfield far below. Players from both varsity and alumni were staring up at the press box, metaphorically tapping their feet. I was certain I could hear them pleading, "What are you waiting for?" Wendell was anything but eager, wasn't sure he was allowed to say anything other than how many yards the halfback had just gained, and whether or not it was enough for a first down.

I managed to say, "If you don't read it, the players say they will not continue the game." Wendell looked at the man sitting next to him, then again at the players' statement. He looked down at the players, who stared back from midfield. Wendell turned to his microphone and his booming voice reverberated throughout the historic horseshoe stadium and out across Lake Washington.

"Ladies and gentlemen, may we have your attention for a very important announcement. The football team at the University of Washington wishes to take this moment to express its concern over the present situation in Vietnam. Toward this end, the team will now delay the game for a couple of minutes."

As Wendell's words echoed throughout the stadium, a loud symphony of boos arose from the seats on the stadium's south side, where the alumni donors and wealthy season ticket holders sit. The boos were unremitting, and they grew as Wendell continued.

"The players basically have one thing to say: they feel the war and the killing should be ended immediately. The team wishes you would take these few minutes to think about what has happened in the world this week and what consequences they may have. Thank you."

As Wendell concluded, a massive cheer erupted from the north side stands, where thousands of students had leapt to their feet, shouting, waving arms, answering the boos and catcalls with applause for the players. Their cheering intensified. Because the visiting team's bench was directly in front of the south side seats, the alumni players could hear the boos and catcalls quite clearly.

Reese Lindquist, who coached the alum squad that Saturday, re-members having to restrain Dave Kopay. Kopay, a running back, had captained Owens's 1964 Rose Bowl team, and then gone on to play in the NFL with San Francisco, New Orleans, Washington, Detroit and Green Bay. "He was really tough," Lindquist said. 'When the alumni started booing, I had to grab Dave—with both arms—to keep him from charging up into the stands. I was afraid he would tear some people apart. Oh, he was mad. He thought the war was completely wrong." (Kopay later made history as the first retired male pro athlete to come out of the closet.)

In the press box, time stood still. After a couple of minutes, I spotted the sign from the players at midfield, and told Wendell he could now finish reading the statement. He sighed, and then an-nounced: "The game will now resume; the team thanks you for your patience."

Decades later, memory unclear, I can only assume the varsity won the game. They usually did. But of one thing I remain certain: those players pulled off one of the best antiwar actions in the na-tion that week. The entire team lined up against its coaches, the alums that helped bankroll the athletic department, a football-fanatic president, and the war they all believed in with a zeal that routinely crushed small countries—and they won. It's not often that football jocks, routinely lionized by pro-war hooligans, get a public chance to run with a message of peace and sanity, get to carry it straight at half a stadium of captive Nixon supporters, stuck in their seats, unable to ignore their idols' antiwar beliefs. In a game whose context was military escalation and presidential saber-rattling, they called the perfect play.[16]

The New Sportswriting

A new series of sports books emerged with no resemblance to their puffy predecessors. Jim Bouton's *Ball Four* (1970); Curt Flood's *The Way It Is* (1971); David Wolf's *Foul! The Connie Hawkins Story* (1972), William O. Johnson's *All That Glitters Is Not Gold: The Olympic Game* (1972); Dave Meggyesy's *Out of Their League* (1971); Neil Amdur's *Fifth Down:*

Democracy and the Football Revolution (1971); Lynda Huey's *A Running Start: A Woman, an Athlete* (1976); and Robert Lipsyte's *Sportsworld: An American Dreamland* (1975) all had the effort of scandalizing an industry that would often find itself quite hostile to writers who didn't act like stenographers and athletes who could actually write.

No cows were sacred. The fairy-tale lyricism of Grantland Rice and the grubby street posturing of Jimmy Cannon had given way to a reckless verisimilitude. People such as Lipsyte, Ira Berkow, Jerry Izenberg, Sandy Padwe, and Leonard Schecter wanted to expose sports and explicate what sports say about ourselves.

Lipsyte, a sportswriter of great repute at the *New York Times* for fifteen years, wrote in *SportsWorld*:

A man must prove his faith in sports and the American Way by whipping himself into shape, playing by the rules, being part of the team, and putting out all the way. If his faith is strong enough, he will triumph. It's his own fault if he loses, fails, remains poor. Even for ball games, these values, with their implicit definitions of manhood, courage, and success, are not necessarily in the individual's best interests. But for daily life, they tend to create a dangerous and grotesque web of ethics and attitudes, an amorphous infrastructure that acts to contain our energies, divert our passions, and socialize us for work, war or depression. I call this infrastructure SportsWorld. . . .

A great deal of the angry energy generated in America through the coming apart of the 1960s was absorbed by SportsWorld in its various roles as socializer, pacifier, safety valve; as a concentration camp for adolescents and an emotional Disney Land for their parents. . . . SportsWorld is a buffer, a DMZ between people and the economic and political systems that direct their lives.[17]

Bouton said years later:

I think the '60s affected everybody. Part of what was really good about it was that it just called everything into question—all the assumptions, all the rules, all the ways of doing things, and tossed them all up in the air, and forced everybody to take another look at questioning authority, and you know, it was really a necessary thing to do because we had just sort of inched our way and then leapfrogged into Vietnam without a lot of public discussion about it, taking the word of a handful of leaders. . . .

That was the driving force. That, and racism. Blacks were challenging the white status quo, and so there was all that going on. I don't think any of us at the time—certainly not myself—thought this was going to be some sort of pivotal time in American history. When you're living through history, it just seems like the most natural thing in the world. I don't think it occurred to me that "Gee, all these other people are kicking up a fuss, maybe I should write a book that does the same thing." That thought never occurred to me, but you're part of your environment. I don't know if I would have or could have even thought of writing *Ball Four* during the Eisenhower years.[18]

Bouton's *Ball Four* is a tender look at the complex, at times charming, and often infantile relationships that make up a typical baseball team. He included looks at the drinking, partying, and boredom that pervade a typical locker room.

After the book was released, one would have thought he'd paraded around Havana wearing an American-flag G-string. He became a baseball pariah, with Pete Rose standing on the dugout steps and yelling, "Fuck you, Shakespeare!" Dick Young called Bouton and his sportswriting advisor Leonard Schecter "social lepers." Most baseball officials proudly proclaimed that they hadn't read it and that it was a disgrace.[19]

Commissioner Bowie Kuhn called Bouton to his office and said, "This is a horrible piece of writing! You've done the game a grave disservice. Saying players kissed on the Seattle team bus—incredible! Or that some of our greatest stars were drunk on the field. What can you be thinking of?"[20]

"I don't know," said Bouton years later.

I think for them it was just one more nail in the coffin, just more questioning of authority. The whole edifice was shaking from all the assaults on it and this was just one more instance—gee whiz, even in baseball! Not even baseball can be sacrosanct! That was part of it. I think baseball, football—they've always felt the need to be patriotic, to be on the side of America and might, supporting wars no matter what, and so that conservative bent, to have a break in their ranks: this was a little too much for them. And the truth of it is they hadn't read the damn book. They would have realized if they had read it that the things that they claimed bothered them were just in the context of a larger story. Baseball fans easily absorbed this concept. So many people picked up that book to read it and get angry about it, started reading it, and were saying, "What the hell are they making such a big deal about?" I mean, that was the tone of 99 percent of the letters I received. "I read your book, I kept waiting for this, and waiting for that, and I never saw it. There was nothing in the book that turned me off of the game or the people involved or anything." It was just a love letter. It's just the opposite of what baseball was saying.[21]

The shift over the last ten years was seismic. If in 1960 we had Willie Mays defensively speaking about the right to not protest, in July 1970 we had all-star slugger Richie "Dick" Allen tell *Ebony* magazine, "I wouldn't say that I hate whitey, but deep down in my heart, I just can't stand whitey's ways, man. . . . I get right mad."[22]

Protest in sports was still a very dicey and polarizing act, but it was also legitimized. Bill Walton, who opposed the war and believed in the hippie aesthetic, went into practice and said to his legendary coach, John Wooden, that he wouldn't be shaving his beard because it would conflict with his belief system. John Wooden expressed his respect for Walton's sense of principle and said, "We're sure going to miss you around here, Bill."[23]

In 1972, Frank Deford wrote the following about West Point's clean-cut football star Pete Dawkins:

There is real comfort to be had waking up one fine, polluted, polarized morning and discovering that there is still a Biltmore clock
and a YMCA and a Pete Dawkins. Perhaps each morning one last
hero should be assigned to stand under the Biltmore clock so we
can hear the ticks from the good old times when peace and prosperity were both lit up at this end of the tunnel and the only
shaggy-haired perverts were the four who were making noise in a
Liverpool cellar.[24]

Black Struggle in the 1970s

The very public hand-wringing over whether to be a John Carlos or a
Pete Dawkins, whether one should throw one's lot in with athletic revolution or the "establishment," affected every corner of sports.

In 1972 no less a person than Jesse Owens wrote *I Have Changed*, a
remarkable, and remarkably underread, story of his own radicalization
as he was pushing sixty years of age. The same man who said to the
sprinters in 1968, "The black fist is a meaningless symbol," wrote, "I realized now that militancy in the best sense of the word was the only answer where the black man was concerned, that any black man who
wasn't a militant in 1970 was either blind or a coward."[25]

It is hard to believe that this was the same Jesse Owens who had written in his 1969 book *Black Think*: "The memory [of oppression] may still
be painful. . . . But, by god, it's only a memory. . . . Believe it or not, most
black men today start just about equal with the white. We may not begin
with as well-off a set of parents and we may have to fight harder to make
that equality work. But we can make it work. Because now we have the
one all-important gift of opportunity. . . . If the Negro doesn't succeed in
today's America, it is because he has chosen to fail."[26]

It became an assumption that African American pro jocks needed to
be a part of the struggle. As Jesse Jackson said in a 1975 interview:

Black athletes are not off limits to the struggle; they have an obligation to participate in it. If they think that because somebody
is screaming for them tonight and their picture is in the paper

that they have it made, you wait until the day when there's a choice between a white boy with equal or less ability and see what happens.[27]

In the same interview Jackson said:

One hundred years ago we brought the cotton bales to the store-house and we got a pat on the back and they told us we were the strongest Blacks in all of the county. We made all-county cotton-picker and went back down to our little shack. We pick the cotton, white people pick the money.

One hundred years later, we take the basketball to the hoop or the football to the goal line and we get a pat on the back and we are all-county, all-state, All-American, all-pro and we get a trophy and a percentage of the money but the little white people upstairs get the bulk of the money. They choose who can play, who can't play. They determine who will be blackballed.[28]

There was much to still be angry about. In April 1974 Henry Aaron of the Atlanta Braves broke Babe Ruth's seemingly unbreakable home run record when he hit his 715th off Al Downing. The racism that sur-rounded Aaron was off the charts. In 1973, as he closed in on the record, the U.S. Postal Service reported that Aaron received 930,000 letters, the most of anyone not named Richard Nixon. Much of it was in the cate-gory of death threats. Samples read, "Dear Hank Aaron, How about some sickle cell anemia, Hank?"; "Dear Nigger, You black animal, I hope you never live long enough to hit more home runs than the great Babe Ruth." Aaron later wrote, "The Atlanta fans weren't shy about letting me know what they thought of a $200,000 nigger striking out with men on base."[29] When Aaron finally broke the mark, baseball commissioner Bowie Kuhn didn't show. Aaron was never particularly political as a player, but his experience left scars.

In 1976, James Harris was the only African American quarterback di-recting an NFL team. Issues such as this began to be discussed openly for the first time. Harris later said, "[Blacks] get two types of opportunities to play QB in the NFL. A chance and a 'nigger' chance." Jim Brown firmly agreed that blacks were being confined. "There are black positions. A lot of coaches are kind of stupid. They don't know anything about black people or black players. We obviously know they don't want blacks at quarterback because that takes brains. Every time you hear them talk about a black leader, they say he leads by example. If he's smart, 'Well, he's a troublemaker.'"[30]

Death of Clemente

The proud politicization of sports took a terrible blow in 1972 with the death of baseball icon Roberto Clemente. Clemente's legend has only mushroomed over time. As David Maraniss wrote in his book, *Clemente: the Passion and Grace of Baseball's Last Hero*, "Forty public schools, two hospitals, and more than two hundred parks and ballfields bear his name, from Carolina, Puerto Rico, where he was born, to Pittsburgh, Pennsylvania, where he played, to far-off Mannheim, Germany." Maraniss could have added a bridge in Pittsburgh to that list, as well as countless children. Much of Clemente's lasting legacy has to do with the way he died, but it is also intimately connected with who he was as a player. He wasn't the first Latino, but he was the first Latino star. He was the first to wear his Latin heritage proudly. He was the first to speak out on the way racism in the United States affected Latino ballplayers. He was the first Latino to find the hearts of white baseball fans, but never by checking his culture, language, or heritage at the door.[31]

Clemente's last season, 1972, started with a players' strike, the first of the new, more confrontational Players Association, under the leadership of former steel union organizer Marvin Miller. It was a strong victory. The Pirates, in a union town, were united as a team in support of the strike.

This position was helped by Clemente, who lived with the rookies in spring training—before the strike was official—and talked union to young players. That last season included Clemente's three thousandth hit, a frozen-rope double on September 29. Clemente was only the eleventh player to reach that number. It was a guarantee that he would become the first Latino to be enshrined in the Hall of Fame. He also won his twelfth Gold Glove that year and became the all-time leader in games played for the Pirates, surpassing Honus Wagner. There were rumors that Clemente would retire, but he said that, whatever he did, it wouldn't be for the money. "The only thing I worry about is being happy . . . If I can for example have my health I can work. I don't care if I'm a janitor. I don't care if I drive a cab. . . . I can be a person like me—I make a lot of money, but at the same time I live the life of the common fellow. . . . I just worry that I be healthy and live long enough to educate my sons and make them respect people. And to me this is my biggest worry: to live for my kids."[32]

That December 23, an earthquake gutted Nicaragua. It hit 6.5 on the Richter scale, crushing 350 square blocks while killing and injuring thousands. The horror of this natural disaster was compounded by the relationship between Richard Nixon and Nicaragua's military leader, Anastasio Somoza. Somoza was an anticommunist zealot whose family had stolen 25 percent of Nicaragua's wealth, murdering and torturing anyone who got in their way. All of this was done for decades with the full financial and moral support of the U.S. government. It was Somoza's father about whom, legend has it, President Franklin D. Roosevelt remarked, "Somoza may be a son of a bitch, but he's our son of a bitch." Somoza junior was certainly Nixon's SOB. Somoza had even written a letter earlier in 1972 nominating Tricky Dick for the Nobel Peace Prize.

Thanks to Nixon's elaborate obsession with audio technology, we know that his immediate concern after the earthquake was not the horrific loss of life in Nicaragua but rather that the country would "go communist" in the ensuing chaos. Instead of providing relief, he sent in paratroopers to help the Nicaraguan National Guard keep order. Somoza had issued shoot-to-kill orders against anyone foraging for food, but not before shutting down all the service agencies that were feeding people. One doctor reported, "I had more individuals that I treated who were shot [than who were injured by effects of the earthquake]. They were shot for looting. It was amazing. Young kids. I remember operating on young kids to remove bullets."

Roberto Clemente had many friends in Nicaragua. He also was haunted by the thoughts of the children he had visited there over the years. In twenty-four hours' time, he had set up the Roberto Clemente Committee for Nicaragua. Fear for his friends was supplanted by fury when he heard stories of Somoza's troops seizing aid for their own enrichment. One friend returned to Puerto Rico with a story that he stopped Somoza's troops from seizing his supplies by saying that if they didn't let the supplies through, he would tell the great Roberto Clemente what was taking place. Clemente took from this that he himself would have to go to Nicaragua to make sure the aid got where it was supposed to go.[33]

On December 31, 1972, he boarded a ramshackle plane overloaded with relief supplies. A friend tried to warn Clemente that it was unsafe, but in the urgency of the crisis Clemente's phobia of planes seemed to have left him. He could even die riding a horse, he told his friend. The plane went down a thousand yards out to sea and Clemente's body was never recovered. His young boys were six, five, and two. The outpouring of emotion was overwhelming, and thousands of mourners flocked to the home of Clemente's wife, Vera. Eleven weeks later, Clemente was elected to the baseball Hall of Fame, joining Gehrig as one of the only players who didn't have to wait five years for enshrinement. Vera gave the speech, her three sons looking on. One writer said of Clemente that the "things he did on a ball field . . . made me wish I was Shakespeare." Puerto Rican poet Elliott Castro wrote, "That night on which Roberto Clemente left us physically, his immortality began."[34]

In the days after Clemente's death, an obituary ran in the newspaper of the Black Panthers. The Panthers thanked Clemente for supporting the breakfast programs and health clinics operated by their Philadelphia chapter. They wrote, "Roberto unhesitatingly donated to the Survival Programs and showed a keen interest in their progress." The obit ends this way: "It is ironic that the profession in which he achieved 'legendry' knew him the least. Roberto Clemente did not, as the Commissioner of Baseball maintained, 'Have about him a touch of royalty.' Roberto Clemente was simply a man, a man who strove to achieve his dream of peace and justice for oppressed people throughout the world."[35]

Jack Scott's Athletic Revolution

One of the true visionaries of sport in the 1970s was a man named Jack Scott. A former athlete, and author of the influential book *Athletics for Athletes*, Scott's vision was for sport "to be run in a democratic manner and all of those involved would have a say. . . . Unlike today's static, authoritarian, tradition-bound athletic programs, it would allow radical change in order to serve properly each group of athletes." He called for greater inclusion of women and people of color on teams and for giving both college and pro athletes a voice in team management. Scott's mission, he said, was not to "deemphasize" sports but to "democratize" them. The goal of sports, he believed, should be geared toward getting more to play, not more to watch. As he said, "The beauty is in the classic struggle of man against man, man against nature and man against himself. . . . If you don't struggle well, you should feel badly. But you shouldn't feel badly just because you lose. The final score should be almost incidental."[36]

Scott was a vocal critic of esteemed authoritarian coaches such as Vince Lombardi, Adolph Rupp, and Bear Bryant. After Scott criticized Bryant, Vice President Spiro T. Agnew called Scott an enemy of sport, a "perma-critic," and a "guru from Berkeley."[37]

Criticism from Agnew only burnished Scott's credentials. He was given the position of athletic director at Oberlin College in 1970 to see if he could make his vision a reality. When the liberal arts college made the hire, a coach told *Time* magazine anonymously, "Sports will be destroyed at Oberlin."[38]

This was part of a broader report *Time* did on the changes Scott brought to the liberal-arts college's athletic department. Scott hired two women coaches to encourage more coed sports and, as he put it, "break down the machismo atmosphere." He stopped selling tickets to all sporting events—everything would be free. He also allowed athletes to have veto power over all coaching hires. "There's more of a team feeling now,' said Marty Dugan, basketball team co-captain. "It's not just the coach telling you to do something. There's room for questioning."[39]

Scott also believed in a radically new athletic ethos that saw physical fitness and striving for "personal bests" as an end in and of itself. Jogging, hiking, and exercising for the fun of it were all part of taking sports away from the experts or attacking the line between participants and observers.

Scott's early returns were very promising. Exercise classes doubled in size and several dozen students signed up to major in physical education. College president Robert Fuller was supportive and hopeful that Scott's way would be the way of the future. As he said to *Time*, "If it does work, I'm sure many other schools will adopt the approach.' "[40]

Not everyone was thrilled with this. When Ohio State football coach Woody Hayes heard about Oberlin's adding a women's sports program he said, "You can bet your ass if you have women around—and I've talked to psychiatrists about this—you aren't going to be worth a damn. . . . Man has to dominate."[41]

One of Scott's moves was hiring Tommie Smith as track coach. Of Smith, Scott said, "He's a pretty quiet, dignified guy. He is not a black-power person who's going to blow up the gymnasium with a hand grenade. He wants to build winning teams."[42]

Scott, a tempestuous personality, didn't last more than two years at Oberlin, but his impact was still felt. Phoebe Jones ran at Oberlin under Smith's tutelage. As she writes, it was inspiration from Smith, and by extension from Jack Scott, that gave her the confidence to devote her life to sport and come out of the closet.

> I was a student at Oberlin College from 1972 to 1976. Although I was involved in sports from my early tomboy days, I would never have considered coming out as a [lesbian] athlete without the influence of Tommie Smith and Jack Scott. . . . Until Jack Scott— who I don't think I ever met—wrote *The Athletic Revolution*, and until he and other athletes starting agitating for athletes' rights, being involved in sports was like saying you were for the Vietnam War. I didn't know Jack Scott, but I did know Tommie Smith. He was my coach in a running class. Coach Smith was very encouraging— he would say, "You're not bad, Jones." But by then I was a senior

and it wasn't until after I graduated that I got serious as a runner and started competing. I wound up getting a Ph.D. in physical education partly due to his influence. But what I mainly learned from Coach Smith was that nothing is outside of politics, not sports or women's housework, or anything—that there is no level playing field unless you make it happen, and that by taking an action, an autonomous action, you lay the way for others to take action. So when I got involved in a women's organization, the International Wages for Housework Campaign, the same year I started running (1974, and thirty-three years on I am still involved in both). I knew that women moving on our own behalf is a power to all people, and figuring out and demanding—yes, demanding—what we need is the only way for all of us to move forward. One of our first acts as the Wages for Housework Campaign was to support Tommie Smith's bid for tenure, which he unfortunately didn't get. The sixties were over and other forces predominated. It was Oberlin's loss.[43]

South Africa

If there were a Mount Rushmore of political athletes, tennis star Arthur Ashe would be a first-ballot choice. Thanks to the efforts of Ashe, the issue of apartheid in South Africa came to the forefront of Americans' consciousness. Ashe was the first person of African descent to win a grand slam tennis title, winning the U.S. Open in 1968. He also won at Wimbledon and the Australian Open. But Ashe is better known for his political acumen. This is a man who said, "For every hour spent on the playing field, two should be spent with a book."[44]

He made international news in 1969 when he applied for a visa to play in the South African Open and was denied. He also said, in a rare moment of anger for the pacific Ashe, that he wouldn't mind seeing a "hydrogen bomb" dropped on the capital, Johannesburg. He called for South Africa to be expelled from the tennis tour and Davis Cup play. His bold stand began to raise the world's awareness of South Africa's apartheid government. Ashe later said, "South Africa was testing the credibility of Western civilization. If you didn't come out against the most corrupt system imaginable, you couldn't look yourself in the eye."[45]

Four years later, South Africa granted Ashe a visa, and he became the first black man to play a tennis tournament in that country. This also met with tremendous criticism from the left, some of whom said his appearance would give credibility to the country.

An antiapartheid activist, the South African poet laureate Dennis Brutus, expressed to me,

Arthur consulted with me first and I say, "don't go." I say, "Arthur, it doesn't matter what these guys tell you, and they may even give you a visa. There's going to be segregation everywhere you go. They may make you an 'honorary white' just as they made wealthy Japanese "honorary whites," to avoid problems." He says, "No, they promised me, there will be no segregation at any event where I play." He goes to Johannesburg and what does he see? A little zoo in the corner for blacks and the rest is all whites. So in spite of what they'd told him they'd not kept their word. And the way they got around it was to sell two colored tickets: a black one and a yellow one. If you got a yellow ticket you sat in the white stand, but if you were black you got a black ticket. So he looks around and he's astonished to see the segregation. We disagreed on that, because I'd told him. I said, "Well, look, I think there's a mistake." An unforgivable mistake, because it was possible to anticipate what they would do and I had predicted it.[46]

Brutus's critiques notwithstanding, there were benefits to making the trip to South Africa. Ashe was able to visit with dissidents, including Nelson Mandela on Robben Island. He devoted much of his life to raising awareness around apartheid, including getting arrested in front of the South African embassy in 1985.

In 1976, Ashe visited South Africa for a documentary about sports in the area. He wanted to build tennis courts in black Soweto. He was given a rude awakening from Tsietsi Mashinini, a militant black student from South Africa who had coordinated the "children's demonstration" in Soweto a few months earlier. Mashinini said, "We [black South Africans] don't want tennis courts. We want our land back."[47]

The Black Revolt Becomes a Women's Revolt

In the 1970s, the push for peace in Vietnam and civil rights at home sparked a struggle for the rights of women, gays, and lesbians. The social movements had irrevocably changed the terrain. In 1964, feminist and sociologist Alice Rossi said, "There is practically no feminist spark left among American women." If there wasn't a spark, there was anger: anger articulated by Betty Friedan in her landmark 1963 book *The Feminine Mystique*: "Just what was the problem that has no name? What were the words women used when they tried to express it? Sometimes a woman would say 'I feel empty somehow . . . incomplete.' Or she would say, 'I feel as if I don't exist.' Sometimes . . . 'A tired feeling . . . I get so angry with the children it scares me. . . . I feel like crying without any reason."[48]

A transformation from despair to action was under way. This especially came into play when NOW—the National Organization for Women—was formed in 1966 after Lyndon Johnson left the issue of gender discrimination out of the Civil Rights Act. They filed a thousand sex discrimination suits the following year. In 1967, after lobbying by women's groups, President Johnson signed an executive order banning sex discrimination in federally connected employment. Women's liberation groups were organized across the country. On August 26, 1970, more than fifty thousand people took part in the "Women's Strike for Equality," a day of action for women's rights. In 1973, the women's movement won a victory when the Supreme Court made abortion legal with its *Roe v. Wade* decision.[49]

This was the terrain upon which women competed (or didn't compete) until the late 1960s, when a growing women's movement made demands for equality in the world of sports. Their roar was demonstrated in dramatic fashion on September 20, 1973, when Billie Jean King faced off against Bobby Riggs in their "Battle of the Sexes" tennis match, called by the London *Sunday Times* "the drop shot and volley heard around the world."[50] Riggs, a 1939 Wimbledon champion, had already swept the court with women's champion Margaret Court on Mother's Day in 1973. King, who previously had rejected Riggs' dare to play, accepted his latest challenge.

It all sounds like fun and games, but for Riggs and King it was more than that. King's was a voice for a very concrete kind of feminism: one that demanded equal pay, more endorsements, better training and locker room facilities. Riggs kept upping the ante, saying, "Hell, we know there is no way she can beat me. She's a stronger athlete than me and she can execute various shots better than me. But when the pressure mounts and she thinks about fifty million people watching on TV, she'll fold. That's the way women are."[51] Riggs also said, "She's a great player for a gal. But no woman can beat a male player who knows what he's doing. I'm not only interested in glory for my sex, but I also want to set women's lib back twenty years, to get women back into the home, where they belong."[52]

Riggs was not alone in this view. Tennis pro Gene Scott said, "Women are brought up from the time they're six years old to read books, eat candy, and go to dance class. They can't compete against men."[53]

King read every quote and was understandably concerned. "I thought it would set us back 50 years if I didn't win that match. It would ruin the women's tour and affect all women's self esteem."[54]

The "Battle of the Sexes" match reached a Super Bowl level of anticipation. On Sept. 20, 1973 in Houston, King was carried out on the Astrodome court like Cleopatra, by four muscled "ancient slaves." Riggs was escorted by women he called, "Bobby's Bosom Buddies." Their entrances turned out to be the most competitive part of the day as King, then twenty-nine, ran Riggs ragged, winning 6–4, 6–3, 6–3.

As Neil Amdur wrote in the New York Times, "Most important perhaps for women everywhere, she convinced skeptics that a female athlete can survive pressure-filled situations and that men are as susceptible to nerves as women."[55] And Frank Deford wrote in Sports Illustrated, "She has prominently affected the way 50 percent of society thinks and feels about itself in the vast area of physical exercise."[56]

King was far more than a symbol or an athlete. She was an activist and participant in the women's movement for equal rights. In the words of

Martina Navratilova, she was "a crusader fighting a battle for all of us. She was carrying the flag; it was all right to be a jock."[57]

King fought for a women's players' union and co-founded the Women's Tennis Association. She was elected its first president in 1973. King, who received $15,000 less than Ilie Nastase did for winning the U.S. Open in 1972, called for a strike by women players if the prize money wasn't equal by the following year. In 1973, the U.S. Open became the first major tournament to offer an identical winners' purse for men and women. She allowed her name to be used in a feature in the first issue of *Ms.* magazine that said simply, "I had an abortion."[58] But the Riggs match was her defining moment, proving that the representative power of sports can at times dwarf the actions themselves.

"All her life, King had been battling for equal rights for women, not only in tennis and in sports, but in society," wrote Anthony Holden. "But all of her hard work and dedication were dwarfed by what she accomplished in the two hours and four minutes it took to dismantle Riggs."[59]

King understood this. "On college campuses women were hanging out of their dorm windows celebrating. The match had enormous symbolic importance. It helped women stand taller. . . . Before that, women were chokers and spastics who couldn't take pressure. Except, of course, in childbirth."[60] This is why she is remembered for this match more than her incredible thirty-nine Grand Slam singles, doubles, and mixed doubles crowns. One gets the feeling she wouldn't have it any other way. It was for her role in the movements of the day that *Life* magazine named her one of the "100 Most Important Americans of the 20th Century," the only female athlete on the list.

Title IX

King's victory is inextricable from the passage of Title IX, which guarantees equal funding for men's and women's educational opportunities. Its greatest impact has been seen in spurring girls' and women's participation in sports. According to the Women's Sports Foundation, one in twenty-seven high school girls played sports twenty-five years ago; more than one in three do today. Before Title IX, fewer than 32,000 women participated in college sports; today that number exceeds 150,000.[61]

Women who play sports, according to one study, are far less likely to be involved in abusive relationships or have eating disorders. In other words, it is a reform that has improved the quality of life for tens of millions of women around the country.

Yet when Title IX was passed, the critiques from the world of sports were ample. Father Edmund Joyce, the head of almighty Notre Dame University, called the legislation "asinine." Longtime autocratic executive director of the National Collegiate Athletic Association, Walter Byers, described Title IX as carrying with it the "impending doom" of college athletics.[62] Sports columnist Furman Bisher of the *Atlanta Journal-Constitution* expressed much of the conventional wisdom of the sports page when he argued against expanding athletic opportunities, writing, "What are we after, a race of Amazons? Do you want to bring home a companion or a broad that chews tobacco? What do you want for the darling daughter, a boudoir or a locker room full of cussing and bruises?"[63]

But not all men were so threatened. As David Auxter, an educational psychologist at Slippery Rock State University, wrote in *Time* magazine, "We value athletics because they are competitive. That is, they teach that achievement and success are desirable, that they are worth disciplining oneself for. By keeping girls out of sports, we have denied them this educational experience. Better athletic programs will develop more aggressive females, women with confidence, who value personal achievement and have a strong sense of identity. I think that would be a good thing for us all."[64]

A recent study by scholars R. Vivian Acosta and Linda Jean Carpenter illustrates the impact of Title IX on the collegiate level. In 2002 the average number of women's teams per school hit an all-time high of 8.34, compared with a little over 2 per school when Title IX was enacted in 1972, and 5.61 in 1978, when schools were expected to be in compliance. In just a two-year period, 2002 to 2004, 270 women's teams were added. Soccer has increased the most in twenty-seven years, and is now on nearly 88.6 percent of campuses compared to only 2.8 percent in 1977. Basketball, volleyball, and cross-country are the three most frequently offered sports for women, followed by soccer, softball, and tennis.[65]

Curt Opens a Flood

The radicalization in society was spreading into not only the politics but also the very economics of sport. The pioneer of this approach was major league baseball union leader Marvin Miller, a former United Steelworkers official who became head of the players' union in 1966. As Reggie Jackson said, "Miller had more influence on major league baseball than anyone ever."[66]

As Miller remembered to me,

[The players] had an organization—a fake union—called the Players Association that had been formed by the owners. This was a company union in every sense of the word, the employers had formed it back in 1947 as basically a response to two things. One, there was a drive to organize players into a union, and two, there had been an attempt by two wealthy Mexican businessmen to start a major league in Mexico and they offered larger salaries. That was also the year of Jackie Robinson coming to the Dodgers and the year of a man on his own trying to organize the players. A man named Robert Murphy went from Spring Training site to site—and the owners saw this and said, "We need to head this off and form a company union."

A segment of players were ready for a more aggressive approach.

One was that the pension had not kept pace over eighteen years of progress. Also, they picked up strong rumors that the owners were wanting to change it. Television, by 1965, had grown tremendously. [L.A. Dodgers owner] Walter O'Malley saw this and wanted to alter the benefit plan. But beyond that, I was also learning that it was like pulling teeth learning what else made them unhappy. This was because they were a workforce basically unschooled in working conditions. They had all undergone a bunch of brainwashing that being allowed to play Major League Baseball was a great favor. That they were the luckiest people in the world. They were accustomed never to think, "This stinks. We need to change this." You have to remember, baseball players are very young, and, with few exceptions, have no experience in these matters."

But Miller's genius was that he understood the way social movements were cross-pollinating with the world of sports. The black power movement had radicalized African American players, and he courted them to challenge the reserve clause. As Miller said, after the civil rights movement, "you now had at least some people who were able to think in terms of what was wrong with the society."

Miller found such a player willing to stand up in the St. Louis Cardinals' Curt Flood. Flood was born and raised in Oakland and was fighting mad after making it through a southern minor league system of segregated hotels and eating out of the kitchen on road trips.

In October 1969, the Cardinals traded Flood to Philadelphia and Flood just said no. The All-Star contacted baseball commissioner Bowie Kuhn, writing:

Dear Mr. Kuhn:

After 12 years in the major leagues I do not feel that I am a piece of property to be bought and sold irrespective of my wishes. I believe that any system that produces that result violates my basic rights as a citizen and a human being. I believe that I have the right to consider offers from other clubs before making any decisions. I, therefore, request that you make known to all the major league clubs my feelings in this matter, and advise them of my availability for the 1970 season.

It sounds polite, but at the time this was political TNT. Kuhn didn't take Flood seriously at all, replying: "Dear Curt: I certainly agree with you that you, as a human being, are not a piece of property to be bought and sold. That is I think obvious. However, I cannot see its application to the situation at hand." As the great columnist Red Smith put it in a beautiful pro-Flood piece, "Thus the commissioner restates baseball's labor policy any time there is unrest in the slave cabins. 'Run along, sonny, you bother me.' "[67]

Support came to Flood in the form of a physically ailing Jackie Robinson. Flood recalled their discussion. "I said, 'I really appreciate your taking the time and effort to do this.' And he said, 'Well, you can't be out there by yourself.' I remember these words very well: 'You can't be out there by yourself and I would be remiss if I didn't share these burdens with you.' "[68]

In this context, Flood was the ideal candidate to step forward and risk all. As Miller said:

> To me, Flood epitomized the modern player who began to think in terms of union, to ask questions like "Why is baseball an exception to how labor is treated in other industries? Why should we be treated like property? Why should we agree to have a reserve clause?" Basic questions that had gone unasked. . . . Black and Latin players like Roberto Clemente were at the forefront. This was not just the color of their skin. Flood, for example, did not grow up in the South. He grew up in Oakland, California. He was an outstanding high school athlete, he was drafted to play in the majors, and was promptly sent to the South. He wasn't old, but he wasn't a child. What I am about to say is not a fact but I have always felt that when a player of his temperament and pride was sent to the South, not being able to stay in the same hotels and motels, playing in Georgia and Mississippi, I think it made a very big difference in his outlook on the world.

At first the union's executive board feared this dynamic. As Miller recounts it:

> Finally a board member asked Curt, "The motivation here—why are you doing this?" Was it to attack the reserve clause to stop the

owners from trading a player where he didn't want to go? Or was this a sign of "Black Power"? And Curt looked at him and said, " 'I wish it was, but we are dealing with an issue that affects every player. Color has nothing to do it. We are all pieces of property.' "[69]

On June 6, 1972, Curt Flood lost his struggle in a 5–3 Supreme Court decision. However, his stand opened the way for the eventual destruction of the reserve clause. He paid a terrible price, though: he was shunned and cast aside. The lifetime .293 hitter and Gold Glove center-fielder found himself shut out of the 1970 season. The following year Flood returned with the Washington Senators but quit after eighteen games of mistreatment by major league baseball and antiunion team-mates. He was never to play major league baseball again. As he once said, "I am pleased that God made my skin black but I wish he had made it thicker."[70]

Although Flood, who passed away in 1997, never achieved the financial gains of the next generation of players, his stand benefited everyone. One player said anonymously, "Ten percent of Alex Rodriguez's check should go to the family of Curt Flood."[71]

The Brewing of Backlash 3.0

As sports was demonstrating itself as yet another sphere where the seeds of democratic anarchy were starting to flower, efforts were being made to roll it all back. Think-tank theorist Samuel Huntington wrote in a piece titled "The Governibility of Democracy":

> The essence of the democratic surge of the 1960's was a general challenge to existing systems of authority, public and private. In one form or another, this challenge manifested itself in the family, the university, business, public and private associations, politics, the governmental bureaucracy, and the military services. People no longer felt the same obligation to obey those whom they had previously considered superior to themselves in age, rank, status, expertise, character, or talents. . . .
>
> To the extent that the United States was governed by anyone

during the decades after World War II, it was governed by the President acting with the support and cooperation of key individuals and groups in the executive office, the federal bureaucracy, Congress, and the more important businesses, banks, law firms, foundations, and media, which constitute the private sector's "Establishment."[72]

The backlash was bipartisan in character. When Jimmy Carter became president in 1976, the United States continued to support some of the nastiest regimes in the world: in the Philippines, in Iran, in Nicaragua, and in Indonesia, where the inhabitants of East Timor were being slaughtered in genocidal fashion.[73]

Carter also signed a law making abortion not covered by Medicaid, saying, "Well, as you know, there are many things in life that are not fair, that wealthy people can afford and poor people cannot."[74]

The bitter national coal strike of 1977–78 forced union leaders such as UAW president Doug Fraser to acknowledge the kind of counteroffensive that was under way. Fraser said:

The leaders of industry, commerce and finance in the United States have broken and discarded the fragile, unwritten compact previously existing during a past period of growth and progress. . . . [That compact] survived in part because of an unspoken foundation: that when things got bad enough for a segment of society, the business elite "gave" a little bit—enabling government or interest groups to better conditions somewhat for that segment. . . . But today, I am convinced there has been a shift on the part of the business community toward confrontation, rather than cooperation. . . .

Fraser sums it up this way: "I believe leaders of the business community, with few exceptions, have chosen to wage a one-sided class war today in this country."[75]

Months later, Chrysler demanded givebacks from the UAW to avoid bankruptcy. Fraser agreed to wage and benefit cuts (and a seat on

Chrysler's board) while the company received huge government loan guarantees.

BusinessWeek put it even more bluntly: "It will be a hard pill for many Americans to swallow—the idea of doing with less so that business can have more. . . . Nothing that this nation, or any other nation, has done in modern economic history compares in difficulty with the selling job that must be done to make people accept the new reality."[76]

After a decade that had seen unprecedented efforts to politicize sports, to use sports as a platform for other ideas, to break down the participant/spectator divide, a backlash was coming against this as well. Anyone trying to connect with the spirit of the 1960s and 1970s in sports would find themselves entering a minefield.

As politics in sports was poised to take a major hit, globalization and technology were poised to take sports to a place never before seen. The millions would become billions; the history would be either forgotten or made shiny and palatable for a new audience. But this was little seen in 1979. Few noticed when, a father and son, both unemployed, bought a twenty-four-hour satellite feed to broadcast sports into their home state of Connecticut. They called the low-budget venture Entertainment Sports Programming. It would soon add an N, and with all the ceremony of a forlorn tree falling in the forest, the boo-yah had begun.[77]

·9·

The 1980s: Welcome to Hell

There is no fire like passion, there is no shark like hatred,
there is no snare like folly, there is no torrent like greed.

—Buddha (or Charles Barkley)

Driven by twenty-four-hour cable television and an expanding global audience, the 1980s saw a deluge of dollars flow into sports. But it's hard not to see sports in the 1980s following a pattern we have already seen in the 1920s and 1950s. In those decades, the sports explosion occurred against a backdrop of a nation weary from war, well heeled from economic recovery, and enjoying the spread of new leisure technologies: radio in the twenties and television in the fifties. The eighties held similar dynamics, with cable television being the techno-bauble of the decade. But while all three eras share similar terrains, the stronger thread is an environment feeding on political backlash.

Before the election of Ronald Reagan began what became known in labor circles as the "looting decade," with the federal government doling out millions in corporate tax breaks amid an atmosphere of corporate and stock market scandal, sports had already set the scene for a period of nationalist ascendancy.

If there was one sport other than soccer that the United States could legitimately claim to be an underdog in, it would be hockey. So when the 1980 U.S. Olympic hockey team won gold, it did so in a context that was catnip for those on the right seeking to bury the previous decades' work to democratize society. It was a propaganda tonic, a counterweight to the "shame of losing Vietnam," the USSR's invasion of Afghanistan, the energy crisis, and the fact that as the Olympics opened, fifty-two Americans were held hostage by student radicals in Iran.[1]

The line endlessly repeated was that "it gave the country a reason to feel good again." The victory over the Soviet Union in the semifinals was particularly wrapped in Cold War regalia. Mark Johnson, who had scored two of the U.S. goals, said, "I can't believe it. I still can't believe it. We beat the Russians!" A sister of one of the U.S. hockey players shouted "The Russians! I can't believe we beat the Russians!" She also said that she hadn't seen so many flags since the sixties. "And we were burning them then."[2]

Reagan, the former sports announcer, the man who played George Gipp in *Knute Rockne, All-American,* had a unique ability to connect with sporting themes. But if Reagan's supporters saw a hearty jock making America feel good again, for others he symbolized the counteroffensive—both in the United States and internationally—against the social reforms and the spirit of struggle that had dominated the preceding years. In the 1960s Reagan said of antiwar protestors, "The last bunch of pickets were carrying signs that said 'Make love, not war.' The only trouble was they didn't look capable of doing either." Of a hippie he said, "His hair was cut like Tarzan, he acted like Jane and he smelled like Cheetah."[3]

Reagan was the smiling face calling for a new "Morning in America." But there was nothing new about his agenda: making the rich richer, attacking unions, promoting U.S. imperial power, and abusing the most vulnerable in society.

"It was the truly wealthy, more than anyone else, who flourished under Reagan," as former Republican strategist Kevin Phillips put it, "The 1980s were the triumph of upper America . . . the political ascendancy of the rich, and a glorification of capitalism, free markets, and finance."[4]

New requirements eliminated free school lunches for more than one million poor children, who depended on the meal for as much as half of their daily nutrition. Millions of children entered the ranks of the officially declared "poor" and soon a quarter of the nation's children—twelve million—were living in poverty. In parts of Detroit, infants were dying at the same rate as children in Bangladesh, and the *New York Times* commented in an editorial: "Given what's happening to the hungry in America, this Administration has cause only for shame."[5]

The eight years of Reagan in the White House during the 1980s dragged mainstream politics to the right and launched a new era of bigotry as well. "The Great Communicator" announced his presidency in Philadelphia, Mississippi—the infamous site where three civil rights workers were murdered in 1964—with the rallying cry of "states' rights." Myths of welfare queens riding around in Cadillacs were spun out of Pennsylvania Avenue, and well-funded think tanks included young comers such as future imprisoned lobbyist Jack Abramoff and 1988 George H.W. Bush campaign chief Lee Atwater.[6]

"By the end of the 1980s, the U.S. had achieved the dubious status as the most unequal society among Western industrial countries," writes Sharon Smith in *Subterranean Fire: A History of Working-Class Radicalism in the United States*. "An end-of-decade report on salaries in 10 leading companies showed that while the average CEO earned 34 times more than his employees in the mid-1970s, he earned 110 times more by the late 1980s."[7]

The 1984 Los Angeles Olympics

The 1984 Olympics were supposed to symbolize the vibrancy and virility of Reagan's America. The games were actually opened by a speech from Reagan, the first time a president had ever done so. The games were an absolute gold glut for the United States. This surprised no one, as the countries behind the Iron Curtain boycotted in protest of the U.S. boycott of the 1980 games in Moscow. Even more than other Olympics, it was an event stylized by Olympic organizer Peter Ueberroth to promote not internationalism but a side in the new Cold War. (For his trouble, Ueberroth was *Time* magazine's Man of the Year.) Los Angeles hosted the Olympics because no other city even bid for the privilege. It was a privilege no one wanted to be saddled with after the financial debacle that accompanied the 1976 Summer Olympics in Montreal. Those games were a financial nightmare. It took the people of the city of Montreal and the province of Quebec thirty years to pay off the debt that piled up from the games. But the Los Angeles Games, appropriately for the Reagan era, were the first privately financed games in history. They ended with an announced surplus of over $200 million. But the Olympics weren't a dream for everyone.[8]

Organizers of the Los Angeles Olympics operated with the carrot and the stick. Police sweeps were undertaken (later immortalized in the NWA video for "Straight Outta Compton"). Old antisyndicalism laws were put back on the books to jail young people with ease and deny them due process, though the overwhelming number of people arrested were never charged.

Ueberroth's Olympic Committee also pledged to have a policy of "equal opportunity and affirmative action" that guided its every act of decision making, hiring, contracting, and subcontracting.[9] They publicly pledged that "surplus profits" from the games would go to poor communities. (While there is no word where the "surplus profits" went, the games did create more than seventy thousand temporary service-oriented jobs.) Ueberroth even met with Dr. Harry Edwards to get his blessing. Then, as the final act, the committee hired John Carlos himself to act as "special consultant on minority affairs."[10]

Campanis Revelations

Racism in sports may be ever-present, but it is rarely if ever discussed. Usually it takes a gaffe of titanic proportions to incite an open discussion. And there were few gaffes in the 1980s in any field like the moment of ugly honesty that came from the mouth of L.A. Dodgers' general manager Al Campanis.

Campanis, speaking on ABC's *Nightline* to commemorate the fortieth anniversary of Jackie Robinson's entry into the major leagues, spoke without stutter or stammer that blacks "may not have some of the necessities to be, let's say, a field manager, or, perhaps, a general manager."

Nightline host Ted Koppel tried repeatedly to get Campanis to alter or clarify his comments, to throw in some spin, but Campanis just continued with this line of thought.[11] His words struck a bitter chord, since eighteen years earlier, in 1969, Jackie Robinson had refused to participate in Old Timers' Day at Yankee Stadium, citing baseball's failure to hire black coaches and managers.[12] The furor that erupted over Campanis's remarks resulted in his being fired two days later, but little else. In the five years after Campanis's comments, twenty-eight major league teams hired forty-eight managers, only six of whom were people of color.[13]

In the aftermath, Frank Robinson, baseball Hall of Famer and its first African American manager, spoke in bitter terms:

> Baseball has been hiding this ugly prejudice for years—that blacks aren't smart enough to be managers or third-base coaches or part of the front office. There's a belief that they're fine when it comes to the physical part of the game, but if it involves brains they just can't handle it. Al Campanis made people finally understand what goes on behind closed doors—that there is racism in baseball. . . .
>
> Speaking up could be damaging. Someone will get buried. The ownership might think, "He's mouthing off. Who needs him?" I won't say that today they could blackball a smart player. But they could make it tough for him. At the end of his career, he might not get to play those extra years if they feel he's a troublemaker."[14]

The NBA Rises to a Beat

The early 1980s saw the rise of an angry form of rap music that was far from party music. Grandmaster Flash and the Furious Five's "The Message" let loose with lyrics like

> *Broken glass everywhere*
> *People pissing on the stairs, you know they just don't care*
> *I can't take the smell, I can't take the noise*
> *Got no money to move out, I guess I got no choice*
> *Rats in the front room, roaches in the back*

Junkies in the alley with a baseball bat
I tried to get away, but I couldn't get far
Cause the man with the tow-truck repossessed my car
Don't push me, cause I'm close to the edge
I'm trying not to lose my head
It's like a jungle sometimes, it makes me wonder
How I keep from going under.[15]

The rise of hip-hop came at a time when the NBA was on its deathbed. Basketball was played inside half-empty arenas, the finals were shown on tape delay, and most people associated the game with drugs, violence, and decrepitude. The league was seen as both too thuggish and too dominated by black players to cross over. Concurrently, hip-hop was emerging in the South Bronx at a time when unemployment was 80 percent in a borough that had lost 600,000 industrial jobs over the previous generation. The South Bronx defined despair, even garnering a visit from Mother Teresa.[16]

Conditions in the South Bronx characterized urban life across the country. Recreation centers were shuttered, after-school and jobs programs became as passé as the Bee Gees and bell bottoms, and African Americans in places such as the South Bronx were invisible. But invisibility had its privileges. Without state-sponsored employment or grant-funding for the arts, a protective hothouse developed where, unencumbered by the reach of commercialism, the holy trinity of hip-hop—MCing, break dancing, and graffiti writing—was able to gestate future legends such as Kool DJ Herc, Afrika Bambaataa, and Grandmaster Flash. They made history every weekend before a crowd of dozens. As Jeff Chang wrote in his *Can't Stop Won't Stop: A History of the Hip-hop Generation*, "If blues culture had developed under the conditions of oppressive, forced labor, hip-hop would arise from the conditions of no work."[17]

This dynamic also began to have a seismic impact on African Americans and sport. With the destruction of rec leagues, youth teams, and public school phys ed programs, the once thriving culture of urban American baseball suffocated.

The "beneficiary" of the starving of urban sports was basketball: cheap, easy, and creative. These two uniquely urban art forms found their first synthesis in the rhymes of the legendary Kurtis Blow. In 1984, Blow recorded the classic anthem "Basketball," in which he extols his love of all things hoop and rhymes "microphone" with "Moses Malone." Hip-hop was in its swaddling clothes, but that didn't stop the floundering NBA from using Blow's rallying cry at games. They even created a video that pieced together clips of every player mentioned on Blow's track, from Earl Monroe to Tiny Archibald, Larry Bird, Bernard King, and "number 33, my man Kareem, the center on my starting team." Also on the 1983–84 NBA Entertainment–produced season retrospective, the execs financed their own song: "14 Johnsons," a tribute to the fourteen players with the last name Johnson.[18]

The rhyme redefines terrible, but it was the equivalent of the NBA buying shares of Microsoft when Bill Gates was working out of his garage. The NBA, led by an ambitious young commissioner named David Stern, saw how hip-hop—at the time being dismissed by most as a fad or gimmick—came from the same earth as a new generation of players lighting up the league.

The hip-hop/basketball connection took a quantum leap forward the very next season when a bald-headed Brooklyn-born kid with a wagging tongue took the court and redefined the parameters of gravity. His name was Michael Jeffrey Jordan. Jordan's talent would have captured people's imagination in any era. But the corporate synthesis of a struggling shoe company called Nike and a director named Spike Lee sent him into the commercial stratosphere. The commercials, filmed in the arty black-and-white style of Lee's indie film hit *She's Gotta Have It*, and starring not just Jordan but Lee as his character from that film, Mars Blackmon—branded the catchphrase "it's gotta be the shoes" for eternity. As Chang wrote, "Spike and Mike's ads helped propel Nike past Reebok and the company never looked back. Not only did Nike's success confirm that niches were the future, it also confirmed that a massive shift in tastes was occurring—from baby boomer to youth, from suburb to city, from whiteness to Blackness."[19] The NBA, more than any other league, recognized this trend and ran with it. With Stern pulling the strings, the league was set to become the "hip-hop league"—not running from associations with urban culture but marketing them to death.

In the late 1980s, rap music transitioned in the eyes of the U.S. culture czars from dismissible fad to political TNT: a wellspring of debate, polarization, resentment, and racial resistance. In other words, it wasn't something you merely "liked" or "disliked." It was something you were either for or against. The top stars—from Public Enemy to Ice-T to NWA—were attacked by Congress, police organizations, parents, and religious groups. The stars themselves thrived on controversy and lived by the Jungle Brothers line of wearing "black medallions, no gold." The NBA once again was ahead of the curve. While hip-hop was under siege, they arranged to have Michael Jordan host the season premiere of *Saturday Night Live* in 1991. The musical guest? Public Enemy.

The Frustration of Jim Brown

NBA's new superstars, with their hip-hop cachet, had more economic clout and cultural capital than any athletes, particularly African American athletes, in history. But instead of using this platform to pick up the torch from the athletes of yesteryear, narcissism became the obsession of choice.

Jim Brown expressed his frustration in his 1989 autobiography *Out of Bounds*:

> When I look at the black stars today, I wonder if they ever study history. How do they think they got the position they're in? Blacks who came before them paved the way, blacks who had to do more than just play good football, who had to endure some bitter cruelties. A lot of them did more than endure. They spoke out, provoked some thought, took some damn chances, instead of saying, "Hey, I've got mine. Everything is cool." If we had done that, the guys today would be starting from scratch.
>
> And that is my crucial point: it's thirty years later, but everything is not cool. If blacks start taking their gains for granted, future generations will have serious trouble. I don't want the guys today to

give me their damn time and money. I want them to wake up. To look around, realize the struggle is only beginning.

I look at athletes today, black and white, wonder if they watch anything but MTV. They're Very Nice, Very Rote, everyone says they're Wonderful. Maybe so. But I can't help thinking. They're not that wonderful. They won't say a word about South Africa. It's the worst country there is. They have apartheid. They're terrorists, killing people in the name of white superiority. These Wonderful Guys, particularly when they're at the peak of their visibility, are the ones who can get people's attention. Why don't they speak up?[20]

Martina

But not every player was silent. One who did speak out wasn't the male athlete of Jim Brown's dreams but a woman and a lesbian: Martina Navratilova. Her career started at age fifteen in 1972, and she won her first title at seventeen. Navratilova started her epic tennis career out of shape, awkward, and shy. Tennis commentator Bud Collins called her "The Great Wide Hope." But after defecting from the Eastern bloc at age eighteen, she blossomed as a player. Navratilova was unique in her adoption of a training regimen that made grown men weep. It was designed by former basketball superstar Nancy Lieberman-Cline. Navratilova, along with McEnroe and Connors, was more intense than any player of her age.

By 1985, Navratilova had racked up millions of dollars in tournament winnings and international celebrity for her towering talent. She was the victor in six consecutive Grand Slam events, a feat never touched. At the time she had won more money than any player in tennis history, male or female. While Navratilova won her share of admirers, she also faced a barrage of criticism for being "too good." Much of this criticism was shorthand for looking, playing, and acting "manly." Rather than enjoy her celebrity, Navratilova had to constantly ward off homophobic attacks—such as one article that quoted a player saying she "must have a chromosome loose somewhere." As Susan Cahn writes, "Some wondered whether Navratilova even belonged on the women's tour anymore, given her apparent invincibility. Noting her high-tech, precision-oriented training methods, they characterized her as a 'bionic sci-fi creation' of her training team—a kind of unnatural, even monstrous 'Amazon' who 'has the women's game pinned to the mat.' "[21]

Navratilova wasn't deterred by this and instead helped push this discussion forward by coming out as a proud lesbian and even giving her partner a prominent spot in the "family section" at matches. She has spoken out consistently against antigay legislation and spoken at gay rights marches. In an interview with Connie Chung, Chung quoted the following comment by Navratilova from a German newspaper: "The most absurd part of my escape from the unjust system is that I have exchanged one system that suppresses free opinion for another. The Republicans in the U.S. manipulate public opinion and sweep controversial issues under the table. It's depressing. Decisions in America are based solely on the question of how much money will come out of it and not on the questions of how much health, morals or environment suffer as a result."

Chung had a follow-up question ready: "Can I be honest with you? I can tell you that when I read this, I have to tell you that I thought it was un-American, unpatriotic. I wanted to say, go back to Czechoslovakia. You know, if you don't like it here, this a country that gave you so much, gave you the freedom to do what you want."

Navratilova responded, "And I'm giving it back. This is why I speak out. When I see something that I don't like, I'm going to speak out because you can do that here. And again, I feel there are too many things happening that are taking our rights away."[22]

By confronting the homophobia around her, Navratilova has transcended the pantheon of great women players to earn a place among those like Ali and Jackie Robinson who were not content to let their play do the talking for them. As she said, "I hope, when I stop, people will think that somehow I mattered."[23]

Women's Sports Feels—and Feeds—the Backlash

But Navratilova, with her full frame and ropy muscles, was never the 1980s icon for women's sports. In the 1980s, that meant gymnastics. As Joan Ryan writes in her harrowing book, *Little Girls in Pretty Boxes*:

In 1956 the top two Olympic female gymnasts were 35 and 29 years old. In 1968 gold medalist Vera Caslavska of Czechoslovakia was 26 years old, stood 5 feet 3 inches and weighed 121 pounds. Back then, gymnastics was truly a woman's sport. It was transformed in 1972 when Olga Korbut, 17 years old, 4 feet 11 inches, 85 pounds, enchanted the world with her pigtails and rubber-band body. Four years later 14-year-old Nadia Comaneci clutched a baby doll after scoring the first perfect 10.0 in Olympic history. She was 5 feet tall and weighed 85 pounds. The decline in age among American gymnasts since Comaneci's victory is startling. In 1976 the six US Olympic gymnasts were, on average, 17 and a half years old, stood 5 feet three and a half inches and weighed 106 pounds. By the 1992 Olympics in Barcelona, the average US Olympic gymnast was 16 years old, stood 4 feet 9 inches and weighed 83 pounds, a year younger, 6 inches shorter and 23 pounds lighter than her counterparts of 16 years before.[24]

This change in size came with an epidemic of eating disorders that afflicted all of women's athletics. A 1986 study of female college athletes in the Midwest found that 74 percent of gymnasts—and a third of all women athletes—practiced some form of bulimia or took laxative or diet pills without the supervision of a physician or trainer. As Kathy Johnson, silver medal Olympic gymnast, said in a comment that garnered media admiration, "When I ask myself if I want an ice cream soda, I answer, 'Not as badly as I want a gold medal.' "

Joan Ryan reveals the shock of her final findings:

What I found was a story about legal, even celebrated child abuse. In the dark troughs along the road to the Olympics lay the bodies of girls who stumbled on the way, broken by the work, pressure and humiliation. I found a girl whose father left the family when she quit gymnastics at the age of 13, who scraped her arms and legs with razors to dull her emotional pain and who needed a two-hour pass from a psychiatric hospital to attend her high-school graduation. Girls who broke their necks and backs. One who so desperately sought the perfect, weightless gymnastic body that she starved herself to death. Others who became so obsessive about controlling their weight that they lost control of themselves instead, falling into the potentially fatal cycle of bingeing on food, then purging by vomiting or taking laxatives. One who was sexually abused by her coach and one who was sodomized for four years by the father of a teammate. I found a girl who felt such shame at not making the Olympic team that she slit her wrists. A skater who underwent plastic surgery when a judge said her nose was distracting. A father who handed custody of his daughter over to her coach so she could keep skating. A coach who fed his gymnasts so little that federation officials had to smuggle food into their hotel rooms. A mother who hid her child's chicken pox with make-up so she could compete. Coaches who motivated their athletes by calling them imbeciles, idiots, pigs, cows.[25]

The most disturbing part of all of this was what didn't happen after Ryan's study was revealed. No calls for reform. No organizing from an embattled women's movement feeling the full weight of the backlash. Only glory being heaped upon "pretty girls in little boxes," a perversion of what Title IX was supposed to bring: women comfortably athletic in their own bodies.

The Gay Games

As dark as the 1980s could seem, there were some surprises. In 1982, former 1968 Olympian and decathlete Tom Waddell started what he called the Gay Olympics in San Francisco. The idea was that they would be open to everyone, regardless of skill and of course sexual orientation. The first one drew 1,600 people. Today it draws upward of 15,000. But in 1982, it was a very daring idea. This was a time when AIDS was still referred to as "the gay cancer." A roadblock was immediately thrown up when Waddell and the other organizers were sued by the International Olympic Committee (IOC) and the United States Olympic Committee (USOC) to prevent them from using the word Olympics. This was the first time the IOC had ever sued for the usage of a word that had been adopted across the country from the Special Olympics, to the Police Olympics, to the Nebraska Rat Olympics. But Waddell was undeterred. To promote the Gay games he did everything from traditional advertising to passing out flyers himself on street corners.[26]

Waddell, in outlining his mission early in the process, said, "The Gay Games are not separatist, they are not exclusive, they are not oriented to victory, they are not for commercial gain. They intended to bring a global community together in friendship, . . . to elevate consciousness and self-esteem, and to achieve a form of cultural and intellectual synergy." Waddell also formed a women-led Women's Outreach Committee to put out the word that the Games were not an exclusively male activity.[27]

Eight thousand people attended the opening ceremonies in 1982. The Gay Games didn't launch with the pomp and nationalism typical to games. Instead, they were greeted by a performance from the immortal Tina Turner. That set the stage for a very different kind of Olympic experience. Representative Phil Burton (D.-Calif.) and San Francisco supervisor Doris Ward gave speeches that defied a court-ordered ban on using the word *Olympic* in connection with the event. Ward unveiled a proclamation declaring "Gay Olympics Day."[28]

The games were structured with age categories so that athletes in their thirties and forties could compete. Lesbian athletes also participated in high numbers: of 1,300 athletes, 600 were women. Women competed in all events except wrestling. As Stephen Kulieke and Pat Califia wrote on the Gay Games for the *Advocate*:

> Competition was tough, often fierce, but what struck participants and spectators alike was the prevailing sense of camaraderie and community. "The events were competitive and at the same time supportive, exhilarating, loving and caring," said Karen Kiss, the announcer at the swimming competition. Richard Boner, a Los Angeles swimmer, said: "The last placed competitor gets the most applause because he or she had the guts to do it. . . . That's what it's all about. Not winning, but doing your best."

The Gay Games were certainly different from Brundage's vision of what Olympics were supposed to be—and not just because participants had names like Kiss and Boner. Take the description of the open wrestling match from the *Advocate*. "The scene was the Monday night wrestling preliminaries at Kezar Pavilion. The two opponents had fought long and hard and were drained of energy. Finally, one man pinned the other's shoulders to the mat, winning the match. As the loser exhaled a deep breath of resignation, the winner leaned over and kissed him on the lips."[29]

More than ten thousand attended the closing ceremonies on September 5. *Tales of the City* author Armistead Maupin and *Rubyfruit Jungle* author Rita Mae Brown were masters of ceremony. In Brown's speech she "slammed the professional athletes, 'who make millions of dollars lying about being gay. You have your integrity and honor and you carry ours as well. When we look at you, we see the best that we can be.' "[30]

In 1986, even though the IOC held a lien on Tom Waddell's house as part of its lawsuit against the unauthorized use of the word *Olympics*, the games went on as scheduled. It was triple the size of the 1982 games, with three thousand athletes attending from eighteen countries to compete in seventeen different sports.

There were three times as many women as men in the power-lifting events, and featured participants who were openly HIV-positive. Sean O'Neil, for example, a tennis player from San Francisco, said, "I'm playing for all the other people with AIDS."[31] As the *Advocate* wrote about AIDS and the Games:

> You can't be in San Francisco long without knowing that this city is going through a terrible ordeal. In the San Franciscans who repeat a litany of lost and dying friends in a continuing service of remembrance. In the *Bay Area Reporter*'s page of treacly obituaries, which would seem kitschy were they not so utterly sincere and so unutterably sad. In the emotion that swept the physique contest audience for competitor Christian Heren, who'd fought off AIDS paralysis through an improbable regimen of bodybuilding.

But I also think that we—the athletes and friends and writers and tourists—gave the city something back. The Castro that week was packed with swaggering athletes, young men and women sure they could set a goal, work hard and attain it. Natives talked about how the street was "like it used to be." Physique judge and Detour bartender James Hamrick looked around his Market Street barroom and, in the manner of publicans quick to scent a mood, summed it up: "This has been a good season; our spirits needed a lift. . . . For the athletes the closing ceremony was one long good-bye. I found myself sandwiched between Seattle and Boston. I chatted with Seattle physique contestant Debby Carricola. She was in a serious mood, so I asked her what had meant the most to her. 'Seeing men display affection toward each other,' was her reply. 'You don't see much of that in Seattle.' "[32]

Wrote Ann Meredith in 1986 for the magazine *Off Our Backs*:

Even the language was different. There were "participants" as opposed to "competitors." Women and men competed side by side in the same events with the emphasis on victory defined as one's personal best. There was such a feeling of warmth and commonality. The person who finished last received as loud an ovation as the one who came in first. We were all applauding our existence; our gayness; a camaraderie and our love of life. I saw many older gays in their 60s beaming as they paraded by with a gold or a silver or a bronze medallion ribbon around their necks. I came out 17 years ago and have attended literally hundreds of events and you know, I have never quite seen, never felt such a cohesiveness in the gay community. We are very special people. We are wonderful. Our hearts and our minds are very open. It is important to us that our world include both women and men; that it include people of color, older gays and people who are physically challenged. Our spectrum is a broad and inclusive one.[33]

The Gay Games also opened themselves up to parents and friends of gays and lesbians.

> One woman I met was from South Carolina and came to swim in show of her support of her lesbian sister who swam on the San Francisco team. Families from across the country came with placards and buttons reading: "We Love Our Gay Children." I sat next to some parents from Portland, Oregon, who came to cheer on their lesbian daughter, a firefighter in Dayton, Ohio, through twelve grueling hours of powerlifting. The opening and closing ceremonies, sporting an audience of 20,000 were enough to send chills up and down anyone's spine. The Parade of Athletes women and men together: hugging, smiling, walking arm-in-arm: the strength of Triumph in '86![34]

Strike!

James Reston, longtime editor for the *New York Times*, once wrote that journalists are far better at covering revolution than evolution. The evolution was seen in the growth of ESPN and twenty-four-hour sports coverage. It started innocuously enough, with logrolling and exercise shows providing most of the filler. But 1,440 minutes a day of sports coverage began to slowly change the relationship between the consumer and the product. The need developed for more information about people's favorite stars, more analysis, more filler. The added coverage meant added interest. Added interest translated into even more revenue streams and the explosion of player salaries beyond the wildest dreams of those from earlier eras. The questions of how to divide this new pie manifested itself in strikes as bitter—or at least as high-profile—as any seen during the 1980s. In the NFL, there were strikes for free agency in 1982 and 1987. In 1982, the players had slogans like "No freedom, no football," "Fifty-five percent of the gross," and "Because we are the game."[35]

During the 1987 NFL strike, the union was far from united: there was a Quarterbacks' Club that separated itself from the union for marketing purposes. Fights broke out on picket lines as 15 percent of the players crossed. Mark Gastineau, the record-setting defensive end of the Jets, was punched as he tried to wade through a picket line. Players in the South carried rifles. The NFL started scab football, hiring players off the streets to cross the picket line and play for peanuts. One high-profile person highly critical of this was Irv Cross, Emmy-winning announcer for *NFL Today*, who had worked with the Negro Economic Forums started by Jim Brown in the 1960s.

Columnist Mickey Spagnola tells one dramatic story involving two future Hall of Famers in Dallas:

> As vivid as yesterday is the day when several of the "real" Cowboys players were forced to cross the picket line if they wanted the team to continue funding their annuities, which at the time, were fancy mechanisms included in contracts for delayed payments. One of the first was Randy White, and he pulls up in his pickup truck with fellow defensive lineman teammate Don Smerek alongside.
>
> Well, the picket line was in progress, and the guys made White, of all people, wait patiently for an opening to drive through. Finally, White, nicknamed "Manster" for very good reasons, crossed the sidewalk into The Ranch entrance. But by then, Tony Dorsett and a couple of the other guys walked in front of White's truck. There was a standoff. White was burning. Know that Smerek once suffered a gunshot wound to his leg. And let me tell you, Randy White is the last guy you want burning, especially back in the day. The game of chicken was on.
>
> Finally, White smashed the clutch in and raced his engine, sticking his head out the window. He then briefly popped the clutch. The truck slightly lurched forward. Teammates, you know. This was ugly. They were ready to go at it. That's what labor differences can instigate.
>
> Dorsett and gang finally moved. White raced down the driveway to the players' entrance, tires smoking. Funny thing was, Randy White wasn't the only guy who crossed the picket line to keep his annuity funded. So did Danny White and Ed "Too Tall" Jones and . . . Dorsett.[36]

To this day, the bitterness lingers. "It made me angry," said Tim Irwin, a former Minnesota Vikings player representative. "Some of the guys crossing the line were superstars making the bucks. It was selfish."[37]

In baseball, the Players Association was one of the few unions in the country that actually gained strength in the 1980s. In 1981, it struck for the fifth time since 1972. It led to the canceling of almost 40 percent of the games. Players collectively lost $4 million a week in salary but hung together and once again humbled an ownership group Orioles boss Edward Bennett Williams called "a den of idiots." *Sports Illustrated* had a headline that read, "Strike! The Walkout the Owners Provoked."[38]

Players were making more than ever. Stadium attendance records were being set. Sports coverage was becoming an omnipresent media operation. But lost in the celebrations of sport was what had almost entirely ceased to exist by decade's end: the legitimate use of sports for political ends by the athletes themselves.

· 10 ·

C.R.E.A.M.

The 1990s began with the slogan that launched a thousand unreadable doctoral dissertations. A State Department intellectual named Francis Fukuyama alerted the world that we had reached "the end of history." The fall of the USSR and the Berlin Wall meant that globalization and market economies would dominate every corner of the globe. The time of great ideological or military struggles was past. As Margaret Thatcher noted, the new watchword was TINA—"there is no alternative."

As the introduction to the 1989 edition of the annual Economic Report of the President proclaimed, "The tide of history, which some skeptics saw as ebbing inevitably away from Western ideals . . . flows in our direction." [1]

But the talk of "peace dividends" and ending history was upended by the 1991 war on Iraq. As Zinn wrote, "It was given the name Desert Storm. The government and the media had conjured up a picture of a formidable military power, but Iraq was far from that. The US Air Force had total control of the air, and could bomb at will." [2]

The war unleashed anti-Arab chauvinism, where Arab lives were seen as being worth less than U.S. lives. Dan Rather, reporting on seeing a laser-guided bomb hitting a marketplace and killing civilians, said, "We can be sure that Saddam Hussein will make propaganda of these casualties."[3] Bumper stickers sprouted up with slogans such as "I don't brake for Iraqis" and "Take their gas and kick their ass."

Sports played a prominent role in hyping the war. Many associate the start of the war with Whitney Houston's muscled rendition of the national anthem at the 1991 Super Bowl. As radio stations were pounded with requests for Houston's version, we had clearly come a long way from Jose Feliciano's mellow, abstract version from the 1968 World Series, which ended with his voice over acoustic strings saying, "Oh yeah." (Then again, in 1968, Feliciano had his life threatened for his performance, which was ridiculed in some corners. Ernie Harwell, the avuncular Hall of Fame Tigers announcer who invited Feliciano, was derided as a communist. One distraught listener wrote in to the Detroit *Free Press*, "No wonder our country has lost its dignity.") Houston and George H.W. Bush seemed determined to bring the dignity back, one glass-shattering note and laser-guided missile at a time.[4]

In such an atmosphere, antiwar athletes found very little oxygen. One of the few examples of athletes trying to take even a silent stand, and the price they could pay, was the case of Marco Lokar. Lokar was an Italian-born guard for the Seton Hall Pirates' basketball squad. He had set their freshman scoring record, dropping 40 points in one game. When the team regulated that players wear American flags on their uniforms for the duration of the war, he refused. Lokar's life was threatened by anonymous phone calls and letter. His pregnant wife's life was threatened as well. "I know you have to pay a certain price for taking unpopular positions during a war," he said, "but I never expected anything like what happened to us in America, a country everyone looks to as a house of individual freedom."[5]

The *New York Times* wrote months later,

> It is saddening when even a few Americans use the flag as a license for persecution. Yet persecution is the word that most captures the trials of Marco Lokar. . . . Just last year the Supreme Court rebuffed those who tried to set the flag above the Constitution. . . .

The dark patriotism to which Mr. Lokar was subjected is a troubling reminder of other efforts to extort conformity in a nation built on free speech and diversity. Though Mr. Lokar was persecuted by a rabid few, he is due an apology from all Americans who love freedom."[6]

Marco Lokar was forced to leave the country. As he said on July 4, 1991, "Before a war, there's always a lot of talking. And after a war, they always have peace conferences. So why don't we just eliminate the war in the middle?"[7]

It wasn't just the little-known Lokar. Craig Hodges was a three-point specialist for the 1991 champion Chicago Bulls. His basketball career came to an ugly halt because he dared demonstrate dissent. In a league enslaved by corporate correctness, Craig Hodges felt he couldn't just stand in silence for a White House photo op with President George Bush after the Bulls won their ring, not with 150,000 corpses in Iraq still being bulldozed into mass graves. Craig Hodges, a Muslim, in a gesture of quiet grace, handed President Bush a letter detailing his opposition to Operation Desert Storm and expressing his concern about racism in the United States. He thought he was doing the right thing. But Craig Hodges found that three-point role players of principle were eminently expendable. And just like that, he was gone.[8]

AIDS

In 1991 AIDS hit the world of sports not once but twice. That fall, it would be Magic Johnson with his famed press conference announcing he was HIV positive. But in January, Alan Wiggins died in a Los Angeles hospital of complications due to AIDS. Wiggins played major league baseball for seven years. He was the starting second baseman for the pennant-winning 1984 San Diego Padres. The sports world barely noticed, and didn't even shed a public tear. The only people to attend his funeral from the baseball world were his former teammates Steve Garvey and Lee Lacy. AIDS was still a mystery, still the wages of sin.[9]

How this changed in the fall, when Magic Johnson, at age thirty-two, announced to a packed news conference that he was retiring. In one of two front-page articles, the *Los Angeles Times* said public reaction to the news had been like "an icon had been shot down in mid-stride. . . . The news was treated like the death of a head of state or the outbreak of war."[10]

Johnson said he intended to remain active in basketball off the court and that he would become a spokesman for AIDS prevention. "I plan to go on living for a long time," he said. But it was seen as a no-brainer that he would retire. It was still thought that the virus could be spread through any kind of physical contact. Following Johnson's announcement, rules were instituted that any open cut would result in a player immediately leaving the game until the wound could be closed.

Johnson also felt the need to emphasize repeatedly that he had contracted the virus by having a lot of unprotected heterosexual sex. Unlike Wiggins, Johnson was embraced. President George H.W. Bush gave him a ceremonial position as head of AIDS Awareness. But one person who bucked this warm embrace was Martina Navratilova. She said, "There have been other athletes who died from AIDS and they were pushed aside because they either got it from drugs or they were gay." She also said, "If it had happened to a heterosexual woman who had been with 100 or 200 men, they'd call her a whore and a slut and the corporations would drop her like a lead balloon. And she'd never get another job in her life." Her reaction prompted outrage from the mainstream press.

"I certainly don't want him to take it personally because it is not meant as an offensive thing to him," Navratilova said in follow-up comments "But the double standard is there, and it makes me mad as hell. . . . This Magic thing is another example of women losing power, and we are taking steps backwards."[11]

Navratilova said she does not wish to judge anyone. "And I don't want people to judge me . . . and you know, I am not great. But we can all do better, I think. And the male athletes can certainly do better in their sexual habits. . . . If I can make a difference in preventing some of that [double standard], then I will. But it is not a personal thing against Magic in any way. I don't wish this on him or anybody else. I've had some friends that have died from this disease."

Navratilova said she was "astonished" by the response to what she had said. "I am sure I could have said that President Bush is a closet cross-dresser and I wouldn't have got this much. . . . Nobody deserves to get AIDS, nobody deserves to get cancer, but that's the breaks. You can prevent AIDS a whole lot better than you can prevent cancer. But I think the message should be don't be promiscuous and use a condom. It is not going to cut it, as Dan Quayle was suggesting, that you just don't have sex until you get married."[12]

Fires in Los Angeles

In 1992, the chickens of Reaganism came home to roost when the Los Angeles riots became the largest urban uprising in the history of the United States. It was so big, professional sports had to notice as Los Angeles teams were forced to cancel games, including the NBA playoff game between the Clippers and the Utah Jazz, and the match-up between the Dodgers and the Philadelphia Phillies.

It was sparked by the acquittal—by an all-white jury—of four police officers who had viciously beaten unemployed black construction worker Rodney King. The beating was videotaped and endlessly replayed on television screens across the world. The upheaval's center was in South Central Los Angeles, which had been stricken especially hard by the recession that began in 1990—the recession that turned into the longest economic downturn since World War II. Unemployment for young blacks in the city jumped to 45 percent. Extreme poverty in combination with police corruption and racism in the criminal justice system produced intense desperation and anger. This accounts for the fact that the Los Angeles rebellion involved not just blacks but also Latinos, whites, and Asians. Los Angeles mayor Tom Bradley, himself black, said, "Most of the people who were engaged in the violence were young whites."[13] Fifty-two percent of those arrested in the riots were Latino, 10 percent white, and 38 percent black.

The riots also revealed that the election of a black mayor had not ameliorated the circumstances endured by poverty-stricken African Americans in Los Angeles—nor of blacks living under black mayors in New York, Chicago, or Atlanta. In many cases conditions not only didn't improve but also deteriorated.[14]

The rebellion certainly showed just how out of touch President George H.W. Bush was. The man who didn't know how much a carton of milk cost—the man born, as Ann Richards so memorably said, "with a silver foot in his mouth"—couldn't comprehend the anger and insanity that had led to the National Guard having to protect Frederick's of Hollywood. Now Bush, who had been riding high with 90 percent approval ratings after his victory in the 1991 Gulf War, suddenly found himself in a fight for his political life as the economy crumbled. This played right into the hands of a little-known governor from Arkansas.

The recession coupled with the Los Angeles rebellion delivered the 1992 elections to Bill Clinton. Clinton used the rebellion to attack Bush and shore up his own campaign. He walked through South Central Los Angeles. There, Clinton played off hatred of Bush at the same time as he castigated the "looters" whose children "are growing up in a culture alien from ours, without family, without neighborhood and without church, without support." The solution, as Clinton would trumpet repeatedly for eight years, was "personal responsibility."

Black political leaders backed Clinton, painting the Los Angeles rebellion as a consequence of Bush's policies, but also acquiescing to Clinton's rhetoric about "personal responsibility." Under Clinton, however, America's prison population rose astronomically. By the end of the 1990s, blacks made up 13 percent of the population but 50 percent of those in prison. At the end of 2000, 791,600 black men were behind bars and 603,032 were enrolled in college. By contrast, in 1980—before the prison boom—black men in college outnumbered black men behind bars by a ratio of more than three to one.

And, as promised, "personal responsibility" became the order of the day, with Clinton adopting a Republican plan to dismantle the welfare system. Three months before the 1996 elections, Clinton signed the Personal Responsibility and Work Opportunity Reconciliation Act, saying he was "ending welfare as we know it." The bill was celebrated because it pushed 2.5 million people off the welfare rolls. But there was far less discussion about what happened to people when they landed. The combination of deindustrialization, outsourcing, and the prison boom created a situation in the cities where sports programs withered on the vine.

This has tangentially affected the world of sports. South Central Los Angeles was once a cradle of black baseball talent, producing players such as Eric Davis and Darryl Strawberry. No more. The first reason is economic. As longtime major leaguer Royce Clayton said, "Many black families can't afford for their children to play the sport, which requires the purchase of gloves, balls, bats and other equipment as well as money to maintain playing fields."[15] A low-priced set of baseball gear—a bat, a ball, some spiked shoes, glove—costs about $75, while a $20 basketball or football can serve ten or more players. Then there is city upkeep of fields and leagues. In Washington, D.C., the public baseball diamonds are nobody's idea of a field of dreams. More likely, they're swamped in broken glass and neglect, with kitten-sized rats waddling around the bases, always heading for home.[16] Baseball's owners could have stepped in at any point in the last thirty years and made modest private investments in youth programs and upkeep. But they didn't, because MLB was growing fat on the influx of "cost-effective" players from Latin America.

Harry Edwards said, "I'm convinced that the increase in Latin players is not because all of a sudden the leadership and hierarchy of baseball developed a love for Latins. It's about money. . . . I'm convinced, as Michael Corleone used to say, it's not personal. It's just business."[17]

Baseball has now belatedly attempted to start programs in the inner cities, opening a "factory" in South Central Los Angeles, but this may be a case of too little too late. As Edwards said of such programs, "It's like pumping air into the lungs of a dead man. He needs life; he doesn't need air."[18]

Byron Jones, a Little League coach in Gary, Indiana, said to me:

It breaks my heart seeing our pitchers dodging large indentations in the mound to keep from breaking their ankles—pitchers including my own son. Yes, it's definitely the economics that is keeping African Americans on the outside looking in. There's a lot of lip service from corporations and major league teams about fields they have built or refurbished, but that isn't even a drop in the bucket. Even on a small scale, it's a losing battle. I don't have to look further than the Gary SouthShore Railcats Stadium. The Railcats, to their tremendous credit, established the Homefield Advantage Foundation, which has been invaluable in keeping baseball alive in Gary. Last year they donated $50,000 to Gary Youth Baseball, money that was desperately needed. But the Railcats play in a stadium that cost over $50 million. For a minor league stadium. Let that marinate for a moment . . . $50 million! With an *m*! For just 1 percent of that we could build a centralized youth complex for baseball and softball. When they play in such luxury while we wallow in the muck and mire of fields decades old, it just leaves a bitter taste in my mouth. The bottom line is we just want to provide our kids with a decent place to learn and play this game, a game I love and respect. We just want to give our kids the same chance as anyone, a level playing field, pun definitely intended.[19]

End of Days

The moment for many that signaled the end of Clinton's short-lived honeymoon was when he backed off on a campaign promise to offer asylum to HIV-positive Haitian refugees. One person fought against this injustice until his last days: Arthur Ashe. The former tennis great was dying of AIDS. Despite his terribly weakened state, in the last days of Bush's presidency Ashe had demonstrated to support Haitian refugees, even getting arrested in front of the White House. His actions inspired another athlete to act. Two months after Ashe's death, NBA basketball player Olden Polynice protested outside the Krome Detention Center in Miami in an effort to check in on the condition of detained Haitian refugees. He was inspired to become more active after watching Ashe led off in cuffs in opposition to the Bush administration's policy on Haiti.

"That's what really got me going," he said. "Emotionally, I have a tie with Haitians because I'm one of them. But Arthur Ashe didn't know them. . . . This is about giving of yourself."[20]

In one of Ashe's last speeches he said, "Living with AIDS is not the greatest burden I've had in my life. Being black is." In his last speech, given a week before he died, he said, "AIDS killed my body, but racism is harder to bear. It kills the soul."

Before his death at age forty-nine, Ashe told a friend, "You come to realize that life is short, and you have to step up. Don't feel sorry for me. Much is expected of those who are strong."[21]

Jordan Inc.

Much is also expected of those with power. And no athlete has ever had more and done less than Michael Jeffrey Jordan.

The 1990s in sports saw the corporatization of the game gain an even stronger hand. The fall of the Berlin Wall meant there were new markets to conquer and new products to shill. Athletes on the whole didn't want to take a stand and become the next Craig Hodges. As basketball all-star Chris Webber said,

"People will be so worried about how they will be seen by history or how their commercials are going to be taken away. Now the thing is, 'Don't step out of line.' Now the cool thing is, 'I don't want to be looked at. Don't separate me; don't pick on me.' I've even felt that way a couple of times, too—and that's not good. We have so much influence; I don't think we know how much we have."[22]

The role model for all athletes—and particularly African American athletes—was Michael Jordan. Jordan's basketball resume needs no hype. He is a five-time Most Valuable Player, and a six-time finals MVP. He is the all-time leader in points per game and became the only person over forty years to ever average 20 points per game. He has also been named by ESPN and the *New York Times* as the "athlete of the twentieth century," in both cases besting Muhammad Ali. While Ali shone so brightly for his acute social conscience, Jordan shines as the ultimate salesman.[23]

If Ali's most iconic quote is "I ain't got no quarrel with them Viet

Cong," then Jordan's was his response in 1990 to why he wouldn't endorse Black North Carolina Democrat Harvey Gantt in his Senate campaign against the notorious racist Republican Jesse Helms by saying, "Republicans buy sneakers, too."[24]

Michael Crowley of the *Boston Phoenix* wrote:

> If Ali's persona dramatically overshadows Jordan's, perhaps that's what we should expect. Maybe Michael Jordan reflects our times no less than Ali reflected his own. Just as Ali was a vessel for the social chaos and spiritual liberation of his day, so Jordan symbolizes the political apathy and cultural shallowness of ours. Ali was a 1960s archetype in that he was a passionate and incendiary rebel. Michael Jordan is a 1990s archetype in that he is a value-neutral brand name.[25]

Forbes estimated "his Airness's" commercial value to corporate America in 2000 at $43.7 billion. When in March 1995 he was rumored to be returning to the NBA in one of his many comebacks, the stocks of the companies he endorsed increased in value a combined $3.84 billion. Jordan has shilled proudly for Nike, Coke, McDonald's, Hanes, Ball Park franks, and pretty much everything short of Be Like Mike menthol cigarettes. In the process, he is the first modern athlete, along with perhaps Magic Johnson, to make the transition from corporate mouthpiece to being part of the corporate world himself. Jordan's net worth is estimated in the nine figures, he has made several efforts to buy an NBA team, and he runs his own division of Nike: Jumpman23.[26]

Yet his careful efforts to model himself as a modern pitchman and avoid social issues haven't escaped criticism. Several well-known pro athletes—including Jim Brown, Hank Aaron, and the late Arthur Ashe—have knocked Jordan for standing on the sidelines. "He's more interested in his image for his shoe deals than he is in helping his own people," Brown said of Jordan in 1992.[27]

What has so frustrated older athlete/activists such as Brown is the power Jordan could wield if he wanted to. When Nike's sweatshop labor practices in Southeast Asia received international exposure, a press conference from Jordan could have made a real difference. Instead Jordan said it wasn't his problem. Then, in 1997, he changed his tune, saying to the *Sporting News*, "I'm hearing a lot of different sides to the issue. . . . The best thing I can do is go to Asia (in July) and see it for myself. If there are issues . . . if it's an issue of slavery or sweatshops, [Nike executives] have to revise the situation." It was a trip his Airness never took.[28]

Jordan in his own defense said, "I don't think I've experienced enough to voice so many opinions. . . . I think people want my opinion only because of the role model image that has been bestowed on me. But that doesn't mean I've experienced all those things."[29]

Sportswriter William Rhoden expressed the irony of Jordan's situation. "Had he said 'jump,' had he said 'protest,' most athletes would have jumped; most would have protested. . . . His right to remain silent is what we won. Jordan didn't have an obligation to speak up on racial injustices, but he had an unmatched opportunity."[30]

Abdul-Rauf: The Anti-Jordan

Certainly if players were looking for role models, Jordan was a far more appetizing vision than Mahmoud Abdul-Rauf. Born Chris Jackson in Gulfport, Mississippi, Rauf was an All-American at Louisiana State University, an unstoppable six-foot shooting guard with a jump shot so quick on the release, it looked like he was whipping a slingshot. As a member of the Denver Nuggets, Rauf refused to stand before games during the singing of the national anthem, saying at first that doing so would be in contradiction with his Muslim beliefs. The media asked him how he could refuse to stand when the flag was a symbol of freedom and democracy. He responded by saying that while it may be that for some, in many countries in the world it was a symbol of "tyranny and oppression." On March 12, 1996, the NBA suspended Abdul-Rauf for his refusal to stand, but the suspension lasted only one game. Two days later, the league, eager to get the headlines off the front page, was able to work out a compromise where he would stand during the playing of the national anthem but could close his eyes and tilt his head downward. He usually took this time to recite a Muslim prayer.[31]

The response in Denver was very ugly, as boos rained down on Rauf's head. "Shock jocks" from Denver's KBPI radio were charged with misdemeanor offenses when in response to Rauf, they entered a Colorado mosque playing "The Star-Spangled Banner."[32]

Abdul-Rauf bounced around for several years before he was out of the league. In 2001, his Gulfport, Mississippi, home was burned to the ground. "As far as I'm concerned, this sounds like a hate crime," said Abdul-Rauf, "When a person can't build a home on the property he owns, it's ridiculous. It shows how hateful and how prejudiced people are."

During the home's construction "KKK" was spray-painted on a nearby sign, and the contractor had received calls threatening his life.

"I said before I moved in, it would be burned down," Abdul-Rauf said. "This is just an indication, I think, of how far we've got to go in terms of human relations in this country."[33]

Contrasting Colors

The social crisis in most of black America was in stark contrast to the exploding salaries handed to players, many of whom came from areas experiencing the greatest problems. NBA player Larry Johnson said,

> No man can rise above the condition of the masses of his people. Understand that. So I am privileged and honored by the situation that I'm in, no question. Here's the NBA, full of blacks, great opportunities, they made beautiful strides. . . . But what's the sense of that . . . when I go back to my neighborhood and see the same thing? Everybody [else] ended up dead, in jail, on drugs, selling drugs. So I'm supposed to be honored and happy or whatever, by my success. Yes, I am. But I can't deny the fact of what has happened to us over the years and years and years and we're still at the bottom of the totem pole.
>
> You know what I've come to find out in thirty years? For a black man here in America, there is a struggle and you're either in it, or you're not. You [can] go about your life like it's peaches and cream, and not better the condition of black men and women here, and

better our lives and better our community here, or not. You're trying to just do well by you.[34]

Women, Soccer, and the United States

In much of the world, soccer is more men-only than the bathroom at Au-
gusta National. But this is far less the case in the United States, where it
is the most popular youth sport among girls. It's not difficult to understand why. Not only is it team-oriented, but it is also one of the few team
sports to have produced female athletic role models. The 1999 women's
World Cup team, which included Mia Hamm, Julie Foudy, and the
shirtless one, Brandi Chastain, became an important and historic show-
case for women's sports.[35]

The significance of the 1999 summer of love with women's soccer
has been undermined in two ways. First, in the mainstream press, the
1999 team was dismissed as a fad, as proven by the crash-and-burn demise of the first U.S. women's pro soccer league, the WUSA, in 2003.
Second, as packaged by the press and the president, the spectacle
seemed to carry the queasy message that girls can deliver the jingoistic
goods as well as the boys. Never too shy to ooze toward an opportunity,
Bill Clinton trumpeted the 1999 team with patriotic overkill that developed into a Cold War atmosphere as the United States played China in
the final, with fighter planes flying over a packed Rose Bowl to create a
scene reminiscent of Red Square.

But both perspectives miss the fifteen-year struggle of this team for
recognition and respect, as well as the squad's significance as a physical
representation of the landmark legislation that was Title IX. Even CNN
had to admit, "Team USA's dramatic victory in the women's soccer
World Cup might never have been if not for Title IX." In the last twenty
years alone, the number of women's college teams has nearly doubled.
From 1987 to 1999, the number of girls age six and over playing soccer
increased by 20 percent, to 7.3 million. Women's soccer is now offered
on nearly 88 percent of college campuses compared to only 2.8 percent
in 1977.[36]

Despite this record of achievement, Title IX is subject to constant attack. Like all of the 1960s reforms that improved the lives of women,

people of color, and the poor, Title IX has been the focus of a well-organized and well-funded backlash. Right-wing, bow-tie-wearing columnist George Will used his back-page column in *Newsweek* to brand it "a train wreck."[37]

The members of the 1999 women's soccer team grew up in a time when women's soccer was at best a sideshow. Women's sports meant tennis or golf, country club sports both economically prohibitive and highly individualistic. Team sports were an afterthought. As one member of the team recalls, "Growing up, my idols were eight-foot-tall basketball players and three-hundred-pound football players, and I don't remember ever having a woman that I pointed to and said, 'That's who I want to be someday.'"[38]

In the 1980s, the national team existed without either a World Cup or a spot on the Olympics. They received $10 a day in meal money and practiced on fields in poor condition. "Men's soccer got all the money and respect. That's just the way it was," 1999 team co-captain Michelle Akers said. This began to change with a new generation of teenage players, fifteen- and sixteen-year-olds who grew up with the opportunity to play. The team included Julie Foudy, Joyce Fawcett, Brandi Chastain, and icon-to-be Mia Hamm.[39]

Their breakout finally happened at the 1996 Olympics in Atlanta, but not before a very underpublicized struggle. In the lead-up to the Atlanta games, the players knew that an Olympics on U.S. soil was their best shot at amplifying their sport. They also knew that they were getting a raw deal. The women players were earning $1,000 a month, with a bonus kicking in only if they won the gold. The men were set to get their bonus no matter how they medaled. The players met, and went to get advice from someone who knew about fighting for equal pay and respect: Billie Jean King. King, in addition to her tennis résumé, was also the founder of the first-ever women's athletic union. "I told them, you just don't play," she said. "That's the only leverage you have."[40]

The players unified and basically had what one called a "wildcat strike," refusing to report to practice. As Foudy remembers, "[King] taught us that this wasn't an issue for the federation to handle. The team could handle it ourselves."[41]

The soccer powers—backed by the United States Olympic Committee—brought in a group of scab players, some of whom stayed on the team after the strike ended victoriously. One of those scabs was a player who had left the team and was trying to return: Brandi Chastain.[42]

The 1999 World Cup was the culmination of this struggle. The team sold out Giants Stadium and the Rose Bowl—and did it by marketing the sport straight to fans, in clinics for young girls around the country. The crowd was very young and very female. As Sally Jenkins astutely put it, "One problem with mainstream American sports today is that they have gotten so far from the people who watch them. This team came back to the audience." The final game against China ended, of course, with Brandi Chastain's penalty shot, and the Nike ad heard round the world. The initial popularity of the team was strong. The "reluctant superstar," the painfully shy Mia Hamm, was in Gatorade commercials with the icon of commercialism himself, Michael Jordan. The team became the first group of women ever named *Sports Illustrated*'s Sportsperson of the Year.[43]

There was an effort to capture the popularity of the moment with the creation of the women's pro soccer league, the WUSA, but an absence of corporate sponsorship spelled its doom. This was a profound disappointment, but it shouldn't blind us to the larger significance of that summer. Mia Hamm carried through her play the symbolic weight of everything about Title IX inspiring new generations. In honoring the retiring Hamm, along with teammates Julie Foudy and Joy Fawcett, U.S. national team coach April Heinrichs said, "Think of it this way: imagine that Magic, Larry Bird, Michael Jordan, Shaq, Kobe, and Lebron were all on one team for fifteen years. That's what we have had with our women's national team. They had an impact on America's consciousness, on women's sports, on women's voices." Heinrichs was asked if the feminist movement could in fact take credit for their World Cup triumph, and she said, "Yes. Absolutely."[44]

Women Go to the Hoop

The 1990s also saw the most-viewed basketball game in the history of ESPN, and it didn't involve the Lakers, Knicks, or Bulls. Five million homes tuned in to see the University of Connecticut Huskies trounce the Tennessee Volunteers 70–61 in the 2004 NCAA championship. In front of a raucous sellout crowd, UConn's three-time all-American guard Diana Taurasi played her last collegiate game and went out in style. Taurasi, for those basketball fans who have either missed or avoided her and the women's game, is like Pete Maravich with a ponytail, with a release on her shot so fast it looks like she's setting a volleyball.[45]

The success of this game would seem to bode well for the professional Women's National Basketball Association, founded in 1996. Without question the WNBA has developed a core of fiercely devoted fans, including Norma Havranek of Rockville, Maryland, who hadn't missed a Washington Mystics game since their debut in 1998. "I'm 75 years old, and I've waited for women to get something for a long time," she told the *Washington Post*. "I really don't want this league to disappear because I think if it did, I would go with it."[46]

But while some franchises have found success, others have folded. WNBA TV ratings are microscopic, with little hope for improvement. There are many reasons for this, from the overexpansion of the league to an NBA-style marketing strategy that focuses on individual (and not coincidentally telegenic) players. Lisa Leslie, one of the tapped spokespeople of the new league, said, "When I'm playing, I'll sweat and talk trash. However, off the court, I'm lipstick, heels, and short skirts." The women's game tends to be more team-oriented, similar to the way men play basketball in Europe and South America, with an emphasis on cutting, passing, and a motion offense. Another reason why many franchises suffer is that it has become of a fashion to hold the league up to constant derision and ridicule. Just as the boundaries for sexism have expanded in recent years, from Britney to the mainstreaming of "gentlemen's clubs" to the *Maxim* clones that wallpaper magazine stands in silicone, the WNBA has taken shots that defy belief.[47]

Syndicated national radio host Tom Leykis, for one, suggested that the WNBA should change team names to things like "Denver Dykes," "Boston Bitches," and the "San Francisco Snatch." While Leykis represents the worst of it, the jeers don't spew from men alone.

As Stacey Pressman, a contributing writer for ESPN and the Rupert

Murdoch–owned *Weekly Standard* wrote, "Political correctness has crept out of the academy and into the sports establishment. No one is allowed to say anything negative about women's basketball in fear of coming across as sexist—or worse. . . . In men's sports, ratings are everything. With women's sports, no one cares so long as you're 'on message.' (The WNBA is so political that its website has an entire zone devoted to 'Show Your Support for Title IX.') . . . They're going to jam women's basketball down your throat UNTIL YOU LIKE IT!"[48]

No mention by Pressman that without the women's movement and Title IX women sports journalists—like herself—would still be confined to writing about society teas and zinnia festivals.

Remarks like those of Leykis and Pressman—and the UConn game itself—show that while there is a huge audience for women's sports, we still have far to go before there is equality and fair play, on and off the playing field.

Despite the massive steps forward since the landmark Title IX legislation of the 1970s, sexism still runs through every angle of U.S. sports. Women's scantily clad bodies are constantly used to sell everything from commercial products to the games themselves. Women are systematically marginalized at every level of play, and female athletes face routine and sometimes violent harassment that presents itself drenched in sexism, homophobia, and fear of strong, confident women who don't need an underwire bra to be noticed at a sporting event.

The Williams Sisters

Two women who changed the face of tennis are the sisters Venus and Serena Williams, winners of fourteen Grand Slam singles titles between them. The Williams sisters both turned pro at age fourteen, with the six-foot Venus already a household name. Just like Althea Gibson came up not from the ritzy private academies but from Harlem, the Williams sisters were trained by their father, Richard, at the public courts of Compton, California. Richard Williams has consistently been a public target partly because his has been a booming voice against racism in the country-club world of pro tennis. For someone whose daughters had to walk through, in Venus's words, phalanxes of "guns and gangs" to get to practice, the snooty scions of tennis aren't at all intimidating. That has perhaps been his biggest sin: the refusal to dance. Williams has just re-fused to know his place.

When Venus won her first Grand Slam at Wimbledon, the royal fam-ily was said to be displeased by Richard Williams jumping on the court and yelling, "Straight outta Compton!" And when it became fashionable among sports journalists in 2003 to say that women's tennis "had be-come boring" because it was dominated by Venus and Serena, Richard Williams said, "So women's tennis is getting boring. And you know why? Because two lovely black women dominate it. They're better than the white girls and that's intolerable. They're disturbed by our being there. They've tried everything they could to tame us, to recuperate us and when they couldn't, they said I was a madman."

Richard Williams was quoted as saying he believes racism is rife in women's tennis and within the Women's Tennis Association. "I asked the WTA, 'Does racism still exist with you?' They told me no. They're taking me for an idiot."

Williams has also said he will never salute the flag because of racism in America. "It has no meaning for me." Granted, Williams at times has been his own worst enemy, which stems from his isolation: the pro ten-nis tour is not renowned for its racial sensitivities. His frustration has spurred him at times to give ammunition to his detractors. In March 2001, Venus and Serena Williams experienced problems with referees and fans at the Indian Wells, California, tennis tournament. Richard Williams told CNN that boos directed toward his daughters were moti-vated by racism. Perhaps, but Williams probably stepped over the line when he said, "It's the worst act of prejudice I've seen since they killed Martin Luther King."[49]

But more often than not, the "madman" with the thick Louisiana drawl has gotten the last laugh. His daughters are well-adjusted adults, not ruined tennis prodigies like so many of their peers.

1994 Baseball Strike and Steroids

For many a sports fan, the athletic epoch of the 1990s is inextricably tied to greed. And for many, this "new reality" of greed over games is defined by the 1994 canceling of the World Series. The Fall Classic had survived world wars and economic depressions, and even in 1989 a cataclysmic earthquake. But it couldn't survive the enmity that had built and solidified between baseball owners and the players' union, led by Marvin Miller's protégé Donald Fehr. This was the eighth work stoppage since 1972, all of which had ended with the routing of the owners. The players' union is recognized as the strongest in the country because they don't give an inch. Matt Williams, a recently retired power-hitting third baseman, summed this up well. He was on pace to break Roger Maris's then-record of 61 home runs when the 1994 players' strike ended the season that August. Williams was asked if he regretted missing the opportunity to pass the most hallowed record in the game. He said, "No. The way baseball players think about it is guys before us have sacrificed to enable us to have a healthy game. We're a strong union because we're all on the same page. We need to keep it that way."[50]

DSHEA and the Den of Idiots

Following the strike, attendance took a major hit. Most fans saw the fight as one that was pitting "millionaires versus billionaires," where the fan had to pay the ultimate price. Owners came up with numerous schemes to bring back the fans: interleague play, realignment, and having wild-card teams were all methods to get butts back in the seats. The major league owners—called by late Orioles owner Edward Bennett Williams "a den of idiots"—consciously decided, "We need dingers. Home runs are how people will return to the ballpark."[51]

While the idiots were wringing their hands about how to get more home runs, an amazing piece of legislation passed unanimously in the U.S. Congress at the bipartisan behest of President Bill Clinton and Utah senator Orrin Hatch: the Dietary Supplements Health and Education Act (DSHEA).

Despite focus-tested buzzwords like "health" and "education," DSHEA was little more than a criminal giveback to the pharmaceutical industry. DSHEA's purpose was to shift the burden of proof from the health supplement industry to the Food and Drug Administration (FDA). Previously, a manufacturer had to prove a product's safety before marketing it. After DSHEA passed, the overloaded, underfunded FDA had to prove a product to be unsafe.

"Most people think that dietary supplements and herbs are closely regulated to ensure that they are safe, effective, and truthfully advertised," wrote Dr. Stephen Barrett. "Nothing could be further from the truth. Although some aspects of marketing are regulated, the United States Congress has concluded that 'informed' consumers need little government protection. This conclusion was embodied in the Dietary Supplement Health and Education Act of 1994 . . . which severely limits the FDA's ability to regulate these products."[52]

DSHEA's passage spawned the almost overnight creation of the $27 billion supplement industry and turned the locker room of the average team into a GNC store. Because of DSHEA, teams began to import completely legal weight-lifting and dietary "aids." Many of these are now banned substances. Androstenedione (andro), a highly potent steroid derivative, was legal, available over the counter, and listed as a food supplement. After the 1998 home run race, in which Mark McGwire kept andro in his locker, its sales rose 500 percent to $55 million per year. Substances such as andro were available in every clubhouse. It started with a few teams, but the pressure to keep up pushed other teams to stock it as well. This mentality had deadly consequences. Ephedra, which was completely legal, was linked to the deaths of both Oriole pitcher Steve Bechler and Minnesota Viking offensive lineman Korey Stringer. Now that it has been proven unsafe, it is illegal.[53]

But few were counting the dead because home runs and the media and fan frenzy that accompanied them were making baseball hot on Madison Avenue for the first time since people were doing the Charleston and saying "twenty-three skidoo." Owners milked the new powerball to the hilt and used cartoons of freakishly muscled players as part of ad campaigns. They also embraced the puckishly sexist Nike slogan: "Chicks Dig the Long Ball."

Increased offense and media buzz meant increased money. In 1995, with the sport on life support, the owners sold their broadcast rights for $565 million, which represented a major loss. In 2001, they sold the playoff rights alone for two billion dollars.[54]

Balls were flying over the fence at a record pace. It was far more pervasive than the wildly promoted Mark McGwire/Sammy Sosa home run chase in 1998, in which both players broke Roger Maris's record of 61 home runs in a season. Consider that between 1876 and 1994, the goal of hitting 50 home runs in the course of a single season had been reached eighteen times. From 1995 to 2002, it was done another eighteen times. Slap hitters were hitting 20 homers. Twenty-home-run guys were up to 30. As Joe Morgan said, "There would be times when I would make comments about what I was seeing out there, especially when players had no business driving balls to different parts of the ballpark. I'm talking about guys who had *no business* hitting the ball with that kind of authority. To me, it was just obvious that the nature of the game was different." Morgan was told by his bosses at ESPN not to raise any concerns about this fact. It was a bold new world in athletics: big money and big entertainment propelled baseball toward a frightening future.[55]

Pushing Beyond the Games

A restlessness developed in the 1990s against the big three sports. Other athletic endeavors found space to grow. The nineties saw the explosion of auto racing as well as what became branded "extreme sports" by ESPN. Auto racing drew its strength from the South, the Southeast in particular. Extreme sports, made up of events like snowboarding, street luge, BMX bike racing, and barefoot waterskiing, tended to draw from young people in the West and Northwest, influenced by grunge and surf culture: great athletes alienated from the varsity jock culture. But while on the surface racing seemed to have as much in common with extreme sports as George Strait does with Kurt Cobain, there were similarities. Both were and are overwhelmingly male and overwhelmingly white.

Auto racing, with the ubiquitous Confederate flag, was analyzed by some writers as a refuge for white sports fans alienated by "hip-hop culture" in the big sports. African Americans made up large majorities in basketball and football, with Latinos growing in numbers in baseball. All except the impervious football were leaking ratings. NASCAR's position as refuge for alienated white sports fans was both celebrated and feared by NASCAR officials. As journalist C.W. Nevius wrote, " 'We have," says [one NASCAR official], 'a collection of personalities that people can relate to. They don't seem to be genetic freaks.' The 370-pound football linemen, 7-foot-6 basketball centers and steriod-pumped homerun hitters look nothing like anyone the average couch potato has ever encountered. Meanwhile, NASCAR drivers look like the guy next door." Depends on where you live, I suppose.[56]

The Confederate label is something they earned. As Nevius went on to say,

> Only one black driver has ever won a top NASCAR race. It happened in 1963, when Wendell Scott beat the field in a 200-mile race. But, apparently, officials were concerned about how the mostly white crowd in Jacksonville, Fla., might react to a black man as the winner. Instead of awarding the trophy to Scott, Buck Baker was declared the winner. Then, after the crowd left, a two-hour "review" was conducted, a "scoring error" was discovered, and Scott was declared the winner—to empty grandstands.[57]

It's not just a question of history. When Yahoo! Sports columnist Dan Wetzel wrote a critical but fair-handed examination of the meanings of the Confederate flag at NASCAR events, he received thousands of e-mails. Here is how he started his next column:

> I will answer the two most asked questions.
>
> 1. Calling me a (black person) lover is quite accurate and is not taken as an insult, even though most did not use the term black person. I do indeed love African-Americans.
>
> 2. No, I am not Jewish. Thanks for asking, though. Gee, I can't imagine why that would come up. And for the record, I love Jewish people, too.[58]

For all its image as a rough-and-tumble Rebel sport, no driver approaches the flag issue with a ten-foot carburetor. But on the other hand, NASCAR understood that they would remain a white southern phenomenon, and one defined by celebrating the Confederacy, unless they opened up the doors.

"We need diversity," said H.A. "Humpy" Wheeler, CEO of Speedway Motorsports and president of the Charlotte Speedway. "How are we going to be popular in Southern California without a Hispanic driver?" Good question, Humpy.[59]

In 2003, NASCAR began the NASCAR Diversity Initiative, led by a woman named Dora Taylor. Taylor was a good choice. Her previous job was turning around Denny's after a slew of high-profile racial discrimination lawsuits.[60]

The century was ending with a sports world bigger than ever but badly divided: loving the games but hating the athletes, depoliticized and overcommercialized. The twenty-first century seemed to promise a continuation of these trends. But surprises were in store.

·11·

More of the Same Versus Change

Globalization. The buzzword that defines so much about economics and culture has become the almighty catechism of sports in the twenty-first century. The need for new markets, the prospector's zeal to tap new revenue streams, and the omnipresent media constantly broadcasting the product has put sports in all of our faces, whether we consider ourselves sports fans or not.

The decade has also been defined by war. After the events of September 11, 2001, then national security advisor Condoleezza Rice spoke of "tectonic plates shifting." Vice President Dick Cheney warned of a "war lasting a generation." And the "war president," George W. Bush, asked, "Is our children learning?" This generational "war on terror" had broad appeal following the attacks on the World Trade Center and the Pentagon. Sports played a role in this process. New York Jets quarterback Vinny Testaverde led a push to make sure the Sunday games were cancelled after the attacks. The 2001 World Series, in which the New York Yankees lost in seven thrilling games to the Arizona Diamondbacks, became a place of remembrance and mourning. But as the gongs beat for war, the first post-9/11 Super Bowl was won by the Cinderella-like New England Patriots.

As Steve Serby of the *New York Post* wrote at the time, "Inside a red, white and blue fortress called the Superdome, they let freedom ring last night, and they let freedom sing, and then they played a football game that stands today as tall as the Twin Towers once did, as a defiant statue of liberty. On the night they wrapped a star-spangled banner around the neck of terror and squeezed tight, they played a football game that will be remembered as Patriots' Day." [1]

ESPN joined the fray as well, broadcasting a week's of *SportsCenter* from Kuwait on the third anniversary of 9/11. On a set made to look like a bunker, the executives of Disney (owners of ESPN) were able to do something the Bush administration could not: create a link between 9/11 and the Iraqi occupation. Then *Baseball Tonight* commentator Rob Dibble accepted the perils of their battle mission to Camp Arfijan, saying with the solemnity of Patton, "I know [ESPN talking heads] are risking our lives, but it was the least we could do." [2]

Yet if there was one moment that crystallized the collision of sports and war in a way that would make Donald Rumsfeld blush, it was the tragic case of Pat Tillman. Pat Tillman was a star safety for the Arizona Cardinals, known for his intense style of play. After 9/11, Tillman left millions of dollars on the table to join the Army Rangers along with his brother Kevin. It seemed to be a bonanza for the Pentagon. But Tillman refused to be in any recruitment videos or on a single poster, and soon the story of "NFL player Pat Tillman in the Army Rangers" faded into the next news cycle. A year went by without a mention. No one tracked the day when his shoulder-length hair was shaved to the scalp. No one snapped shots of his time in the Army Ranger indoctrination program. No one knew about his first of two tours in Iraq. But when he died in Afghanistan in 2004, it unleashed a drama that moved from tragedy to obscenity to mystery. [3]

First there was Tillman's death. Because Tillman wasn't the kind of anonymous fallen soldier the Bush administration could blithely ignore, we all bore witness to the tears of his family at a nationally televised funeral.

"Where do we get such men as these? Where to we find these people willing to stand up for America?" asked Republican congressman J.D.

Hayworth as he dived in front of the nearest camera. "He chose action rather than words. He was a remarkable person. He lived the American dream, and he fought to preserve the American dream and our way of life." Senator George Allen of Virginia, the son of the late Hall of Fame coach, sent a letter to NFL commissioner Paul Tagliabue asking the league to dedicate the season to Tillman and other U.S. soldiers "serving in the war on terrorism." Eulogists such as John McCain spoke over Pat Tillman's body about his death in action. And of course Bush jumped into the fray, commenting that "Pat Tillman was an inspiration both on and off the football field." He gave a speech about Tillman over the JumboTron at football stadiums. From the perspective of this administration, Pat died for the noble cause of PR.[4]

This was the tragedy. Then came obscenity: it emerged after Pat's funeral that he had died at the hands of his own troops, in a case of "friendly fire." This bit of information was held back from everyone outside the Pentagon and Oval Office, including Pat's family. It was even kept from Kevin, serving in Pat's battalion.

Finally from obscenity sprung mystery. For Pat's parents, Mary and Pat senior, there were unanswered questions. Why were they fed lies? Why were Tillman's clothes and equipment burned at the scene? Why wasn't Kevin told the truth at the scene? What happened to Pat's journal, which he had kept with him for years?

To pressure army investigators, Mary and Pat senior went public about Pat's true feelings about the war in Iraq. The picture of Tillman they revealed was profoundly at odds with the GI Joe image created by Pentagon spinmeisters and their media stenographers. As the *San Francisco Chronicle* put it, family and friends unveiled "a side of Pat Tillman not widely known—a fiercely independent thinker who enlisted, fought and died in service to his country yet was critical of President Bush and opposed the war in Iraq, where he served a tour of duty. He was an avid reader whose interests ranged from history books on World War II and Winston Churchill to works of leftist Noam Chomsky, a favorite author."[5]

Tillman's close friend Army Specialist Russell Baer remembered, "I can see it like a movie screen. We were outside of [an Iraqi city] watching as bombs were dropping on the town. . . . We were talking. And Pat said, 'You know, this war is so f—— illegal.' And we all said, 'Yeah.' That's who he was. He totally was against Bush."[6] With these revelations, Pat Tillman the PR icon joins WMD and al-Qaeda connections on the heap of lies used to sell the Iraq War.

As Mary Tillman said in May 2007, "They could have told us up front that they were suspicious that [his death] was a fratricide, but they didn't. They wanted to use him for their purposes. . . . They needed something that looked good, and it was appalling that they would use him like that."[7]

Pat's brother Kevin felt he had to speak out, which he did in the piece below:

After Pat's Birthday
By Kevin Tillman

It is Pat's birthday on November 6, and elections are the day after. It gets me thinking about a conversation I had with Pat before we joined the military. He spoke about the risks with signing the papers. How once we committed, we were at the mercy of the American leadership and the American people. How we could be thrown in a direction not of our volition. How fighting as a soldier would leave us without a voice . . . until we get out.

Much has happened since we handed over our voice:

Somehow we were sent to invade a nation because it was a direct threat to the American people, or to the world, or harbored terrorists, or was involved in the September 11 attacks, or received weapons-grade uranium from Niger, or had mobile weapons labs, or WMD, or had a need to be liberated, or we needed to establish a democracy, or stop an insurgency, or stop a civil war we created that can't be called a civil war even though it is. Something like that.

Somehow our elected leaders were subverting international law and humanity by setting up secret prisons around the world, secretly kidnapping people, secretly holding them indefinitely, secretly not charging them with anything, secretly torturing them. Somehow that overt policy of torture became the fault of a few "bad apples" in the military.

Somehow back at home, support for the soldiers meant having a 5-year-old kindergartener scribble a picture with crayons and send it overseas, or slapping stickers on cars, or lobbying Congress for an extra pad in a helmet. It's interesting that a soldier on his third or fourth tour should care about a drawing from a 5-year-old; or a faded sticker on a car as his friends die around him; or an extra pad in a helmet, as if it will protect him when an IED throws his vehicle 50 feet into the air as his body comes apart and his skin melts to the seat.

Somehow the more soldiers that die, the more legitimate the illegal invasion becomes.

Somehow American leadership, whose only credit is lying to its people and illegally invading a nation, has been allowed to steal the courage, virtue and honor of its soldiers on the ground.

Somehow those afraid to fight an illegal invasion decades ago are allowed to send soldiers to die for an illegal invasion they started.

Somehow faking character, virtue and strength is tolerated.

Somehow profiting from tragedy and horror is tolerated.

Somehow the death of tens, if not hundreds, of thousands of people is tolerated.

Somehow subversion of the Bill of Rights and the U.S. Constitution is tolerated.

Somehow suspension of habeas corpus is supposed to keep this country safe.

Somehow torture is tolerated.

Somehow lying is tolerated.

Somehow reason is being discarded for faith, dogma, and nonsense.

Somehow American leadership managed to create a more dangerous world.

Somehow a narrative is more important than reality.

Somehow America has become a country that projects everything that it is not and condemns everything that it is.

Somehow the most reasonable, trusted and respected country in the world has become one of the most irrational, belligerent, feared and distrusted countries in the world.

Somehow being politically informed, diligent and skeptical has been replaced by apathy through active ignorance.

Somehow the same incompetent, narcissistic, virtueless, vacuous, malicious criminals are still in charge of this country.

Somehow this is tolerated.

Somehow nobody is accountable for this.

In a democracy, the policy of the leaders is the policy of the people. So don't be shocked when our grandkids bury much of this generation as traitors to the nation, to the world and to humanity. Most likely, they will come to know that "somehow" was nurtured by fear, insecurity and indifference, leaving the country vulnerable to unchecked, unchallenged parasites.

Luckily this country is still a democracy. People still have a voice. People still can take action. It can start after Pat's birthday.

Brother and Friend of Pat Tillman,
Kevin Tillman[8]

The Break

The Tillmans aren't alone. The country has shifted profoundly against the war in Iraq and the Bush administration. And sports don't exist in a vacuum apart from this.

Take New England Patriots lineman Adalius Thomas. *Sports Illustrated* senior football writer Peter King interviewed him in 2006 and wrote the following:

[Thomas is] politically alert, and not afraid to express his views, which makes him a rarity in the NFL.

"What's the Iraq war all about?" he said, his voice rising. 'If it's about oil, just say that. Don't give us this Weapons of Mass Destruction crap when all you find is three firecrackers."

"You get a little fired up about that," he was told.

"We all have brains," he said. "We should use them."[9]

Thomas is only the latest in a stellar cast of pro players chafing against silence and sounding off against the war. Steve Nash, Etan Thomas, Josh Howard, Joakim Noah, Adam Morrison, Carlos Delgado, Martina Navratilova, Adonal Foyle, and even ultimate fighting champion Jeff Monson, among others, have all spoken out. They are also just the beginning. Stories circulate of teammates and coaches who share their views but don't want to go public. Even some referees whisper covert statements of support. Then there are other stories that largely escape public view. Scott Fujita's grandparents were interned during World War II, and he wants everyone to know about it. His father was born in the Gila River internment camp in Arizona. His grandfather enlisted in the 442nd Regiment. His grandmother received a reparations check and a personal apology letter forty-seven years later.

> The value of telling my story is that the topic of Japanese internment will come up. It helps to educate people, especially in this day and age of heightened paranoia and fear. That kind of thing cannot happen again. There are things going on right now in this country that are just baffling. We may not be taking people and forcibly relocating them but there are many liberties that are being suspended right now. It's a delicate issue. Obviously we are at war and we all have to be smart and observant of our surroundings but at the same time any prejudice has to be unacceptable.[10]

Etan Thomas in particular has been outspoken, delivering political antiwar poetry at demonstrations. At one event in Washington he said:

If he says he's a Christian doesn't mean he follows Christ
Because he's the President doesn't mean that he's bright
Just means you need to research what his speechwriter writes
But through methods of deception he made y'all think that he's right
You owe us
For every mother who will never see their son again
Every husband whose lives you've ruined
Who will never taste the sweet lips of their wife's kiss

Left with the stale bitterness of death to caress their reality
You've created whirlwinds of a widowed future
Causing pain and suffering to give birth to normality
Their blood is on your hands
I hope their pain haunts you while you're sleeping
Wakes you up at night with the cries of the lives you've destroyed
Visions of caskets should dance in your head
I hope your conscience shouts in your ears that our heroes deserved
    better
Rest in peace to the abundance of lives you've ceased
Mr. Commander in Chief
You owe them more
They put their trust in you
Riding in a ship that we all knew would sink
A medal of honor to put in their grave is a slap in the face
Human life is precious no matter what you think
And even after all that. . . .
You're still committed to continuing a winningless battle
You don't know when to say when
You can't even admit that you made a mistake
So how can the healing possibly begin?[11]

The bigger question is why more athletes who share these ideas don't speak out themselves. Of the players I have spoken with, two main reasons emerge. The first is pessimism. Like most people in this country, pro athletes don't believe that they have any power to determine the course of this war. The thought is that the media might give them some coverage, but in the end, nothing would change and they would just earn ESPN Radio's "Just Shut Up Award" for their trouble. One said to me, "The quickest way to win that Just Shut Up award is to have something to say."

The other roadblock is straight-up fear: fear that taking an unpopular stand would mean a quick ticket out of the sports world along with its attendant privileges. All NBA players know the cautionary tales of Craig Hodges and Mahmoud Abdul-Rauf. Taking a stand against U.S. foreign policy could be a toboggan ride to unemployment. Most athletes came up poor and it is not a life anyone wants to revisit.

As Jim Brown said in a recent interview with Yahoo! Sportswriter Charles Robinson,

> The Civil Rights movement is over. Individuals can buy homes wherever they want, travel first class wherever they want, eat wherever they want. All of these things now are part of the everyday lives of players. But the discrimination and racism in the world now is very subtle. It's poor people that are really suffering from a lack of inclusion. Poor people live in a part of town that most players don't go into, and those people aren't an issue as far as the league is concerned. Basically, the players have become part of the elite part of society. And I mean regardless of their color or anything like that. They are part of the elite part of our society because of money and status. So there's not discrimination based on black and white; it's more of a discrimination based on the rich and the poor.[12]

Rich and Poor: Stadium Edition

Brown is correct that wide gaps between rich and poor define today's United States. They define our politics. They also define how sports is used. This was laid bare for the world in August 2005 after Hurricane Katrina flattened the Gulf Coast. The Louisiana Superdome, the largest domed structure in the Western Hemisphere, morphed into a homeless shelter from hell, inhabited yet uninhabitable for an estimated thirty thousand of New Orleans's poorest residents. It took Hurricane Katrina for them to actually see the inside of the Superdome, a stadium whose ticket prices make entry restrictive. At the time of the hurricane, game tickets cost $90, season seats went for $1,300, and luxury boxes for eight home games ran more than $100,000 a year. But the Katrina refugees' tickets were courtesy of the federal and local government's malignant neglect.

It was only fitting, because these thirty thousand people helped pay for the stadium in the first place. The Superdome was built entirely on the public dime in 1975, as a part of efforts to create a "new New Orleans" business district. City officials decided that building the largest domed stadium on the planet was in everyone's best interest. Instead, it set a path that has seen money for the stadium but not for levees; money for the stadium but not for shelter; money for the stadium but not for an all-too-predictable disaster.

The tragedy of Katrina then became farce when the Superdome's inhabitants were finally moved: not to government housing, public shelters, or even another location in the area, but to the Houston Astrodome.

Barbara Bush walked among the dispossessed and said without shame: "Almost everyone I've talked to says, 'We're going to move to Houston.' What I'm hearing, which is sort of scary, is they all want to stay in Texas. Everyone is so overwhelmed by the hospitality. And so many of the people in the arena here, you know, were underprivileged anyway, so this—[she chuckles slightly] is working very well for them."

Today so much in New Orleans remains shuttered—so much except for, you guessed it, the Superdome. This came at a price of $185 million. This has been sold as priority one because it walks hand in glove with the idea that the road back for New Orleans begins in the Dome: with tourist dollars greasing the path back for all residents.

Stadiums are sporting shrines to the dogma of trickle-down economics. In the past ten years, more than $16 billion of the public's money has been spent for stadium construction and upkeep from coast to coast. Their building has become the substitute for anything resembling an urban policy in this country. The stadiums are presented as a microwave-instant solution to the problems of crumbling schools, urban decay, and suburban flight. Reports from both the right-wing Cato Institute and the more centrist Brookings Institution dismiss stadium funding as an utter financial flop, yet the domes keep coming.[13]

As Neil DeMause, co-author of the book *Field of Schemes*, said to me, "The history of the stadium game is the story of how, by slowly refining their blackmail skills, sports owners learned how to turn their industry from one based on selling tickets to one based on extracting public subsidies. It's been a bit like watching a four-year-old learn how to manipulate his parents into buying him the new toy that he saw on TV. The question now is how long it takes our elected officials to learn to say no."[14]

But our elected officials have been more like the children, as sports owners tousle their hair and set the budget agendas for municipalities around the country with a simple credo: stadiums first and people last.

Ball Four author Jim Bouton has become an agitator against stadium construction.

> It's such a misapplication of the public's money. . . . You've got towns turning out streetlights, they're closing firehouses, they're cutting back on school supplies, they're having classrooms in stairwells, and we've got a nation full of kids who don't have any health insurance. I mean, it's disgraceful. The limited things that our government does for the people with the people's money, to spend even a dime or a penny of it on ballparks is just a crime.
>
> It's going to be seen historically as an awful folly, and it's starting to be seen that way now, but historically that will go down as one of the real crimes of American government, national and local, to allow the funneling of people's money directly into the pockets of a handful of very wealthy individuals who could build these stadiums on their own if it made financial sense. If they don't make financial sense, then they shouldn't be building them. If I was a team owner today, asking for public money, I'd be ashamed of myself. Ashamed of myself. But we've gone beyond shame. There's no such thing as shame anymore. People aren't embarrassed to take—to do these awful things.[15]

Stringer

Bigotry continues to be unchallenged. Hurricane Katrina destroyed a majority-black city, which continues to die from naked neglect. Women face a constant barrage of sexism in our "girls gone wild" culture, and if you challenge it, then you must be a humorless prig. The pent-up anger about these things was released in 2007 on two fronts, both of which connected with sports. One was the case of Don Imus, who called the Rutgers women's basketball team "nappy-headed hos."

"There's nothing rare about Imus's vile attacks," wrote *Washington Post* sportswriter Michael Wilbon. "This is what he does as a matter of course. Imus and his studio cohorts have painted black people as convicts and muggers and worst of all, apes. Not only do they find it funny, they expect everybody else will as well."[16]

Wilbon is correct. Yet it took Rutgers coach C. Vivian Stringer and her team to remind the media that Imus's comments weren't just racist but sexist. As she said, "I would ask you . . . who amongst you could have heard the comments and not been personally offended? It's not about the Rutgers women's basketball team, it's about women. Are women 'hos'? Think about that. Would you have wanted your daughter to have been called that? It's not about they as black people or as nappy-headed, it's about us as a people—black, white, purple or green."[17]

It didn't surprise anyone in the world of women's hoops that Stringer stood so tall. For more than three decades she has been building her reputation as one of the most accomplished coaches in basketball history. Stringer is the only coach in NCAA history to have led three different schools to the Final Four. One of those schools, the historically black college Cheyney University, provided one of the most improbable Cinderella stories in NCAA history. Her lifetime record over thirty-five years is an unbelievable 750–251. This is also the thirty-fifth anniversary of Title IX. Title IX was supposed to level playing fields between men and women. In many respect, as discussed earlier, the results have been remarkable. But for women—especially African American women— sports remains a place of denigration, not celebration. Swimsuit issues, cheerleaders, and beer-commercial sexism define women in the testosterone-addled sports world. There is an arsenal of homophobia and mockery sprayed at those who dare sweat, compete, and play hard. Every woman who has played sports and every man with a female athlete in the family felt Imus's words in a way that cut deeply.

But why did this comment, in a career of ugly statements, finally break the camel's back? Some of the answer partly lies in how we are taught to understand sports. Rush Limbaugh felt the biggest backlash of his career when he said that the media overhyped Philadelphia Eagles football star Donovan McNabb because of their "social concern" to see a successful African American quarterback. After thousands of angry calls and e-mails Limbaugh was bounced from ESPN. Both Imus and Limbaugh built careers on this kind of bile, but when they cross-pollinated their bigotry with sports, a new level of anger exploded. We are relentlessly sold the idea that our games are a space safe from this kind of political swill.

We are also told that sports are a "field of dreams," a true meritocracy where hard work always meets rewards. But when the playing field is shown to be unlevel, it stings. This sporting reality can wake people up and reveal the hidden inequities in our society that otherwise go unnoticed. When a Rutgers team defies the odds, makes the NCAA finals, and gets called "nappy-headed hos" for their trouble, it presses a very all-too-raw nerve.

Imus reaped the whirlwind because Coach Stringer and the Rutgers team refused—like so many of Imus's targets—to be silent. As team captain Essence Carson said, "I know we're at a young age, but we definitely understand what is right and what should get done and what should be made of this. We're happy—we're glad to finally have the opportunity to stand up for what we know is right."[18]

But the bull's-eye reason Imus was canned like a tuna is because the political climate in this country in recent years has shifted. All the "red state, blue state" blather is so much bunk. Bush has as of this writing an approval rating of 29 percent, slightly lower than Nixon's corpse. His popularity among African Americans in one recent poll was 2 percent. Which means beyond Condi Rice and her family, the cupboard is bare.

On issue after issue, consciousness in the United States has shifted left, as revealed by a recent Pew Research Center poll. Two-thirds of the country disapproves of Bush's handling of Iraq, 59 percent support a path to citizenship for undocumented workers, and 73 percent agree with the statement that the rich are getting richer and the poor poorer. According to a Gallup poll, 75 percent of people believe it is the responsibility of government to make sure everyone has health care. This shift comes out of people's lived experiences.[19]

Coach Stringer spoke beautifully about how to understand the response to Imus. Speaking at warp speed to MSNBC's Keith Olbermann, she said,

> We've become so desensitized that we've allowed a lot of things to pass, and we've not been happy. . . . Too often politicians, leaders, and . . . religious leaders . . . speak for us, and we sit back and don't realize the power in numbers, and that when we have had enough is enough. . . . We see [injustice] over time, you know, a kid that steals something with a plastic cap pistol, to spend ten years in jail, and yet you see . . . the white-collar workers, you know, thieves that steal millions of dollars [get off]. . . . And I do think that if people stood up, politicians [wouldn't] wait for a poll but [would be] strong enough to make a decision and stand . . . You know I happen to be the daughter of a coal miner. My father lost both his legs in a mine. He worked hard each and every day. He only stayed out of the mine six months until he got prosthetics. I know what it is to work hard and this has been a lifelong pursuit and passion. I've coached for thirty-six years. . . . As a person of conscience, I . . . have seen so much, you know, that I would like to see changed. . . . I would gladly exchange winning a national championship if we, as young ladies, would stand and allow the country to somehow be empowered and that we take back our country.[20]

Jena

The issue by now has become well known, discussed on CNN and in the pages of *USA Today*. At Jena High School in Jena, Louisiana, a black student received permission from school authorities to sit underneath what was known as the "white tree" (it's remarkable that he felt he had to ask). The next day, in retribution, three nooses hung from the branches.

In protest, black students collectively decided to sit under the tree.

This was a bold and beautiful act, in the spirit of the best traditions of the 1960s. They refused to comply with racist terror, even when those threats are as drastic as being lynched for simply not staying in your place.

And just like in the old South, the state made clear which side it was on. The town DA, Reid Walters, actually had the audacity to threaten only the black students, telling them that he had the power to ruin their lives with the stroke of his pen if they continued to make trouble.[21]

Tensions escalated over the course of the semester. Two black students were beaten by a white student, while another group of black students was threatened with a shotgun by a former classmate. Surprisingly, none of the white students or former students was punished in any way for these incidents. But the following Monday, when a white student was beaten up by six black classmates, the black students were immediately arrested and charged with attempted murder and conspiracy to commit murder, charges that would put them in jail for one hundred years without parole. The "Jena 6" range in age from fifteen to seventeen. The white student spent three hours in a hospital emergency room and required no further medical care.

This particular case resonated profoundly in the black community. A march estimated at fifty thousand people filled the streets of Jena, and solidarity T-shirts, beads, and economic boycotts became a staple of African American college life.

It also hit pro athletes. One of the Jena 6 has an uncle, Jason Hatcher, who plays for the Dallas Cowboys. Others of the Jena 6 are athletes themselves, with one, Mychal Bell, one of the most highly recruited players in the state.

People in the sports world spoke out about the case, As Billy Hunter, the head of the NBA Players Association, said, "The situation in Jena, Louisiana, is abominable and rotten to the core. The actions of the district attorney demonstrate that racism and bigotry are live and well in Jena. As a former U.S. attorney for the Northern District of California and assistant chief in the S.F. district attorney's office, it is my opinion that the district attorney has severely overcharged the case, revealing his bias against the six black Jena youth. His actions should serve as a wake-up call for all Americans who believe in an impartial and fair criminal justice system."[22]

What makes this group of socially conscious athletes so interesting is that it combines familiar names (athlete activists like Washington Wizards center Etan Thomas and Dr. John Carlos) with new names like Saints linebacker Scott Fujita, writers like ESPN.com's Jemele Hill and Scoop Jackson, and NBA rookie Joakim Noah. We will see more athletes serious about reclaiming politics from the "experts" that have so thoroughly failed us.

Sports has often acted as a reflection of the national life. At different times it has also been a fetter holding back the tide of change. In other instances, it has been a Taser, sending an electric jolt into the body politic. Today sports is something both altogether familiar and alien. It affects our lives whether we consider ourselves sports fans or not. It also still has the capacity to inspire. But one thing is certain: we can pretend sports isn't political just as well as we can pretend there is no such thing as gravity if we fall out of an airplane. The truth remains obstinate as a mule. Sports are what we make of them. If we sit back and let political messages be casually pumped through our play, it will be the death of us. If we challenge sports to be as good as they can be—a force to break down walls that divide us, a motor for inclusion—they can propel us toward a better world, a world worth playing in—and worth fighting for.

Notes

1: UNTIL THE TWENTIETH CENTURY

1. "George Catlin Describes a Choctaw Lacrosse Match. c. 1830s," quoted in Steven A. Riess, *Major Problems in American Sports History* (Houghton Mifflin, 1997), 27–31.
2. Elliott J. Gorn and Warren Goldstein, *A Brief History of American Sports* (University of Illinois Press, 2004), 5.
3. Ibid., 9.
4. "King James I Identifies Lawful Sports in England," quoted in Riess, 23.
5. Ibid.
6. John Cox and Dave Zirin, "Hey Guys, It's Just a Game," *The Nation*, June 20, 2006, http://www.thenation.com/doc/20060703/zirin.
7. Gorn and Goldstein, 11.
8. Ibid., 31.
9. Nancy Struna, "The Sporting Life in Puritan America," quoted in Riess, 40.
10. Gorn and Goldstein, 33.
11. Ibid., 36.
12. Ibid., 12.
13. Ibid., 13.
14. Ibid., 42.
15. William Rhoden, *Forty Million Dollar Slaves: The Rise, Fall, and Redemption of the Black Athlete* (Three Rivers Press, 2007), 59.
16. Frederick Douglass, *My Bondage, My Freedom* (Biblio Bazaar, 2007), 251.
17. Gorn and Goldstein, 43.
18. Ibid.
19. J.M. Fenster, "A Nation of Gamblers," *American Heritage*, September

1994, http://www.americanheritage.com/articles/magazine/ah/1994/5/1994_5_34.shtml.

20. Howard Zinn, *A People's History of the United States: 1492–Present* (Harper Perennial Modern Classics, Hardcover edition, 2003), 96.

21. Ibid., 97.

22. Gorn and Goldstein, 56.

23. Zinn, 125.

24. "Horace Greeley Decries the Slaughter of Boxer Thomas McCoy," quoted in Riess, 54.

25. Gorn and Goldstein, 61.

26. Arthur Ashe, *A Hard Road to Glory: A History of the African American Athlete, 1619–1918* (Wiley, 1993), 1:10.

27. Zinn, 131–132.

28. Ibid., 110.

29. Ibid., 123.

30. Patricia McKissack and Frederick McKissack, *Sojourner Truth: Ain't I A Woman* (Scholastic, 1992), 121.

31. Gorn and Goldstein, 101.

32. Susan O'Malley, "The Importance of the Bicycle in the Early Women's Liberation Movement," *Cranked Magazine* 4:24 (www.crankedmag.com/womenslib.html).

33. Elizabeth Cady Stanton, "Man Superior, Intellectually, Morally and Physically," September 1848, http://ecssba.rutgers.edu/docs/ecswoman2.html.

34. Reiss, 250.

35. Ron McCulloch, *From Cartwright to Shoeless Joe* (Warwick, 1998), 10.

36. Ibid., 14.

37. Ibid., 11.

38. Ibid., 17.

39. Ibid., 22.

40. Ibid., 24.

41. "The Doubleday Myth," www.hickoksports.com/history/doublday.shtml.

42. Albert G. Spalding, *America's National Game* (New York, 1911), 3–14.

43. Michael Aubrecht, *Baseball and the Blue and the Gray,* Baseball Almanac, July 2004, http://www.baseball-almanac.com/articles/aubrecht2004b.shtml.

44. Ibid.

45. Zinn, 240.

46. Ibid., 238.

47. Gorn and Goldstein, 82.

48. Ibid, 91.

49. Clifford Putney, *Muscular Christianity: Manhood and Sports in Protestant America, 1880–1920*, new ed. (Harvard University Press, 2003).

50. Ibid.

51. Gorn and Goldstein, 90.

52. Spalding, 3–14.

53. McCulloch, 36.

54. Ibid., 44.

55. Ibid., 39.

56. Ibid., 48.

57. John Montgomery Ward, "Is the Base-Ball Player a Chattel," quoted in Riess, 216.

58. Gorn and Goldstein, 101.

59. McCulloch, 57.

60. Gorn and Goldstein, 126–27.

61. McCulloch, 57.

62. Ashe, 71.

63. Rhoden, 82.

64. Moses Fleetwood Walker, *Our Home Colony*, 1908.

65. Ibid.

66. James Riley, *The Biographical Encyclopedia of the Negro Baseball Leagues* (Carroll & Graf, 2002).

67. Zinn, 245.

68. Ibid., 251.

69. Ibid., 283.

70. Ibid., 267.

71. Ibid., 277.

72. Ibid., 281.

73. Gorn and Goldstein, 103.

74. Ibid., 104.

75. Rhoden, 72–73.

76. Ibid., 77.

77. Ibid., 70.

78. Ibid.

79. Ibid., 77.

80. Ibid.

81. David Remnick, *King of the World* (Vintage, 1998), 221.

82. Gorn and Goldstein, 113.

83. Ashe, 23.

84. Ibid.

85. Ibid., 27.

86. Susan K. Cahn, *Coming on Strong: Gender and Sexuality in Twentieth-Century Women's Sports* (Harvard University Press, 1998), 86.

87. Caspar W. Whitney, "Evolution of the Country Club," Annals of American History, www.america.eb.com/america/article?articleId=386350&query=sports.

88. Theodore Roosevelt, "Professionalism in Sports," *North American Review*, 1890.

89. Theodore Roosevelt, *Value of an Athletic Training*, privately printed, 1929.

90. Spalding, 11.

2: ROUGH RIDING

1. Theodore Roosevelt, *The Rough Riders*, 1899, (accessed from Bartleby.com).
2. Howard Zinn, *A People's History of the United States: 1492–Present* (Harper Perennial, 2008), 297.
3. Ibid., 299.
4. Ibid.
5. Ibid., 300.
6. Thomas E. Woods Jr., *Theodore Roosevelt and the Modern Presidency*; http://www.lewrockwell.com/woods/woods79.html.
7. Elliott J. Gorn and Warren Goldstein, *A Brief History of American Sports* (University of Illinois Press, 2004), 176.
8. Theodore Roosevelt, *"The American Boy,"* 1900, quoted in Gorn and Goldstein, 148.
9. Dan Daly, "Danger, Football Go Back," *Washington Times*, September 1, 2005.
10. Gorn and Goldstein, 157.
11. Gorn and Goldstein, 158.
12. Michael Oriard, quoted in Gorn and Goldstein, 159. (University of North Carolina Press, 1998).
13. Gorn and Goldstein, 159.
14. Richard P. Bookowski, *The Life & Contributions of Walter Camp to American Football* (Temple University, 1979).
15. Ibid., 154.
16. Jeremy Schaap, *Triumph: The Untold Story of Jesse Owens and Hitler's Olympics* (Houghton Mifflin, 2007), 63–64.
17. Gorn and Goldstein, 165.
18. Harry Edwards, "His Political Legacy to the 20th Century Gladiator," in *Paul Robeson: The Great Forerunner* (International Publishers, 1998), 18.
19. Ibid., 19.
20. Ibid.
21. Ibid., 20.
22. Ibid.
23. James D. Carr, "Concerning the Snubbing of Paul Robeson," quoted in David Kenneth Wiggins and Patrick B. Miller, *The Unlevel Playing Field: A Documentary History of the African American* (University of Illinois Press, 2003), 177.
24. Edwards, 21.
25. Zinn, 355.
26. E.V. Debs, "The Canton Ohio Speech," www.marxists.org/archive/debs/works/1918/canton.htm.
27. E.V. Debs, "Statement to the Court," www.marxists.org/archive/debs/works/1918/court.htm.
28. Gorn and Goldstein, 178–79.

29. Ibid.

30. *Encyclopedia Britannica Guide to Black History*, www.britannica.com/blackhistory/article-9023985.

31. Arthur Ashe, *A Hard Road to Glory: A History of the African American Athlete, 1619–1918* (John Wiley, 1993), 102.

32. William Rhoden, *Forty Million Dollar Slaves* (Three Rivers Press, 2007), 226.

33. David Remnick, *King of the World* (Vintage, 1998), 221–223.

34. "Jack Johnson Believes He's Jeff's Master," *Philadelphia Inquirer*, July 4, 1910.

35. "Negroes Praying for Johnson," *Dallas Morning News*, July 4, 1910.

36. Geoffrey Ward, *Unforgivable Blackness: The Rise and Fall of Jack Johnson* (Vintage, 2006), 201.

37. Ibid.

38. Remnick, 226.

39. " 'Papa Jack': In the Ring and Out," in Wiggins and Miller, 74, 77.

40. "W.E.B. Du Bois and Jack Johnson: The Scholar's Pugilist and the Heavyweight Champ as Folk Hero," in Wiggins and Miller, 79.

41. Remnick, 223.

42. *Jack Johnson: In the Ring and Out*, in "Booker T. Washington and Jack Johnson: Race Men and Respectability," in Wiggins and Miller, 77.

43. Ibid., 79.

44. Ibid., 78.

45. Lawrence W. Levine, *Black Culture and Black Consciousness: Afro-American Folk Thought from Slavery to Freedom* (Oxford University Press, 2007), 82.

46. W.E.B. DuBois, "The Prize Fighter," *The Crisis*, August 1914.

47. W.E.B. DuBois, "The Problem of Amusement," quoted in Wiggins and Miller, 40.

48. "Judge Landis Hears Stories of the I.W.W.; Some Plead for Mercy, While Others, Including Haywood, Prove to Be Defiant," *New York Times*, 1918.

49. Shirley Povich, *All Those Mornings . . . at the Post* (Public Affairs, 2005), 13.

3: SPORTS AND LEISURE

1. Howard Zinn, *A People's History of the United States, 1492–Present* (Harper Perennial, 2005), 380.

2. Sharon Smith, *Subterranean Fire: A History of Working Class Radicalism in the United States* (Haymarket Books, 2006), 82.

3. A Mitchell Palmer, "The Case Against the 'Reds,' " *Forum* 63 (1920): 173–85.

4. Transcribed from Merritt Brunies and His Friars Inn Orchestra; vocals by Lew King; recorded March 2, 1926, from *Can't Help Lovin' That Man*, Art Deco Columbia Legacy CK 52855.

5. Bruce Bliven, "Flapper Jane," *New Republic*, September 9, 1925.
6. H.L. Mencken, "On Being an American," in *Prejudices, Third Series* (Knopf, 1922).
7. Richard Wright, *Black Boy* (Harper Collins, 1945), 177.
8. Ruth's statistics and biography are available at www.babe-ruth.com.
9. Marshall Adesman, "A Babe Retrospective," http://www.thediamond angle.com/archive/jan04/baberuth.html.
10. Grantland Rice, *New York Herald Tribune*, quoted from the Notre Dame Archives, http://archives.nd.edu/rockne/rice2.html.
11. Shirley Povich, *All Those Mornings . . . at the Post* (Public Affairs, 2005), 171.
12. Rice, quoted from the Baseball Almanac, www.baseball-almanac.com/quotes/quodean.shtml.
13. Judith Stein, *The World of Marcus Garvey: Race and Class in Modern Society* (Louisiana State University Press, 1991).
14. "Nelson George on the Harlem Globetrotters," quoted in Dana K. Wiggins and Patrick B. Miller, *The Unlevel Playing Field* (University of Illinois Press, 2003), 232.
15. "James 'Cool Papa' Bell Remembers Negro League Baseball in the 1920s and 1930s," quoted in Steven A. Riess, *Major Problems in American Sports History* (Houghton Mifflin, 1997), 284.
16. Ernest C. Withers, *Negro League Baseball* (Harry N. Abrams, 2005), introduction.
17. "James 'Cool Papa' Bell Remembers," 285.
18. Withers, introduction
19. William Rhoden, *Forty Million Dollar Slaves* (Three Rivers, 2007), 104.
20. Ibid., 102.
21. Ibid., 105.
22. Baseball Library, www.baseballlibrary.com/ballplayers/player.php?name =Rube_Foster_1 888.
23. Ibid.
24. Susan K. Cahn, *Coming On Strong* (Harvard University Press, 1998), 32.
25. Ibid., 39, 60.
26. Molly Jay, *Winning Woman: 500 Spirited Quotes About Women and Their Sport* (Running Press, 2001), 33.
27. Ibid., 199.
28. Cahn, 116.
29. Cahn, 33.
30. Jay, 17.
31. Cahn, 25.
32. Ibid., 52.
33. Ibid., 73, 77.

4: NO DEPRESSION

1. Howard Zinn, *A People's History of the United States, 1492–Present* (Harper Perennial, 2005), 387.
2. Ibid.
3. Studs Terkel, "Hard Times: An Oral History of the Great Depression," www.studsterkel.org/htimes.php.
4. "Phyllis Bryant Remembers Her Christmas Doll Bed," *Michigan History Magazine*, January–February 1982, www.michigan.gov/hal/0,1607,7-160 -17451_18670_18793-53511—,00.html .
5. Sharon Smith, *Subterranean Fire: A History of Working-Class Radicalism in the United States* (Haymarket Books, 2006), 111–14.
6. Genora (Johnson) Dollinger, as told to Susan Rosenthal, *Striking Flint: Genora (Johnson) Dollinger Remembers* (Haymarket, 1998).
7. Zinn, 387.
8. Mark Naison, *Communists in Harlem*, new ed. (University of Illinois Press, 2004), 41.
9. Baseball Almanac, www.baseball-almanac.com/yearly/yr1933a.shtml.
10. Richard Wright, *Black Boy* (HarperCollins, 1945) 315.
11. William J. Baker, "Muscular Marxism and the Chicago Counter-Olympics of 1932," cited in S. W. Pope, ed., *The New American Sport History: Recent Approaches and Perspectives* (University of Illinois Press, 1997), 284.
12. Ibid., 285.
13. Ibid., 294.
14. Dave Zirin, "An Interview with Lester "Red" Rodney," www.counter punchorg/zirin04032004.html, April 3, 2004.
15. Irwin Silber, *Press Box Red: The Story of Lester Rodney, the Communist Who Helped Break the Color Line in American Sports* (Temple University Press, 2003), 3.
16. Ibid., 4.
17. *WMNF*, 40. Zirin, *Counterpunch*.
18. Jeremy Schaap, *Triumph* (Houghton Mifflin, 2007), 45.
19. Shirley Povich, *All Those Mornings . . . at the Post* (Public Affairs, 2005), 41.
20. Ralph Wiley, *Serenity: A Boxing Memoir* (University of Nebraska Press, 2000).
21. David Remnick, *King of the World* (Vintage, 1998), 227.
22. Schaap, 17.
23. Jesse Owens: Track and Field Legend, www.jesseowens.com/quotes.
24. Schaap, 159.
25. Ibid., 84.
26. Ibid., 90.
27. Walter White to Jesse Owens, December 4, 1935, quoted in David K. Wiggins and Patrick B. Miller, *The Unlevel Playing Field* (University of Illinois Press, 2003), 165.
28. Schaap, 57.

29. Ibid., 98.
30. Mark Rhoads, "Illinois Hall of Fame: Avery Brundage," *Illinois Review*, http://illinoisreview.typepad.com/illinoisreview/2006/08/illinois_hall_o_ 20.html.
31. Schaap, 72.
32. Ibid.
33. Ibid., 85.
34. Ibid.
35. Ibid., 64.
36. Justus D. Doenecke, *In Danger Undaunted: The Anti-Interventionist Movement of 1940–1941 as Revealed in the Papers of the America First Committee* (Hoover Institution Press, 1990), 14–15.
37. Schaap, 76.
38. Ibid., 161.
39. Ibid., 124–25.
40. Ibid., 153.
41. Arnold Rampersad, *Jackie Robinson: A Biography* (Ballantine, 1998), 15.
42. Schaap, 172.
43. Ibid., 195.
44. Ibid., 211.
45. Ibid., 186.
46. Ibid., 192.
47. Clint Wilson, *LA Sentinel*, Olympics Hero and Humanitarian Jesse Owens Dies; Brad Pye, Jr. "Bye Jesse!" March 31, 1980 (www.blackpress usa.com/history/archive_essay.asp?NewsID=295&Week= 13)
48. Schaap, xii.
49. Remnick, 224.
50. Arthur Ashe, *A Hard Road to Glory: A History of the African American Athlete 1619–1918* (Wiley, 1993), 12.
51. Joe Louis's Official Career Record, http://www.boxrec.com/list_bouts .php?human_id=009027&cat=boxer.
52. Marcus Garvey, "The American Negro in Sport," in Wiggins and Miller, 167–68.
53. Author interview with Lester Rodney.
54. Richard Wright, "High Tide in Harlem: Joe Louis as a Symbol of Freedom," quoted in Wiggins and Miller, 170–171.
55. New York *Daily News*, June 23, 1938.
56. Willis P. Armstrong, "A Toast to Joe Louis," Wiggins and Miller, 174.
57. Quoted in Remnick, 227.
58. Good overview on sportswriters and the black press: Brian Carroll, *When to Stop the Cheering? The Black Press, the Black Community, and the Integration of Professional Baseball* (Routledge, 2006).
59. William Brower, "Has Professional Football Closed Its Door?" in Wiggins and Miller, 198.

60. "Tuskegee and 'Force' Rapped for Tribute to Knute Rockne," in Wiggins and Miller, 134.

61. Wendell Smith, "'A Strange Tribe': On the Loyalties of Black Fans," in Wiggins and Miller, 135–37.

62. Harry Levette, "Eddie Tolan Is the Fastest Human—But," in Wiggins and Miller, 155–56.

63. Roy Wilkins, "That Old Southern Accent," in Wiggins and Miller, 191–92.

64. Povich, 64.

65. Quoted in Ashe, 36.

5: WAR AND ITS DISCONTENTS

1. Shirley Povich, *All Those Mornings . . . at the Post* (Public Affairs, 2006 paperback edition), 95. 71.

2. Ibid., 112–13.

3. Martin Glaberman, *Wartime Strikes: The Struggle Against the No Strike Pledge in the UAW During World War II* (Bewick Editions, 1980).

4. Charlie Vascalleros, "Nisei: The Early Japanese-American Ballplayers," http://www.thediamondangle.com/archive/aug01/nisei.html; Gary T. Otake, "A Century of Japanese American Baseball," www.njahs.org/research/bbnist.html.

5. Quoted in Vascalleros.

6. Earl Brown, "American Negroes and the War," *Harper's Magazine*, April 1942, cited in Lawrence Wittner, *Rebels Against War: The American Peace Movement, 1941–1960* (Columbia University Press, 1969), Zinn, 410.

7. Zinn, *A People's History of the United States, 1492–Present* (Harper Perennial, 2005), 419.

8. Ibid.

9. Ibid., 415.

10. Lisa Krause, "Black Soldiers in WW II: Fighting Enemies at Home and Abroad," National Geographic News, February 15, 2001, http://news.nationalgeographic.com/news/2001/02/0215_tuskegee.html.

11. Ibid.

12. Official Web site of the All-American Girls Baseball League, http://www.aagpbl.org.

13. Interview with Jeanie Des Combes Lesko, pitcher, Grand Rapids Chicks, 1953–54, by Leanna Kamrath, San Dimas, CA, January 14, 2005, http://www.aagpbl.org/articles/interviews.cfm?ID=1.

14. www.aagpbl.org/league/charm.cfm.

15. Women's Sports Foundation, www.womenssportsfoundation.org/cgi-bin/iowa/sports/article.html?rec ord=89.

16. Arthur Ashe, *A Hard Road to Glory* (Wiley, 1993), 2:6

17. Steven Goldman, "The Motives: Rickey Had Several Reasons to Sign Robinson," MLB.com, http://mlb.mlb.com/mlb/history/mlb_negro_leagues_story.jsp? story=rickey_branch

18. Povich, 65.

19. August Wilson, *Fences* (Plume, 1986), 9.

20. Ashe, 3:7.

21. Jules Tygiel, *Baseball's Great Experiment* (Oxford University Press), 59–62.

22. Ibid.

23. Harvey Frommer, *Rickey and Robinson: The Men Who Broke Baseball's Color Barrier* (Taylor, 2003).

24. Goldman.

25. Harvey Frommer, "Branch Rickey and Jackie Robinson," http://www.baseballlibrary.com/baseballlibrary/submit/Frommer_Harvey16.stm.

26. Povich, 153.

27. Arnold Rampersad, *Jackie Robinson: A Biography* (Ballantine, 1998), 127.

28. Ibid., 147.

29. Ibid., 141.

30. *The People's Voice* [New York], October 5, 1946, 29.

31. Elliot J. Gorn and Warren Goldstein, *A Brief History of American Sports* (University of Illinois Press, 2004), 215.

32. Walter White, *Jackie Robinson on Trial,* quoted in David K. Wiggins and Patrick B. Miller, *The Unlevel Playing Field* (University of Illinois Press, 2003), 209.

33. Ibid.

34. *People's Voice*, Nov. 16, 1946, 28.

35. Larry Schwartz, "A Hero for Generations," ESPN, December 1999, http://espn.go.com/sportscentury/features/00107091.html.

36. Richard O. Davies, *America's Obsession: Sports and Society Since 1945* (Wadsworth, 1994), 11.

37. Ibid., 16.

38. Jackie Robinson, *I Never Had It Made: An Autobiography* (HarperCollins, 1995), 58–60; Rampersad, 157.

39. Rampersad, 187.

40. Roger Kahn, *Boys of Summer* (Harper Perennial, 2006), xvii.

41. Davies, 41.

42. Sam Lacy, "Campy, Jackie as Dodgers," in Wiggins and Miller, 211.

43. Rampersad, 237.

44. Povich, 150.

45. William Rhoden, *Forty Million Dollar Slaves* (Three Rivers, 2007), 119.

46. Gerald Early, "*American Integration, Black Heroism, and the Meaning of Jackie Robinson,*" in Wiggins and Miller, 216–20.

47. Effa Manley, "Negro Baseball Is at the Crossroads," in Wiggins and Miller, 215.

48. Ibid., 214.

49. Ibid., 214–15.

50. *People's Voice*, Dec. 7, 1946, 28.

51. Rick Hurt, *"The Sports Train," Washington Afro American*, January 11, 1947.

52. Davies, 40.

53. William A. Brower, "Has Professional Football Closed the Door?" in Wiggins and Miller, 200.

54. Ibid., 199–201.

55. *People's Voice*, Oct. 12, 1946, 28; Davies, 12.

56. John Keim, "Remembering Marion Motley," *Pro Football Weekly*, June 29, 1999, http://archive.profootballweekly.com/content/archives/features_1999/keim_062999.asp.

57. Ibid.

58. Ibid.

59. Ibid.

60. Davies, 39.

61. "The Alice Coachman Foundation: A Worldwide Olympic First," www.alicecoachmanonline.com.

62. "African American Women Make Their Marks in Sports," in Wiggins and Miller, 115.

63. Rhoden, 198.

64. A good book to learn the basics of NASCAR, where it is, and where it is going is Joe Menzer's *The Wildest Ride: A History of NASCAR (or, How a Bunch of Good Ol' Boys Built a Billion-Dollar Industry out of Wrecking Cars)* (Simon and Schuster, 2002).

6: "HAVE WE GONE SOFT?"

1. John Steinbeck, "Have We Gone Soft?" *New Republic*, Feb. 15, 1960, 11–15.

2. David Halberstam, *The 50s* (Ballantine, 1993), 587.

3. On McCarthyism, see Victor Navasky, *Naming Names*, rev. ed. (Hill and Wang, 2003).

4. Ellen Schrecker, *Many Are the Crimes: McCarthyism in America* (Boston: Little, Brown, 1998), x.

5. Halberstam, 59–61.

6. Ibid., 331.

7. Elizabeth Schulte, "The Execution of Ethel and Julius Rosenberg,' June 20, 2003, http://www.socialistworker.org/2003-2/458/458_06_Rosenbergs.shtml.

8. Ibid.

9. Miriam Zahler, "A Poisoned Childhood," in *Red Diapers: Growing Up in the Communist Left*, Judy Kaplan and Linn Shapiro, eds. (University of Illinois Press, 1998), 207–8.

10. Ronald A. Smith, "The Paul Robeson–Jackie Robinson Saga and a Political Collision," *Journal of Sport History* 6:2 (Summer, 1979), 16.

11. Robinson, 83, 85–86.

12. Howard Bryant, *Juicing the Game* (Plume, 2005), 177.

13. "Madam Executive," *Time*, Feb. 18, 1974, www.time.com/time/maga zine/article/0,9171,942783-2,00.html.

14. Richard O. Davies, *America's Obsession: Sports and Society Since 1945* (Wadsworth, 1994), 19.

15. Manning Marable, *Race Reform and Rebellion: The Second Reconstruction and Beyond in Black America, 1945–2006*, 3rd ed. (University Press of Mississippi, 2007).

16. Arnold Rampersad, *Jackie Robinson: A Biography* (Ballantine, 1998), 7.

17. Ibid., 281.

18. Ibid., 258.

19. Halberstam, 589.

20. Susan K. Cahn, *Coming on Strong* (Harvard University Press, 1998), 185–87.

21. Shirley Povich, *All Those Mornings . . . at the Post* (Public Affairs, 2005), 176.

22. Ibid., 177.

23. Ibid., 176.

24. "Bowling History," www.hickoksports.com/history/bowling.shtml., cord-house.com/x06/history.htm.

25. Howard Zinn, *A People's History of the United States, 1492–Present* (Harper Perennial, 2003), 441.

26. Ibid., 443.

27. Pete Hamill, *Downtown: My Manhattan* (Little, Brown, 2004), 275.

28. Molly Jay, *Winning Woman: 500 Spirited Quotes About Women and Their Sport* (Running Press, 2001), 59, 112.

29. Alice Marble, *American Lawn Tennis* magazine, 1950, quoted on http://womenshistory.about.com/od/quotes/a/althea_gibson.htm.

30. Rampersad, 335–36.

31. Matt Schudel, "Muckraking N.Y. Reporter Jack NewField Dies at 66," *Washington Post*, December 23, 2004, www.washingtonpost.com/wp dyn/articles/A21116-2004Dec22.html; "The Curse of Brooklyn," baseball fever.com.

32. Luiz Valdez, *Zoot Suit and Other Plays* (Arte Publico, 1992).

33. Peter Dreier and Jan Breidenbach, "Frank Wilkinson's Legacy," January 7, 2006, www.commondreams.org/views06/0107-27.htm.

34. "Chavez Ravine: A Los Angeles Story," www.pbs.org/independentlens/chavezravine/cr.html.

35. Ibid.

36. Ibid.

37. Davies, 28.

38. Joe Goldstein, "Explosion: 1951 Scandals Threaten College Hoops," November 19, 2003, http://espn.go.com/classic/s/basketball_scandals _explosion.html.

39. Jeff Merron, "The List: Basketball Shockers," http://espn.go.com/page2/s/list/basketballshock.html.

40. Stanley Cohen, *The Game They Played* (Farrar, Straus & Giroux, 1977), 156.

41. Bruce Lowitt, "Point-Fixing Scandal Rocks College Game," *St. Petersburg Times*, Nov. 5, 1999, www.sptimes.com/news/110599/news_pf/Sports/Point_fixing_sca ndal.shtml.

42. Povich, 195.

43. Povich, 209.

44. Ibid.

45. Ibid., 150

7: SPORTS ON THE EDGE OF PANIC

1. "John Kennedy on Physical Education," www.jfklibrary.org/Historical+Resources/JFK+in+History/The+Federal+Government+Takes+on+Physical+Fitness.htm.

2. "Pres. Kennedy's Health Secrets," *News Hour with Jim Lehrer*, November 18, 2002, www.pbs.org/newshour/bb/health/july-dec02/jfk_11-18.html.

3. Howard Zinn, *A People's History of the United States, 1492–Present* (Harper Perennial, 2005), 442.

4. Ibid, 453.

5. Ibid.

6. Arthur Ashe, *A Hard Road to Glory* (Wiley, 1993), 16.

7. "Negro Athletes and Civil Rights," quoted from David K. Wiggins and Patrick B. Miller, *The Unlevel Playing Field* (University of Illinois Press, 2003), 274.

8. Richard O. Davies, *America's Obsession: Sports and Society Since 1945* (Wadsworth, 1994), 44.

9. Arnold Rampersad, *Jackie Robinson: A Biography* (Ballantine, 1998), 346.

10. Mike Rampersad, 358.

11. Ibid, 397.

12. Zirin, *What's My Name, Fool?*, 51.

13. David Remnick, *King of the World* (Vintage, 1998), 125.

14. Ibid., 105.

15. Muhammad Ali and William Nack, *My Turf: Horses, Boxers, Blood Money and the Sporting Life* (Da Capo Press, 2003), 175. Hana Yasmeen Ali, *The Soul of a Butterfly: Reflections on Life's Journey* (Simon and Schuster, 2004), 40–41.

16. Remnick, 129.

17. Zinn, 461.

18. David Levi Strauss, "Floating Like a Butterfly . . . ," *The Nation*, January 25, 1999.

19. William Rhoden, *Forty Million Dollar Slave* (Three Rivers, 2007), 17.

20. James Baldwin, "The Fight: Patterson vs. Liston," in Wiggins and Miller, 301.

21. Marqusee, 78, 75.
22. Ibid., 9.
23. Ibid., 9, 76, 57.
24. Ibid., 8, 142.
25. Thomas Hauser, *Muhammad Ali in Perspective* (Harper Collins, 1996), 15
26. Marqusee 133; Hauser, 16.
27. Marqusee, 193.
28. Zirin, *What's My Name, Fool?*, 63.
29. Eldridge Cleaver, *Soul on Ice* (Delta, 1999), 118.
30. Zinn, 477.
31. David W. Zang, *Sports Wars* (University of Arkansas Press, 1999) 78.; Mike Wise, "Olympic Legend Billy Mills: One Man Is Still Going the Distance for Two Nations," *Washington Post*, October 29, 2005; http://www .washingtonpost.com/wp-dyn/content/article/2005/10;sh28/AR200510 2802132.html.
32. Zang, 30.
33. Douglas Hartmann, *Race, Culture, and the Revolt of the Black Athlete: The 1968 Olympic Protests and Their Aftermath* (University of Chicago Press, 2004), 131.
34. Zang, 78, 79.
35. Ibid., 82
36. Robert Lipsyte in Dave Zirin, *The Muhammad Ali Handbook* (MQ Publications, 2006), 286–300.
37. Marqusee, 174.
38. Zinn, 475.
39. Zang, 96–97.
40. Marqusee, 179.
41. Jack Olsen, *Black Is Best: The Riddle of Cassius Clay* (Putnam, 1967), 37.
42. Zang, 19.
43. Zirin, *Muhammad Ali Handbook*, 190.
44. Hauser, 157.
45. Marqusee, 179.
46. Remnick, 290.
47. Zirin, *Muhammad Ali Handbook*, 191.
48. Ibid.
49. Zang, 116.
50. Zirin, *Muhammad Ali Handbook*, 193.
51. Remnick, 289.
52. Marqusee, 210.
53. Ibid., 213.
54. Marqusee, 133.
55. Ibid, 213–15.
56. Ali, *The Soul of a Butterfly* (Simon & Schuster, 2004), 89.
57. Ibid., 89.

58. Hauser, *Muhammad Ali: His Life and Times* (Simon & Schuster), 1992.
59. Hauser, 19.
60. Marqusee, 221.
61. Ibid., 204.
62. Ibid., 175.
63. Ibid., 180.
64. Hauser, *Muhammad Ali in Perspective* (Collins, 1996), 71.
65. Marqusee, 228.
66. Larry Platt, *New Jack Jocks* (Temple University Press, 2002), 102.
67. Hauser, *Life & Times*, 192.
68. Zirin, *Muhammad Ali Handbook*, 166.
69. *Muhammad Ali: Through the Eyes of the World* (Universal, 2001).
70. Marqusee, 246.
71. Zirin, *WMNF*, 151.
72. Ibid., 152.
73. Ibid.
74. Bill Russell, *Go Up for Glory* (Berkley Medallion, 1970).
75. Zirin, *WMNF*, 176.
76. Ibid.
77. Frank Fitzpatrick, "Texas Western's 1966 Title Left Lasting Legacy," ESPN.com, November 19, 2003, http://espn.go.com/classic/s/013101_texas_western_fitzpatri ck.html.
78. Ibid.
79. Ibid.
80. Ibid.
81. Ibid.
82. Harry Edwards, *Revolt of the Black Athlete* (Free Press, 1970).
83. William N. Wallace, *Race Issue Shifts All-Star Game From New Orleans to Houston, New York Times*, January 12, 1965.
84. Ashe, 124.
85. A.S. "Doc" Young, "Rebellion at Cal," *Chicago Defender*, February 1, 1968.
86. Ashe, 124.
87. David Zang, "An Interview with Calvin Hill," in Wiggins and Miller, 365.
88. Chet Walker, "On the Road in the South, 1960," in Wiggins and Miller, 279–80, 282.
89. Ibid., 281.
90. Davies, 52.
91. *Washington Afro-American*, March 9, 1968, 15.
92. David Maraniss, *Clemente: The Passion and Grace of Baseball's Last Hero* (Simon and Schuster, 2006), 220.
93. Mike Towle, *I Remember Arthur Ashe: Memories of a True Tennis Pioneer and Champion of Social Causes by the People Who Knew Him* (Cumberland, 2001), 2.

94. *Washington Afro-American*, April 20, 1968, 15.

95. *Washington Afro-American*, May 11, 1968, 15.

96. *Washington Afro-American*, May 18, 1968, 15.

97. Zang, 5, 78, 79.

98. Robert Lipsyte, *SportsWorld: An American Dreamland* (Quadrangle, 1975), 20.

99. Hartmann, 39.

100. Amy Bass, *Not the Triumph but the Struggle* (Minneapolis: University of Minnesota Press, 2002), 206–7.

101. Ashe, 188.

102. Hartmann, 52.

103. Ibid., 56.

104. Hartmann, 96.

105. Tommie Smith, "Why Negroes Should Boycott," in Wiggins and Miller, 290–92.

106. Hartmann, 84.

107. Ibid., 70.

108. Ibid., 65–66.

109. Rampersad, 438.

110. Ibid., 96.

111. Hartmann, 130.

112. Hartmann, 112.

113. Ibid., 64.

114. Rafer Johnson, "The Decathlete as Community-Builder," in Wiggins and Miller, 350, 349–50.

115. Zirin, *WMNF*, 86.

116. Ibid., 80.

117. *Los Angeles Free Press*, Nov. 1, 1968.

118. Hartmann, 64.

119. *Washington Afro-American*, April 6, 1968, 26.

120. Zirin, *WMNF*, 81–82.

121. Ibid., 76.

122. Hartmann, 157.

123. Allen Guttmann, *The Games Must Go On: Avery Brundage and the Olympic Movement* (Columbia University Press, 1984), 243.

124. Hartmann, 11.

125. Ibid.

126. Zirin, *WMNF*, 88.

127. Ibid.

128. Ibid., 83–84.

129. Amy Bass, *Not the Triumph But the Struggle: The 1968 Olympics and the Making of The Black Athlete* (University of Minnesota Press, 2004), 229–30.

130. Zirin, *WMNF*, 95.

131. Hartmann, 125.

132. Ibid., 8.

133. Ibid., 172, 173.

134. *Washington Afro-American*, Jan. 11, 1969, 1.

135. *Washington Afro-American*, Feb. 15, 1969, Feb. 22, 1969, Sept. 27, 1969.

136. *The South End*, 1969.

137. "College Cager Dropped for Ignoring Anthem," *Washington Afro American*, Dec. 14, 1968, 15.

138. Ashe, 98. Volume 3.

139. Hartmann, 179.

140. Quoted in Robert McCord, *The Quotable Golfer* (Sterling, 2004), 70.

141. Zirin, *WMNF*, 116, 119.

142. Ibid., 118–19.

143. Ibid. 119–21.

144. Author interview with Paul Damato.

145. Robert Lipsyte, *SportsWorld: An American Dreamland* (Quadrangle, 1975), 47.

8: THE FLOOD GATES

1. Howard Zinn, "The Impossible Victory: Vietnam," http://www.history isaweapon.com/defcon1/zinnimvivi18.html.

2. Howard Zinn, *A People's History of the United States: 1492–Present* (Harper Perennial Modern Classics, 2003), 494.

3. Joel Geier, "Vietnam: The Soldier's Revolt," *International Socialist Review* 9, August–September 2000, www.isreview.org/issues/09/soldiers_revolt .shtml.

4. Ibid.

5. *Vietnam GI,* June 1969.

6. Richard R. Moser, *The New Winter Soldiers: GI and Veteran Dissent During the Vietnam Era* (Rutgers University Press, 1996), 41.

7. Ibid., 43.

8. Ibid., 53–54.

9. Geier.

10. Wallace Terry, *Bloods: An Oral History of the Vietnam War by Black Veterans* (Presidio Press, 1985).

11. Zang, 51.

12. Toby Miller et al., *Globalization and Sport: Playing the World* (Sage, 2001), 102.

13. Robert Lipsyte, "A Very Different Shade of Green; 30 Years Later, Don't Confuse Namath's Jets with Today's Team," *New York Times*, January 17, 1999, http://query.nytimes.com/gst/fullpage.html?res=9E05E3D61F31F 934A2 5752C0A96F958260.

14. Kilmer on Nixon, *Uncle John's Third Bathroom Reader* (St. Martin's Press 1990), 45.

15. Robert Lipsyte, "Of Sports, Comebacks and Nixon," *New York Times*, May 1, 1994.

16. Dean Paton's written recollection to the author.

17. Robert Lipsyte, *SportsWorld: An American Dreamland* (Times Books, 1977).

18. Dave Zirin, *Welcome to the Terrordome: The Pain, Politics, and Promise of Sports* (Haymarket, 2007), 199.

19. *Talk* magazine, "Books We Talked About Most: From *Ulysses* to *The Bell Curve*, Titles That Piqued Our Century," December 1999–January 2000, accessible at http://jimbouton.com/talk1_2000.html.

20. *Time*, "Inside Baseball," Monday, June 15, 1970, www.time.com/time/magazine/article/0,9171,909406,00.html.

21. Zirin, *Terrordome*, 197.

22. Ashe, 25.

23. Zang, 15.

24. Ibid., 155.

25. Jesse Owens and Paul Neimark, *I Have Changed* (William Morrow, 1972), 38.

26. Douglas Hartmann, *Race, Culture, and the Revolt of the Black Athlete* (University of Chicago Press, 2003), 235.

27. "Jesse Jackson on Blacks and the Sports $$$," in David K. Wiggins and Patrick B. Miller, *The Unlevel Playing Field* (University of Illinois Press, 2003), 322.

28. Ibid., 320.

29. Dave Zirin, "The Unforgiven: Jack Johnson and Barry Bonds," http://www.zmag.org/content/showarticle.cfm?ItemID=13101.

30. Ashe, 125, 135.

31. David Maraniss, *Clemente: The Passion and Grace of Baseball's Last Hero* (Simon and Schuster, 2006), 2.

32. Ibid., 285.

33. Ibid, 290–304; quote on 304.

34. Ibid, 333, 343, 339.

35. Zirin, *Terrordome*, 50–51.

36. Quoted in Hartmann, 189, and in "Jeremiah of Jock Liberation," *Time*, May 24, 1971, www.time.com/time/magazine/article/0,9171,905113,00.html?iid=chix -sphere.

37. Obituary of Jack Scott in *Footnotes* (publication of the American Sociological Association), April 2000, http://www.asanet.org/footnotes/apr00/departments.html.

38. "Overhaul at Oberlin," *Time*, January 29, 1973, www.time.com/time/magazine/article/0,9171,903775,00.html.

39. Ibid.

40. Ibid.

41. Jay, 118.

42. "Overhaul at Oberlin."

43. Author interview, Phoebe Jones.

44. Margaret Friedenauer, "Tennis Making a Racket," *Fairbanks Daily News–Miner*, January 27, 2007, http://newsminer.com/2007/01/27/4763.

45. Kenny Moore, "Arthur Ashe: Sportsman of the Year," *Sports Illustrated*, December 21, 1992.

46. Author interview, Dennis Brutus.

47. Arthur Ashe, "South Africa's 'New' Interracial Sports Policy: Is It a Fraud? *New York Times*, October 2, 1977.

48. Zinn, 505.

49. Ibid., 510.

50. Larry Schwartz, "Billie Jean Won for All Women, ESPN.com, http://espn.go.com/sportscentury/features/00016060.html.

51. Davies, 160

52. Jay, 8.

53. Ibid., 11.

54. Schwartz.

55. Ibid.

56. Ibid.

57. Ibid.

58. *Ms.* magazine, January 1972.

59. Anthony Holden, "Battle of the Sexes," http://cbs.sportsline.com/u/century/week13.htm.

60. Davies, 161.

61. National Organization for Women stats from the Women's Sports Foundation, http://www.now.org/issues/title_ix/index.html.

62. Davies, 168.

63. Ibid., 171.

64. Ibid.

65. Linda Jean Carpenter and R. Vivian Acosta, "27 Year Study Shows Progression of Women in College Athletics," www.womenssportsfoundation.org/cgi-bin/iowa/issues/part/article.h tml?record=906.

66. David Zirin, "The MLB Strike—25 Years in the Making," www.buzzle.com/editorials/8-18-2004-58021.asp.

67. Dave Zirin, *What's My Name, Fool? Sports and Resistance in the United States* (Haymarket Books, 2005), 103–4.

68. Rhoden, 235.

69. Zirin, *WMNF*, 112–13.

70. Davies, 136.

71. Zirin, *WMNF*, 104

72. Zinn, 558–559.

73. Ibid., 567.

74. Ibid., 570.

75. Howard Zinn and Anthony Arnove, *Voices of a People's History of the United States* (Seven Stories, 2004), 530–531, 530.

76. Dan Clawson, *The Next Upsurge: Labor and the New Social Movements* (Cornell University Press, 2003), 50.

77. Michael Freeman, *ESPN: The Uncensored History* (Taylor, 2002).

9: THE 1980S: WELCOME TO HELL

1. *Do You Believe In Miracles? The Story of the 1980 U.S. Hockey Team*, HBO Sports, 2001.

2. E.M. Swift, "The Golden Goal," *Sports Illustrated*, March 3, 1980.

3. Dan Rather, "Ronald Reagan, Master Storyteller: CBS News' Dan Rather on Former President's Wit and Wisdom," http://www.cbsnews.com/stories/2004/06/07/48hours/main62145 9.shtml.

4. Zinn, 567.

5. Ibid., 566.

6. Bob Herbert, "Righting Reagan's Wrongs?" *New York Times*, November 13, 2007, http://www.nytimes.com/2007/11/13/opinion/13herbert.html?n=Top/Opinion/Editorials%20and%20Op-Ed/Op-Ed/Columnists/Bob%2 0Herbert.

7. Sharon Smith, *Subterranean Fire: A History of Working-Class Radicalism in the United States* (Haymarket, 2006), 234.

8. Robert Ajemian, "Peter Ueberroth: *Time* Magazine's Person of the Year, 1984," *Time*, http://www.time.com/time/subscriber/poy2000/archive/1984.html.

9. Hartmann, 255.

10. Ibid.

11. Ashe, 252.

12. "The Time 100: Heroes and Icons," www.time.com/time/time100/heroes/profile/robinson03.html.

13. Claire Smith, "Baseball: Equality's Hurdles: A Special Report; Too Few Changes Since Campanis," *New York Times*, August 16, 1992.

14. Frank Robinson: "In America's National Pastime . . . White is the Color Off the Field," quoted in Wiggins and Miller, 340–41.

15. Grandmaster Flash and the Furious Five, "The Message," Lyrics available at the Lyrics for All Site, http://www.lyricsforall.com/display/lyric/4998/161869/Grandma ster+Flash/The+Message.

16. Jeff Chang, *Can't Stop, Won't Stop* (St. Martin's Press, 2005), 7–21, quote on p. 13.

17. Ibid.

18. Zirin, *Terrordome*, 111.

19. Chang, 417.

20. Jim Brown and Steve Delsohn, *Out of Bounds* (Kensington, 1989), 51.

21. Jean O'Reilly and Susan K. Cahn, *Women and Sports in the United States: A Documentary Reader* (Northeastern, 2007).

22. CNN Presents Connie Chung Tonight, "Navratilova Sets the Record Straight," July 17, 2002, http://transcripts.cnn.com/TRANSCRIPTS/0207/17/cct.00.html.

23. Jay, 154.

24. Joan Ryan, *Little Girls in Pretty Boxes* (Women's Press, 1996), 3–4.

25. Ibid., 58.

26. *The Advocate*, August 5, 1986.

27. Roger Brigham, "Sports Movement Shines in Face of AIDS," *Bay Area Reporter*, June 1, 2006.

28. Stephen Kulieke and Pat Califia, "In the True 'Olympic' Tradition: The Gay Games," *The Advocate*, October 14, 1982, 29–35.

29. Ibid.

30. Ibid.

31. *The Advocate,* Sept. 30, 1986, 46.

32. Ibid., 108.

33. Ann Meredith, "Gay Games II," *Off Our Backs*, Oct. 31, 1986

34. Ibid.

35. Larry Weisman, "NFL Reflects on Changes at Anniversary of Strikes," *USA Today*, October 6, 2007.

36. Mickey Spagnola, "Don't Do It Again," Dallas Cowboys.com, March 2, 2006, http://lb.dallascowboys.com/news.cfm?editorialAuthor=1&id=BD 89714 7-B8DB-2004-6535F7FAC0F43758

37. Weisman, ibid.

38. "Strike! The Walkout the Owners Provoked," *Sports Illustrated*, June 22, 1981.

10: C.R.E.A.M

1. Paul Damato, "Why Marx Still Matters," *International Socialist Review*, November–December 2006.

2. Zinn, 596.

3. Ibid., 597.

4. Zang, 5–7.

5. Sam Toperoff, "In Pursuit of Peace," *Sports Illustrated*, Feb. 25, 1991.

6. *New York Times* editorial, "Misusing the Flag, Again," February 20, 1991.

7. Toperoff.

8. Steven Wells, "The Search for Integrity," *Guardian Unlimited*, March 15, 2005, http://sport.guardian.co.uk/americansports/comment/0,10160, 143727 4,00.html.

9. "AIDS Killed Alan Wiggins," *Washington Post*, January 15, 1991.

10. "Magic Johnson Tests Positive for HIV," *Los Angeles Times*, Nov. 7, 1991.

11. Thomas Bonk, "Navratilova Says She Will Talk to Magic," *Los Angeles Times*, November 22, 1991.

12. Ibid.

13. Keeanga Taylor, "Ten Years After the Los Angeles Rebellion, No Justice, No

Peace!" April 26, 2001, www.socialistworker.org/2002-1/404/404_08_LA Rebellion.shtml.

14. Ibid.
15. Ibid.
16. Zirin, *WMNF*, 73.
17. Ibid.
18. Ibid.
19. Author interview with Jones.
20. William C. Rhoden, "Dunking and Fasting for Principle," *New York Times,* February 20, 1993.
21. Vivian Chakarian, "Arthur Ashe: Tennis Champion and Civil Rights Activist" (Voice of America, September 18, 2005.) www.voanews.com/spe cialenglish/archive/2005-09/2005-09-18-voa1:cfm.
22. Rhoden, *Forty Million Dollar Slaves,* 183.
23. Sports Century, "Air Supreme," http://espn.go.com/sportscentury.
24. Ira Berkow, "Looking over Jordan," *New York Times*, Jan. 31, 1999, http://www.nytimes.com/books/99/01/31/reviews/990131.31berk owt.html?_r= 1&oref=slogin.
25. Michael Crowley, "Hot Air: The Case Against Michael Jordan," *Boston Phoenix*, January 25, 1999.
26. Zirin, *WMNF*.
27. Crowley.
28. Ibid.
29. Rhoden, *Forty Million Dollar Slaves,* 200.
30. Ibid., 199.
31. Jason Diamos, "Abdul-Rauf Is Calm In Face of Controversy," *New York Times*, March 21, 1996, http://query.nytimes.com/gst/fullpage.html?res= 9C00EFD81739F932A15750C0A960958260&n=Top/Reference/Times %20Topics/People/A/Abdu l-Rauf,%20Mahmoud.
32. "Disk Jockeys Will Apologize for Mosque Incident," *New York Times*, March 31, 1996, http://query.nytimes.com/gst/fullpage.html?res=9B0 DE7DC1239F932A05750C0A960958260&n=Top/Reference/Times% 20Topics/People/A/Abdu l-Rauf,%20Mahmoud.
33. "Fire Engulfs Abdul-Rauf Home," CBC Sports, July 30, 2001, http://www.cbc.ca/sports/story/2001/07/30/abdul-rauf010730. html.
34. Rhoden, *Forty Million Dollar Slaves,* 243.
35. *Dare to Dream: The Story of the U.S. Women's Soccer Team,* HBO Sports, (2005).
36. Dave Zirin, *Welcome to the Terrordome* (Haymarket, 2007), 80.
37. Jean O'Reilly and Susan K. Cahn, *Women and Sports in the United States: A Documentary Reader* (University Press of New England, 2007), 346.
38. *Dare to Dream.*
39. Ibid.
40. Ibid.

41. Ibid.
42. Ibid.
43. Ibid.
44. Ibid.
45. Zirin, *WMNF*, 186–88.
46. Ibid.
47. Ibid.
48. Ibid.
49. Dave Zirin, "The Eclipse of Venus," July 21, 2005, http://www.press action.com/news/weblog/full_article/zirin0721 2005.
50. Zirin, 104.
51. Bryant, 22.
52. Stephen Barrett, "How the Dietary Supplement Health and Education Act of 1994 Weakened the FDA," www.quackwatch.org/02Consumer Protection/dshea.html.
53. Bryant 275, 276.
54. Ibid., 152.
55. Ibid., 150–51.
56. C.W. Nevius, "NASCAR Rising: Why are sports' newest superstars paunchy white men? And how did they take over your TV?" March 9, 2003, *San Francisco Chronicle*, www.sfgate.com/cgi-bin/article.cgi?f=/c/a/2003/03/09/CM16 2371.DTL.
57. Ibid.
58. Dan Wetzel, "Flag Flap Swirls About," http://sports.yahoo.com/top/news?slug=dw-peoplesvoice101906&prov; eqyhoo&type=lgns.
59. Nevius.
60. Ibid.

11: MORE OF THE SAME VERSUS CHANGE

1. Zirin, *Terrordome*, 20.
2. Zirin, *WMNF*, 135.
3. Dave Zirin, "The Unlonesome Death of Pat Tillman," *Counterpunch*, April 29, 2004, http://www.counterpunch.org/zirin04292004.html.
4. Dave Zirin, "Why Pat Tillman's Parents Are No Longer Silent," *Counterpunch*, May 27, 2005, http://www.counterpunch.org/zirin 05272005.html.
5. Robert Collier, "Family Demands the Truth: New Inquiry May Expose Events That Led to Pat Tillman's Death," *San Francisco Chronicle*, September 25, 2005, http://www.sfgate.com/cgi-bin/article.cgi?f=/c/a/2005/09; sh25/MNGD7ETMNM1.DTL.
6. Ibid.
7. Dave Zirin, "Pat Tillman, Our Hero," *The Nation,* October 24, 2005.
8. Kevin Tillman, "After Pat's Birthday," Oct. 19, 2006, http://www.truth dig.com/report/item/200601019_after_pats_birthday.

9. Dave Zirin, "Organizing the Jocks for Justice," Nov. 30, 2006, www
.edgeofsports.com/2006-11-30-212/index.html.
10. Ibid.
11. Reprinted with permission from the author.
12. Charles Robinson, "Q&A with Jim Brown," Yahoo! sports, November 29, 2006, http://sports.yahoo.com/nfl/news?slug=cr-brown112906&prov=yhoo& type=lgns.
13. Zirin, *Terrordome*, 22–26.
14. Author interview with Neil DeMause, April 16, 2007.
15. Zirin, *Terrordome*, 207.
16. Michael Wilbon, "Out of Imus's Bigotry, a Zero Tolerance for Hate," *Washington Post*, April 11, 2007, http://www.washingtonpost.com/wp-dyn/content/article/2007/04; sh10/AR2007041001891.html.
17. "Coach: 'Hos' Comment on Insult to All Women," CNN, April 10, 2007, www.cnn.com/2007/45/04/10/coach.comments/index.html
18. Maria Newman, "Rutgers Women to Meet with Imus Over Remarks," *New York Times*, April 10, 2007.
19. Zirin, *Terrordome*.
20. Interviewed on *Countdown with Keith Olbermann*, MSNSC, April 11, 2007, www.msnbc.msn.com/id/18075483.
21. http://www.johnconyers.com/node/162.
22. Letter to the author.

Index